DOCTRINE AND PRACTICE
IN THE
EARLY CHURCH

Stuart G Hall

DOCTRINE AND PRACTICE
IN THE
EARLY CHURCH

WILLIAM B. EERDMANS PUBLISHING COMPANY
GRAND RAPIDS, MICHIGAN

CONTENTS

PREFACE

This book owes much to various people. It was stimulated by my friends at SPCK who invited it. It was conceived in consultation with colleagues who taught historical theology to London University students as I did, Richard Price and, especially, Anthony Meredith. The latter was originally going to share the work, and, after I became sole author, he generously left me free to use material which he had prepared: some words, phrases and sentences of his have probably got into the text, as have certainly some of his ideas. For his kindness, courtesy and cooperation I am enormously grateful. I am grateful too for those generations of lovable students of theology at Nottingham University and King's College London who have been sounding boards for my ideas, and who constantly stimulated thought and clarification by what they failed to understand as well as by what they understood only too well. If the book in turn stimulates some students of theology and of antiquity to appreciate better the achievement of the creative times it describes, I shall be satisfied. King's College provided me with more than one period of sabbatical leave, and some of that time was dedicated to this work. But beyond that, the contribution of colleagues at King's has over twelve years past been persistent, subtle and benevolent in encouraging theological endeavour and communication. Long may it thrive.

As pious persons of the past in wills bequeathed their souls to Almighty God, I dedicate this book to him whose Word is the substance of all true theology; for how can we speak of him unless he gives us the Word? But as the same pious testators bequeathed their earthly goods to their best and dearest, I dedicate this book above all earthly prizes to my dear wife Brenda Mary. Her steady encouragement and advice enabled me to recognize my academic vocation and has sustained my enthusiasm for this present writing;

her contribution is crowned by her professional skill in indexing it, for which I am immensely grateful.

Stuart George Hall
16 December 1990

O Wisdom, proceeding from the mouth of the Highest, you reach from one end to the other, mightily and sweetly ordering all things: Come and teach us the way to live rightly.

PUBLISHER'S NOTE

This volume makes frequent reference to two companion volumes of early church documents also published by SPCK. Both are standard collections of documents originally edited by J. Stevenson, now available in revised editions edited by W. H. C. Frend. They are *A New Eusebius: Documents Illustrating the History of the Church to A.D. 337* (1987), and its sequel, *Creeds, Councils and Controversies: Documents Illustrating the History of the Church A.D. 337–461* (1989). Both are available in North America from Abingdon Press, Nashville, Tennessee.

The parenthetical citations of these volumes use the abbreviations *NE* and *CCC*. The numbers refer to the pages in the volumes, not to numbered items.

1
GOD AND THE GODS

Religion in the Roman Empire

The gospel of Christ spread in a religious world. Each ancient city-state depended upon its patron deity for prosperity and defence: Athens had Pallas Athene, Rome had Jupiter Optimus Maximus, Ephesus had Artemis. But no god or goddess had a monopoly, and everywhere they multiplied, especially as the Roman Empire expanded.

The focus of cult was usually a particular image of the god, artistically made and adorned with precious metals, which was kept in a shrine or temple. Most of the time the heavy doors would be firmly shut to protect from theft and sacrilege. But at appropriate times, for the god's annual festival, to celebrate a victory or the end of a plague, or to seek help against disaster or adversity, the responsible officers or priests would open the temple in the presence of many people. These would gather in and around the sacred precinct, the reserved grove or garden in which the temple stood. Appropriate ceremonies would follow: often a procession, usually a sacrifice on the altar-stone which stood before the door, appropriate feastings, plays, sports or dancing. Important civic events took place at temples: annual magistrates were inaugurated, war was declared, peace treaties solemnized. Sports, theatres, military life were shot through with religious ceremonial. If the god was not for some reason displeased, he or she prospered what was done in his name.

Gods and goddesses were not ofen jealous as the God of Israel was (Exod. 20.5), and the presiding deity of a city could tolerate the cult of others. Mythology connected gods to each other, and depicted them as a kind of extended family resident on Mount Olympus, discussing, often with passion, the destinies of the human beings below, whom they would help or punish in co-operation or competition with each other. There were several earthly reasons for multiplying deities.

1. First, some were cherished because of their special functions. Juno was useful at Rome; as consort of Jupiter she made marriages prosper. The Greek Asclepios (Latin Aesculapius) was widely popular in the Roman Empire, because of his healing gifts. Demeter was needed in parts of Greece to secure harvests, and Poseidon must be appeased to keep off earthquakes and protect from shipwreck.

2. Secondly wealthy individuals displayed their civic loyalty by erecting temples to gods at their own expense; this was often as the result of a miraculous deliverance, or to fulfil a vow, or as the result of a message from or apparition of the divinity. A good example is the temple of Apollo which the emperor Augustus erected in Rome to rival that of Jupiter; at the battle of Actium in 31 BC he had encamped by a shrine of Apollo, and attributed his victory over Antony and Cleopatra to that god.

3. Thirdly the enlargement of empire promoted the transfer of gods from one place to another. There had always been some community of interest between Greek cities. There were oracular shrines like that at Delphi which served people from all over Greece and beyond, and attracted dedications, some bombastic, others as devout thankofferings for blessings or guidance received. Roman officials and merchants would start paying respects to gods they met in other countries, and might take the cult back home. There was in any case a process of assimilation, so that gods who came from Greece or other parts of the East were identified with Italian gods whom they resemble: Artemis with Diana, Ares with Mars and so forth. Gods could also be physically imported as plunder or works of art, but the sacredness attaching to their figures might linger and grow again in their new home. It was not unusual for a temple precinct to contain minor shrines to gods other than the principal one.

4. Fourthly cults of a more private kind attracted followers and spread from land to land, a process promoted by the good communications in the Roman Empire. Among the more popular were the wine-god Dionysos and the multipurpose goddess from Egypt, Isis. In Christian times Mithras from Persia was spreading especially among the military. In these cases a process

of initiation into the mysteries was involved, but such devotions in no way prevented their adherents from following the public cults.

5. Finally there was a deliberate development of state cults to match the growth of empires. The successors of Alexander's general Ptolemy in Egypt deliberately cultivated a comparatively minor god called Sarapis, who was portrayed with features of the high god Zeus and the healer Asclepios, and was held to be responsible for the seasonal rising of the Nile on which Egypt depended; papyrus letters prove that he was very successful and popular. Augustus, the founder of the Roman Empire, not only promoted familiar gods and deified his official father Julius Caesar, but widely encouraged the cult of 'Rome and Augustus'. This was the dedication (for instance) of an altar and national festival at Lugdunum (Lyons) for the Gallic provinces.

6. Besides the major temples, minor shrines and cult-figures were everywhere apparent in town and village, at road-sides, in gardens, on shopfronts. Minor deities, often referred to as 'divinities' (Greek, *daimones*), lived in woods, hills, springs and rivers; some of these were sinister, evil powers which lurked especially at cross-roads and places of execution. Others might be agreeable or mischievous spirits of wells and woods.

Gods were pervasive as well as numerous. Ordinary people would pray to the gods for help in all kinds of human enterprises, would appease with sacrificial gifts and prayers their malignity or temporary disfavour, and would reward them for services rendered with anything from a bunch of flowers to a large temple. They looked for divine guidance not only through astrology, but through skilled interpreters of the flight of birds, of the arrangement of entrails in slaughtered animals, and in the oracles mysteriously produced by prophets in the depths of the greater oracular shrines. They celebrated family events with feasts at temples where the priest for a fee would slaughter and cook the animal flesh; it might be the ordinary place for the slaughter of beasts for the market. Women visited Juno or Venus before a wedding, or if threatened with divorce might make offerings to an unnamed goddess who placated husbands, *Dea viriplaca*. Temple precincts accumulated gods and religious furniture, the streets of cities displayed their statues, and stories constantly circulated of the appearances, actions, judgements and favours of such gods. As you passed their figures or temples, especially of those you feared or loved, you would kiss your hand in hope of good. It was not only the men of Athens whom a visitor like Paul would see as 'very religious' (Acts 17.22: he was complimenting, not criticizing). Many people in the Empire were in fact genuinely religious, believing that they could improve their prospects in this world by behaving well towards the gods, and hoping for some kind of agreeable after-life. Many others may have been more sceptical, but perceived that social cohesion, the rule of law and the authority of the emperor depended on a proper regard for the traditional gods. Peace with the gods, or the peace of the gods (*pax deorum*) must therefore be a goal of public policy.

Critiques of the gods

With this religion of many gods, this polytheism, the God of Israel was naturally at war. His people were forbidden all other gods beside him, and all idols of gods and goddesses. Their sacred books recorded the fearful punishments which had repeatedly fallen on them for idolatry. 'All the gods of the nations are demons; it is the Lord that made the heavens' (Ps. 96(95).5). The Greek word for a 'divinity', *daimon, daimonion*, has become a sinister word for the malignant forces whose grip upon the world persists by God's permission, or as a punishment of mankind. Men and women are now called upon to turn 'to God from idols, to serve a living and true God, and to wait for his Son from heaven, whom he raised from the dead, Jesus who delivers us from the wrath to come' (1 Thess. 1.10); 'We ought not to think that the Deity is like gold, or silver, or stone, a representation by the art and imagination of man. The times of ignorance God overlooked, but now he commands all men everywhere to repent, because he has fixed a day on which he will judge the world in righteousness by a man whom he has appointed, and of this he has given assurance to all men by raising him from the dead' (Acts 17.29–31).

This message contained the difficult feature of the resurrection of Jesus, and the disquieting or ridiculous one of the impending judgement of the whole world by the God of Israel who sent him. But the primary notion of one only or supreme Deity could ring true to thoughtful Greeks and Romans; philosophers had often questioned the truth of polytheism. Most thinkers held there was one overarching providence (Gk *pronoia*) directing the world. The disciples of Epicurus (4th–3rd century BC) denied it, holding the gods to exist but to be indifferent to the world, which is a fortuitous concourse of atoms. But they were not in favour, and 'Epicurean' is a term of abuse among respectable philosophers in early Christian times; to deny providence is to question the foundation of morality.

Greek and Roman theology combined elements of the three chief philosophical streams of the day:

1. From Plato (428/427–348/347 BC) it derived a strong sense that only the transcendent realm of pure intellect or spirit is stable and permanent. In that realm, everything in this changeable world of transient material beings has its fixed archetype or model (called its 'form' or 'idea'). The intellectual element in the human soul recognizes material things as copies of 'ideas' already innate (inborn), and therefore must have learned those ideas in some previous spiritual existence. That part of the soul must therefore already belong to the unchanging deathless realm, and be immortal. In one much-quoted dialogue, *Timaeus*, Plato describes a Craftsman or Demiurge (Gk *demiurgos*) copying the eternal ideas to make the world. On his own showing this is mythology rather than strict theology, but the Craftsman sufficiently resembled the biblical Creator to provide a bridge to Christianity. Plato also insisted that any true God must share the changelessness of the realm of ideas, and poured scorn on the mythical activities, passions and metamorphoses attributed to the gods by poets.

2. Aristotle (384–322 BC), the second major influence on thoughtful theology, took up this point, and postulated a God absolutely unmoved and occupied with contemplation of his own perfection (since he could not contemplate anything less). Everything else moves and exists out of desire for him, and there is no immaterial realm of ideas transcending the material world.

3. Finally the Stoics, founded by Zeno (*c.* 336–264 BC), identified God with the ordering principle of the universe. He is its rational principle (*logos*), its soul (*psyche*), the refined vapour

(*pneuma* or *aither*) which pervades all things; but whatever his name, he is material (*soma*), which holds the universe in being and will ultimately destroy it as fire. It is man's chief good in Stoicism to be wise by affirming the wise government of the world by this immanent providence of God.

By the time of Christ and the early Fathers it was possible for Greek and Latin philosophers to combine features of these philosophies and to arrive at a form of monotheism: a slightly more active version of Aristotle's God, or a more transcendent version of the Stoic God, might do very well; or else a transcendent Supreme with a secondary assistant directing and creating, called Demiurge or world-soul or *logos* (that is, 'mind' or 'rational principle'). Such monotheisms were compatible with practical observance of ordinary religion, though it was often quietly reinterpreted: sacrifice was offered, not because the gods need it, but as a token of the just man's prayer; the poetic myths of the gods' conduct and misconduct are allegorical fictions which are really about human psychology and morals. Such ideas not only formed a point of contact to which the Christian preacher might appeal, as St Paul does in the speech attributed to him in Athens (he quotes monotheistic sentiments from two Greek writers at Acts 17.28); they would also shape the expression of biblical truth as it was elaborated by Christian thinkers schooled in the classics of Greece and Rome.

A note is perhaps required about education. In spite of the puritan criticisms of such philosophers as Plato, the Greek classical poets, especially Homer and the great tragic poets, continued to constitute a large part of the education of literate minds. For the Latins Vergil and Terence fulfilled the same role. With them would go some reading in philosophical and especially oratorical books, and some history would be studied: Cicero and Sallust were especially popular. Greek education, and even more Latin, while it included grammar, arithmetic, music and astronomy, laid great emphasis on rhetoric, the art of presenting a case, of praising, or criticizing, of accusing and defending. Such skills were essential for anyone engaged in public life, and constantly shaped the forms of expression used by philosophers. There was no other medium of education available. This was why, in spite of the polytheistic beliefs implied, Christians had their children educated in the classics, and continued to function as teachers of this traditional material. When the Emperor Julian ('the Apostate') in 362 banned Christians from teaching classics, the effect on the Churches threatened to be disastrous; it was his most effective measure in his attempt to bring back pagan religion. One way and another Christians tried to vindicate the classical writers, in order to justify their continued use in education: so Clement of Alexandria tried to show the relevance of Greek culture to the meaning of Christianity, and from Constantine onwards Vergil was promoted as one who had (in *Eclogue* 4) predicted the birth and kingdom of Christ. Most Christian theologians were well trained in rhetoric. This often accounts for the way they interpret biblical texts, and for the forms their arguments take; it certainly accounts for the uncharitable vituperation they use about their opponents, which was a skill taught to schoolboys.

Society and government

The society in which the Church spread affected it greatly. The fundamental unit was the family or household (Lat. *familia*, Gk *oikos/oikia*), which affected every person. Most cities were constituted by a number of large households, belonging to persons of distinction who also possessed country houses (villas) as centres of cultivated estates. In such a household the father usually ruled (though we do hear of households apparently headed by women, like Lydia in Acts 16.12–15). His wife and free-born children constituted the kernel of the family. They had privileges and wealth, but also obligations. Their names would be on a municipal list, which required them to perform public functions like repairing buildings and aqueducts or providing a public show with actors and gladiators. There were also land taxes to be met, which would mean exacting money from tenant farmers. To the household would be attached a number of free-born persons with no standing to enable them to constitute a household themselves, though they might in our sense live in families in flats or small houses. These would depend on the wealthier patron for social security and for such things as the education of their sons, and would in return give service of one kind and another when called upon. But the household would largely be run by slaves, and the work on the estates from which the wealth of the family derived was usually done by slaves. The slaves had formally no rights, though they were occasionally protected from harshest abuse by legislation. But owners gained from keeping slaves happy and healthy; all else apart, contented slaves would breed and supply a new generation of home-born servants and labourers. Some slaves progressed educationally, still working for their masters. But many also were allowed to earn money for themselves and buy their liberty: formal legal process existed, based on the temples, for manumission (setting free) of slaves. The manumitted slave usually continued as a member of the family, working for his old owner as a 'freedman'. But treatment varied enormously, and a slave might grow up well treated as one of the family, or might be a recent prisoner of war forced to do unhealthy and disagreeable work under harsh conditions till he died. A poor man's slave was perhaps in the worst predicament, since there was no support if he were ill or too old to work.

The city was the focus of civilized living. It was where the economic resources of the countryside were served by the technical skills of craftsmen, and it was the place for the social and political business of law, commerce, education, religion, theatre, sports and that indefinable human intercourse which made the central square or forum of an ancient city its vital heart. Cities could be free and independent, and there were free cities within the Roman Empire which preserved some elements of self-government, with a council and a budget. Emperors could call upon cities for financial support for the court and the army, particularly when they were passing through or faced with grave emergencies. This in turn led to exactions upon the householders of the city, which were passed down the social chain to become severe hardship for the poor. While many rich persons stumped up, and some even rejoiced to lavish gifts on public statues and buildings to give themselves an everlasting name, there was usually competition to win exemptions from public liabilities. During the early Christian period the rich got richer and the poor poorer most of the time.

The Empire of Rome was huge, extending in most of the early Christian period from north Britain to southern Egypt, from Mauretania (Morocco) to Mesopotamia, and included Asia Minor (most of modern Turkey) and all Europe south and west of the Rhine and Danube, and some beyond. It was in essence a vast military dictatorship. The republican institutions of the ancient city-state of Rome had finally broken under the strain of coping with an increasing dominion. The great generals defied and manipulated its legalities, and finally fought to possess power and protect their own interests. From the deluge of civil wars the adopted son of Julius Caesar, known as Octavian or Caesar, and ultimately given the title Augustus, emerged as sole ruler and restorer of the fatherland. He reigned alone from 31 BC to AD 14, and is regarded as founder of the Empire, having introduced a new constitution in 27 BC. As *Imperator* or Emperor (a military title meaning 'Commander') he was head of the military and directly governor of a number of provinces, ruling them through members of his own household. Other provinces in principle continued to be governed by members of the Roman Senate elected to magistracies and then sent abroad; but here also the Emperor's will prevailed, since as Chief Citizen (*Princeps*) he could not be defied. In the Latin world the title King (*Rex*) was not used, but Caesar's power was absolute, his commands amounting to law, and after death (if he were not damned as a tyrant and all his acts repealed) he was officially deified, and a priesthood and cult set up in his memory. But among the Greek speakers, who predominated especially in the East, he was called King (Gk *Basileus*) as the great rulers of Persia and Macedon had been, and received the divine adulation customary in the past for Hellenistic kings and princes, and for Roman governors of the old republican days. After AD 14 the succession remained within the family of Augustus and his wife, with various complications and misfortunes, until the reign of Nero, 54–68. He was assassinated and regarded as a bad thing, and military chiefs competed for the throne. After him a new dynasty began with Vespasian (68–79).

Two aspects of the system which impinged heavily upon everyday life were the military and the bureaucracy. The military could impose themselves upon ordinary citizens with impunity, officially or unofficially. Passers-by could be forced to carry luggage, cities to provide accommodation. Usually the soldiers lived in separate camps and on retirement were settled in 'colonies', where veterans with land and a civic organization of their own could still be useful in a military emergency. Some important cities were garrison towns, like Caesarea Maritima in Palestine, the chief city of that country. In the third century AD the military were able to make and break emperors too easily, with successful generals from the frontiers being proclaimed by their troops and overthrowing the emperor who had sent them out. Reforms put in hand by Diocletian (284–305) restored stability by dividing power, but the succession continued to be settled by the officer corps, often with some bloodshed. The bureaucracy began ostensibly as a military administration, and certainly served at times to choke the wheels of government. Emperors would repeatedly decree the same thing, because nothing happened, as persons already in local power prevented changes which might affect their position. Such persons also had a way of enriching themselves by using what power they had in response to bribes: there was a great deal of graft, which came to be recognized as normal.

The Empire and Christianity

Roman society coped with other gods quite easily. Philosophers could question the existence or function of the traditional gods; travellers, soldiers and all sorts of others could introduce new cults. The Jews and Samaritans could stay with their ancestral cults without direct interference. In all cases riot, fraud or rebellion could of course provoke the state; but it was not religious persecution as such. With Christianity it was different. For most of its first three hundred years it appears to have been in some sense illegal (see below), and people were at times severely punished for being Christians. But the basis of this before 249 is uncertain, and the pressure varied greatly from place to place and from time to time.

During the first century we have evidence of occasional persecution, but detail is scarce. The sources include some of the earliest New Testament material: 1 Thess. 1.14–16; Rom. 8.35–6; Mark 13.9–13 par.; Acts 6.8 – 8.1; 12.1–3; Rev. 2.13. With this should be taken the case of James the brother of Jesus, known from Josephus, *Ant.* 20.9.1 (*NE* 1), and from apocryphal Christian sources. Like some of the New Testament material, this blames persecution on Jews. There may be truth in that, especially while the context is Palestine. But it was probably exaggerated by defenders of Christianity; to blame the Jews for causing disturbances and attacking Christians is one way of pleading that Christians themselves should be acquitted by the Roman authorities. Such a tendency is already present throughout Acts, where Jews cause persecution and Romans (when honest) prevent it: see for instance Acts 18.12–17.

We have slight evidence from Suetonius of imperial action against Christians about 49 and 64 (*Claudius* 25.4; *Nero* 16.2 [*NE* 1–3]. More interesting is the account by Tacitus of the persecution under Nero (*Ann.* 15.44.2–8 [*NE* 2–3]). This reveals more about the attitudes of Tacitus, an educated official of high birth, than about what actually happened. He says that, after a fire which cleared a large area of Rome for Nero's building schemes, the emperor diverted the blame onto the Christians, and describes the hideous cruelties he inflicted, which shocked the public, even though the Christians were 'hated for their abominations' and deserved punishment. Tacitus is clear that they were convicted of arson: first a few, then an 'immense multitude' informed on by the few. But he says that they were convicted 'not so much of arson as of hatred of the human race'. From this two important points emerge: (1) Nero's persecution provided no legal precedent for persecution, as is often supposed, because it was punishment for a specific crime of arson in Rome (quite apart from the likelihood that Nero's legal acts were invalidated when his memory was damned after his death); (2) an intelligent and serious Roman like Tacitus about 115 believed that Christians hated their fellows and were guilty of 'abominations'. Colour is added to his account from the Christian side by 1 Clement 5–6 (*NE* 4), and the deaths of Peter and Paul in Rome are reported by Eusebius *HE* 2.25.5–8 (*NE* 5); but neither illuminates the causes of persecution.

The most useful documents for this are Pliny's letter 10.96 from Bithynia of about 112 to the emperor Trajan, and Trajan's reply (*NE* 18–21). Pliny seeks clarification of his duty as governor in the matter of Christians. Never having investigated Christianity before, he does not know whether all persons are to be treated alike (or only ringleaders punished), whether to pardon those who stop being Christian, and whether it is the name, or only the 'secret crimes connected with the name', that are punished. He had executed people for persistent, obstinate Christianity. He had released accused persons prepared to prove they were not Christians by sacrificing to the gods, supplicating the emperor's statue with incense and wine, and cursing Christ, 'things which (so it is said) those who are really Christians cannot be made to do'. He then goes on to describe his investigation of the secret crimes, which he has done by questioning ex-Christians and by torturing 'two maid-servants who were called deaconesses' (presumably supposing these would give way easily). He found that when they met they took oaths to behave well, sang a hymn to Christ, and took 'ordinary and harmless food'; he found nothing worse than 'a perverse and extravagant superstition'. We know that one of the popular beliefs about Christians was that they ate human flesh ('Thyestean banquets'; see Eusebius *HE* 5.1.14 [*NE* 36]; Athenagoras *Leg.* 3 [*NE* 67]); doubtless this was the crime Pliny was looking for. In his reply Trajan approves Pliny's action, but says that no official hunt for Christians should be conducted, and anonymous accusations should be ignored. This means that he approved Pliny's action in executing obstinate Christians 'for the name', and releasing those prepared to deny their faith and prove their denial on test. Christianity is therefore itself punishable by death, but not to be prosecuted too vigorously. Perhaps the presence of ex-Christians showed that the superstition might perish of its own accord. Certainly Pliny's investigations reveal that the alleged abominations lacked evidence. If it had not, ex-Christians could not have been acquitted. The allegations perhaps arose because the Christians were secretive and self-isolating, and preached the impending destruction of non-believers by their God; popular resentment would fix rumours of cannibalism and incest upon them, as well as the 'atheism' which led them to repudiate the gods. It becomes a steady theme of Christian apologetic that Christians should not be punished for the mere name, but judged by the quality of their lives.

Various theories have been advanced to account for the apparent illegality of Christianity. The idea that Nero about 64 made a decree against Christianity has little to commend it, popular though it might have been among Christian apologists, who could claim that persecution was begun by that most notorious tyrant. It has been suggested that the punishment was purely for contumacity before the magistrate – contempt of court – partly on the strength of Pliny's remarks about punishing 'obstinacy and unbending perversity'; but although occasionally a Christian provoked a magistrate, usually he would need to be accused of something before the contempt could arise. It could be treason. But the case of the Scillitan martyr is a rare one, who, on being asked to 'swear by the genius of our lord the emperor', replied, 'I do not recognize the empire of this world' (*Pass. Scill.* = *NE* 44). It is nearer the mark to observe that popular dislike of Christians could flare up, especially in times of disaster, stress or danger, and a riot might develop unless the authorities intervened to punish the offenders. This happened because Christians by definition had repudiated the gods, on whom prosperity and peace depended; they were also supposedly guilty of enormities like cannibalism and incest which offended the same gods. Public disaster was a sign that the heavens were displeased, and the Christians were thought to be to blame: 'If the Tiber reaches the walls, if the Nile does not rise to the fields, if the sky does not move [drought] or the earth does [earthquake], if there is famine, if there is plague, the cry is at once, "The Christians to the lion!"' (Tertullian, *Apol.* 40.2 [*NE* 158]). Even educated men like Tacitus and Fronto (see Minicius Felix, *Oct.* 9.6; 31.2 [*NE* 131]) believed in the abominations, but those who did not might still believe that Christianity was fundamentally destructive of a society which depended ultimately on the 'peace of the gods'. Christians were not like Jews, who could be excused for following their ancestral tradition and not taking part in other people's religion. Christians repudiated the gods they belonged to, and sometimes advertised the fact; it would lead them to refuse offerings and oaths if they were tested with them as Pliny tested those who claimed not to be Christians. They might be ignored if inconspicuous; but at the least sign of disorder, or if an accusation were made for private reasons (Justin *Apol.* 2.2 [*NE* 30–31]), they could find themselves before a magistrate having their loyalty and obedience tested, often with fatal outcome. We must consider how people came to adopt this way of life, and how they prepared for it.

2

COMMUNITY AND MORALITY

Conversion and preparation

Many people changed from other religions to Christianity, but as in other ages there is no clear general reason for conversion. Justin could claim about 150 AD that the constancy, patience and business integrity of Christians persuaded others to change their ways and join them (*Apol.* 1.16 [*NE* 59]). There is little reason to doubt that this was so; and the worse the reputation of Christians, the greater the impact of genuine goodness when it was discerned. Tertullian argued that the courage of Christian martyrs caused the conversion of spectators (*Apol.* 50.12-16), an idea already in Justin (*Dial.* 110.3-4 [*NE* 59]), and confirmed by incidents recorded in martyr-stories. Justin traced his own conversion as the end of an intellectual exploration which led him from other philosophies to Platonism and then to the Scriptures, where the fulfilment of the ancient prophecies was the decisive argument. This account is probably in part fictitious, and such an intellectual pilgrimage has never been a common cause of conversions. Celsus, a serious critic of Christianity of the late second century, is critical of the way badly educated Christians won over women and especially children in defiance of their husbands, fathers and schoolmasters, encouraging them to 'go along with the women and little children who are their playfellows to the wooldresser's shop, or to the cobbler's or washerwoman's shop, that they may learn perfection. And by saying this they persuade them' (Origen, *Against Cels.* 3.55 [*NE* 135]). This is a sore point with him, and reflects reality. Women were often converted first (like the wife in the martyr-story, Justin *Apol.* 2.2 [*NE* 30–31]), and tried to bring up their children to believe (like Monnica the mother of Augustine). Some would be converted as the result of an act of charity or a miraculous cure attributed to the God of the Christians. But if anything made an impact on scoffers and unbelievers, it was the fearful warning of judgement. The Christians taught that the whole system of false religion and its adherents were shortly to be swept away by the God of Israel. As the companions of Perpetua were marched into the arena for torture and death they made signs to the judges which unmistakably meant, 'You, us; God, you' (*Acts of Perpetua* 18). The verb to be supplied might be 'watch' or it might be 'kill': either way, the message was unmistakable, and in such circumstances the courage of the martyrs would certainly move some to admiration and fear.

But suppose a non-Christian is seriously interested in the message, whatever the motive, what happens? A better-informed enquirer might attend a 'school' run by a Christian teacher, like that of Justin in Rome (*Martyrdom of Justin* 3 [*NE* 32–33]). Sooner or later he would be regarded as reliable enough to be taken to the place where the Christians assembled: often this could not be done immediately, in case he was an informer. He would then be formally registered as a 'hearer' (*auditor*) or 'catechumen' (= 'under instruction'), and his name recorded with that of his sponsor. Men, women and children would be treated alike, except that little children were obviously dependent on parents or guardians. The enquirer would then be admitted to some kinds of assembly. Practice certainly varied from place to place. In earliest times baptism might follow very rapidly on conversion and repentance, whether of Jews (Acts 2.41, though it does not actually say that the water-baptism was the same day) or of Gentiles (Acts 8.35–8; 16.30–3). But these cases are not easy to parallel after apostolic times, and in any case it is clear that even Apostles passed on rules about conduct to their converts, as Paul did at Thessalonica (1 Thess. 4.1–3). All the evidence after the New Testament suggests a substantial – usually a long – period of instruction before one might be admitted to the fellowship. But it should be said that the catechumen was regarded as a Christian, and was expected to live a good life, even to the point of martyrdom, which would count as his baptism if it should come about.

The catechumen would be expected to attend for instruction. The catechumen in *Didache* had to learn the *Two ways*, a moral code which begins, 'There are two ways, one of life and one of death, and there is a great difference between the two ways.' Most of what follows describes the way of life, beginning with a command to love God and one's neighbour, including snippets from the Sermon on the Mount and an expanded version of the last five of the Ten Commandments; the way of death is a long list of vices of every kind. It is this moral instruction which must be 'recited' before a person may be presented for baptism at the beginning of *Did.* 7 (*NE* 9). This moral instruction is notable for its lack of specific doctrinal content. It should be compared with passages on Christian behaviour in the New Testament, like Matt. 5—7 (to which *Didache* shows close parallels) and Rom. 12.3–21. It is notable that the same document of the *Two ways* appears embedded in the *Epistle of Barnabas* 18–20 as the ways of light and darkness, and in some other Christian documents, and that enough features appear in the document known as *The rule* (or *The manual of discipline:* IQS 3.13-4.26) to show that the *Two ways* derives from Jewish proselyte-instruction. This document comes from the Jewish baptizing sect which had a monastery at Qumran, whose library partly survives in the Dead Sea Scrolls. No doctrinal teaching is mentioned in the baptismal preparation described by *Didache*: the test of readiness for baptism is the upright life, and knowing its rules. But the use of the three names at baptism, and the prayers which are recommended for daily and eucharistic use, imply some such knowledge (*Did.* 7–10 [*NE* 10]).

Though practice varied greatly, one common feature was a division of catechumens into those registered and under instruction in a general way, and those under immediate preparation for baptism. Origen early in the third century implies such an arrangement (*Cels.* 3.51 [*NE* 209–210]). For two or three years a convert would be expected to attend regularly, learning the rules of Christian behaviour, and then would be prepared with advanced instruction and subjected to scrutinies during the months immediately preceding baptism.

The first part of this course would certainly include moral instructions, rather as outlined in the *Didache*, but with more detail. Matters of conduct occupy a surprisingly large proportion of Christian literature in the first three centuries, as witness the *Paidagogos* of Clement of Alexandria and the numerous disciplinary works of Tertullian; this reflects the amount of moral training which went on. It was far more than a matter of a generally good and loving attitude, though that was strongly urged. Some things were completely banned by God's law. Killing human beings in any way was forbidden, including all kinds of abortion, the exposure of babies (then a regular substitute for birth control), taking part in the bloody sports of the arena even as a spectator, and killing on military service. Fornication and adultery were grave offences, including homosexual and pederastic practices and all extra-marital sexual activity, with some variety of views about whether the baptized were required or recommended to stay celibate, and whether sexual intercourse in marriage was permissible only in order to conceive children. Idolatry was banned in any form, which included attendance at sports, theatres and public occasions when gods were invoked; it also meant excluding professions like acting and plastic arts (the standard sculptures mostly representing gods). Integrity with money, and the giving of alms, were essential, and probably commended the faith in a world full of bribery. The elementary instruction included training in regular prayer (the Lord's Prayer three times a day in the *Didache*) and the observance of light fasts each Wednesday and Friday.

But there was always a theological back-drop to this training. It was undertaken because God, the God of Scripture, had stated his will and declared his impending judgement. It thus formed part of the elementary training to hear the words of Scripture and to have them expounded. The ordinary catechumen would hear these readings and expositions Sunday by Sunday at the church meeting or *synaxis*. After what could be a long session of texts and sermons, the catechumens would be blessed and dismissed before the main work of the eucharistic offering began; with them would go some others, such as baptized persons being disciplined for grave sins, and *energumens*, the mentally sick, who were thought to be demon-possessed. City churches, like those in Alexandria, were able to offer weekday teaching. The Scripture would be systematically expounded; Origen as catechist there appears to have begun a cycle of Old Testament homilies intended to last two or three years. Such instruction begins with Genesis, the decisive point where the one Creator and Lawgiver taught by Christians was declared in the face of polytheistic religion and Greek philosophy. It is no surprise to find that the first few chapters are the most discussed and argued-over of the whole Bible, and that exegetes of all schools find there the essential clues to every doctrinal system.

Coming to baptism

After learning morality and the essentials of the Bible, and proving acceptable in conduct, a catechumen might make a request for baptism. We have a description of what happened from a Roman theologian called Hippolytus about AD 200. The candidates are examined individually to see 'whether they lived piously while catechumens, whether they honoured the widows [that is, contributed to charity], whether they visited the sick, whether they fulfilled every good work'; if so they may 'hear the gospel', apparently not previously allowed in this church, and must attend for daily exorcism (for this and what follows, see Hippolytus, *Apostolic Tradition* 20-1). In other churches other tests might be applied. It now seems fairly certain that in much of the Syriac-speaking East candidates for baptism would be expected to commit themselves to celibacy; if already married, they must live continent with their partners after baptism. This practice came to be treated as 'Encratite heresy' by most of the Church, and inevitably where it operated most Christians lived as catechumens, probably getting baptized at the end of their lives.

Hippolytus writes of daily exorcism. Exorcism is casting out evil spirits. Readers of the first three gospels know that possession by evil spirits or demons was widespread. Their presence was felt by all kinds of people. Most acutely it was felt by Christians, for whom all the heathen gods were demons; the protectors, saviours, sponsors of the society they lived in were all malignant spirits who applied pressure through the state, through families, through education, through all the things most people accepted as part of life. Exorcism was performed by directly challenging the demon in the name of Christ to depart, often with some ceremony like blowing on the face or laying on hands. This is probably the 'sign that they have been purified' mentioned by Origen (*Against Cels.* 3.51 [*NE* 209]). Exorcism could be performed by a senior minister, a presbyter or bishop; but most churches had junior officers called exorcists, who might have special gifts for managing the mentally sick or deficient, but were probably in most cases merely competent in the minor ritual of exorcising catechumens.

Most baptisms took place at the Easter Vigil; this practice was not universal, since other festivals and occasions were used. It probably originated as much in the practical educational requirements in larger churches as in the symbolism soon attached to it, since baptism meant participating in the death and rising again of Christ which Easter celebrates. The period of exorcism and instruction became Lent. An intense preparation began with a wash and a fast for two days. 'Before the baptism let the baptizer and him that is baptized fast, and such others as can; and you shall bid the person to be baptized to fast for one or two days before' (*Did.* 7.4 [*NE* 10]). For Easter baptisms two days' fasting coincided with the paschal fast, which lasted through the Friday and Saturday, and was observed by the whole church. On the Saturday Rome had a final exorcism by the bishop: he warned off the spirits, laid hands on the kneeling candidates and 'sealed' forehead, ear and nose. The paschal night of Saturday was spent in vigil and readings. At cock-crow the water was blessed (a flowing fountain was always preferred), and the candidates stripped; there was usually some provision for modesty, chiefly the conduct of baptism in a private room or baptistery apart from the main meeting house of the church; but the oiling and washing were done naked, and one of the recorded functions of deaconesses is assisting at the baptism of women. Children were baptized, that is 'bathed' first, then men, then women (who must put off their jewellery). Our records of full-scale Western baptisms from about 200 agree with Hippolytus, recording that each candidate was first oiled, then bathed three times, then oiled again (see *NE* 141–3). This process resembled that in the public baths so familiar in the Roman world, where a coarser oil was used for cleansing, then the body was washed with hot and cold plunges, and finally refined and scented oil was applied and clean clothes put on. Similarly the church used two oils, one for exorcism used before the washing, and one for thanksgiving afterwards, the washing itself consisting of three complete plunges; and clean festal clothes were put on. In Hippolytus, the candidates were then brought (presumably from the baptistery) to the bishop in the presence of the people, where they received a further token unction with the oil of thanksgiving, and the laying on of hands, and were then admitted to the eucharistic prayer and communion for the first time. Not all this was followed everywhere. The Syrian churches laid more emphasis on the oil, which was applied only once and before the baptism. And in the West, infants were soon being baptized very young, just as the sick and dying might be, in their homes; they might be brought to the bishop for the final ceremonies later, a circumstance which is related to the origin of confirmation.

With the oil of exorcism the candidate makes one very serious statement: 'I renounce thee, Satan, and all thy servants, and all thy works.' The believer has turned away from the old world, never to be compromised again. The great weight laid on moral testings and on exorcisms throughout reflects the sharp break being made with the social environment: the Church was a people apart, and its members must be unbending. This was what was so shocking to their critics, and made the name of 'Christian' decisive for persecutor and matryr alike.

There are questions attached to the three washings. Before each dipping the candidate says 'I believe' to a question, and the questions in Hippolytus together constitute one of the earliest creeds we know, but in interrogative form:

1. 'Do you believe in God, the Father Almighty?'

2. 'Do you believe in Christ Jesus, the Son of God, who was born by the Holy Spirit of the Virgin Mary, and was crucified under Pontius Pilate, and was dead and buried, and rose again the third day, alive from the dead, and ascended into heaven, and sat at the right hand of the Father, and will come to judge the living and the dead?'

3. 'Do you believe in the Holy Spirit, in the holy Church, and in the resurrection of the flesh?'

The obvious feature of this is that it is trinitarian, in the sense that the candidate acknowledges God the Father, Christ Jesus the Son of God, and the Holy Spirit. It conforms to the prescription found in two early texts, Matt. 28.19 and *Didache* 7.1–3 (*NE* 9–10), that baptisms should be 'In the name of the Father and of the Son and of the Holy Spirit', although those words were not used, as they later are, as a formula. Not all baptisms fitted this rule. The Marcosians, whose mission in Gaul prompted Irenaeus to write his *Against Heresies* about 180, are alleged to have used the formula: 'Into the unknown Father of the universe, into truth the mother of all things [= Holy Spirit?], into him who descended on Jesus [= Christ?], into union and redemption and communion with the powers' (Irenaeus, *Adv. Haer.* 1.21.3 [*NE* 91]. More common and perhaps more ancient was the simple, 'In the name of the Lord Jesus [or, Jesus Christ]'. This practice was known among Marcionites and orthodox; it is certainly the subject of controversy in Rome and Africa about 254, as the anonymous tract *De rebaptismate* ('On rebaptism') shows. It is implied by Acts 10.46–8;19.5. The last passage is especially interesting, since its context is 'John's baptism', 'the baptism of repentance'. This is regarded as insufficient, and it is baptism 'in the name of the Lord Jesus' which is associated with the gift of Holy Spirit. Plainly the name of Jesus, and the reference to Holy Spirit, are in this case what make a baptism true and apostolic; so even with the shorter formula the trinitarian thought is implied. In this as well as in the longer Hippolytan baptismal creed the shape of Christian confession is already implied: one God, one Lord Jesus Christ, one Spirit. Finally, we may suppose that the words recorded in Hippolytus have been developed: the references in the third limb to 'the holy Church and the resurrection of the flesh' may reflect the desire to establish the true Church against heretical groups, and to assert the doctrine of bodily resurrection against the (Platonic) belief in some Christian circles in the immortal soul. Some of the words about Jesus Christ may also have been developed to counteract heresy.

When the presbyter anoints the candidate immediately after washing he says, 'I anoint you with holy oil in the name of Jesus Christ' (the bishop later uses a trinitarian formula). This is significant because the title 'Christ' itself means 'Anointed', and for some Christians it is anointing ('chrism') which makes a Christian. Since Christians are also anointed with Holy Spirit, this ceremony can be seen as representing or imparting the gift of the Spirit. The *Gospel of Philip* insists that not water but anointing makes a Christian (*NHC* ii.3; see especially *NHLE* 139 = *NE* 70). But it is never clear whether that (gnostic?) document is distinguishing from water-baptism a spiritual gift, the true knowledge of 'real Christians', or a ceremony of chrismation.

After the bishop's anointing of candidates, they are allowed for the first time to pray with the faithful; until this point that was not allowed. Praying together was limited in this way, because the prayers of the faithful, who are in tune with God's will, are especially potent (see for example Tertullian, *Apol.* 30.5 [*NE* 161]). After the prayers, which might be at some length, a kiss is exchanged, the kiss of peace. Again the catechumens were not allowed to kiss the faithful before baptism, because they were not pure (Hippolytus, *Apostolic Tradition* 18.3; Justin, *Apol.* 1.65 [*NE* 63–64]). One function of the kiss was security: the faithful were members of a family and knew each other like a cluster of Mediterranean people today saluting their uncles, aunts and cousins; a stranger would not be recognized. Clement of Alexandria worried about the scandal the kiss might cause if salaciously abused (*Paed.* III.xi.81.2–3 [*NE* 183]).

The eucharistic offering

Then came the 'oblation'. Hippolytus emphasized that those coming for baptism were not allowed to bring anything with them except their eucharistic offering. This might be bread and wine, but apparently could include all sorts of other produce, as it did for all the faithful. By the middle of the third century the oblation seems to have been limited to bread and wine, and occasionally other things for liturgical use such as oil. But in 200 there was still sufficient memory of an earlier phase of offering when the principal corporate act of Christians was a meal (as in 1 Cor. 11.17–34 and probably *Did.* 9–10 [*NE* 10]). And the point of this meal was that each brought what he had and shared it with the others; that made it the 'Lord's supper', since Christ did the same with the bread and wine on the night when he was given up to death, and his passion itself was a similar sacrifice, a giving for others. Before long the bread was seen as representing Christ's Body and the cup (usually of wine) as representing the Blood, a connection he had himself made in New Testament texts; the meal and other offerings consequently came to be treated as the less important or less serious part of the rite. The faithful of *Didache* 13 were expected to make over a tenth of all produce to their clergy to sustain them and provide opportunity for corporate charity; such gifts would be offered at the assembly, and would be the subject of a thanksgiving (Gk *eucharistia*), and would be shared as the leader decreed. Perhaps originally it was just this kind of giving which constituted the 'Body of Christ', that is the Church as a corporate society, rather than specifically the bread by itself. Certainly the offering had to be pure; the unbaptized and the excommunicate were not allowed to offer.

At the oblation the newly baptized would put in their own

offering with the others, and the bishop would offer the thanksgiving (*eucharistia*), a prayer which might be quite short, or might range widely and include various intercessions. Early accounts are available in *Didache* 9-10 (*NE* 9-10), Justin *Apol.* 1.65 (*NE* 63-64) and Hippolytus *Ap. Trad.* 4-6 (this includes a blessing of oil, cheese and olives, but is a special text for the ordination of a bishop). The prayer gives thanks for the privileges of the gospel, and prays for the protection and consummation of the universal Church. In the early days there was great freedom for prophets and bishops, but custom and the power of the written text came to prevail from the fourth century onwards. Once the gifts had been 'eucharistized' by the thanksgiving, they were distributed to those present, and some was carried by appointed ministers ('deacons') to the sick and other absentees. The newly baptized in some churches had special symbolic drinks of milk and honey (for the promised land) and water (for inner cleansing); but these died out as the Eucharist itself became more uniform.

As the Eucharist became limited to the bread and wine as Christ's sacrificial Body and Blood, features of the original Eucharist were developed in other ways. Common meals without the bread and wine sacrificially offered were held, and especially were arranged as an act of charity by richer members of the church. Such a meal was called an *agape* ('a charity'), and could be quite formal. At the same time the church developed its common purse for charitable purposes, and this had a significant influence on the way it was organized (see Tertullian's defensive comments in *Apol.* 39.5-6 [*NE* 163-64]). In fact the local church was in many ways a charitable society. The vulnerable members of society, such as widows, orphans, surplus babies and elderly slaves, could be sure of a livelihood if they belonged to the church. There the needy had a family which would see that they were not destitute. In 251 a bishop of Rome could boast that his church included not only 162 clergy and servants, but 'above fifteen hundred widows and persons in distress, all of whom are supported by the grace and loving kindness of the Master' (Eusebius *HE* 6.43.11 [*NE* 232]); this means that the gifts of the faithful provided for them all. Similarly Cyprian advised that a converted actor could not be allowed to continue in his profession, but should be found other employment; otherwise the church concerned must give him a pension. In the world where both poverty and riches were increasing, membership therefore had material advantages for many. This had several important consequences: it made the penalty of being deprived of membership (excommunication) a very severe one; it gave great power to those who controlled membership; and it set a high premium on financial integrity as a qualification for office, since any taint of the corruption affecting society at large was intolerable among the saints.

3
THE MESSAGE AND THE MESSENGERS

The canon of Scripture

Christianity was the religion of a book. The training of new Christians and the life of the Community centred on the reading of holy texts. But the Bible was not a single book readily available in bookshops. Its name means 'the books' (Gk *ta biblia*), and it was a collection of different books, commonly referred to as 'the writings' or 'Scriptures' (*hai graphai*). But what books?

When the apostles began preaching Christ their first hearers were Jews, whether in Palestine, where perhaps one in seven of the Jewish population of the Empire lived, or in the much more numerous 'Dispersion', among the Greek-speaking populations of the Empire. Jews occupied a separate quarter of the greatest city of the East, Alexandria, had a shanty-town outside Rome, and were in places considerable country landowners or urban craftsmen. Christian preaching would begin in their synagogues, and from the Scriptures read there. The object of the Christian preacher was to prove that the promised Messiah [= Christ] was Jesus, as in the scene portrayed in Acts 13.14–42 (compare 9.20–2). The synagogue would have the Law, that is the books of Moses (the Pentateuch, the first five books of the present Bible) reverently preserved and honoured. What it had beyond that varied, but would consist of the Prophets (the historical books and prophets as now known), and the Writings, which included the Psalms and books of wisdom like Proverbs. But in these latter categories much variation was possible. The Sadducees who ran the Jerusalem temple acknowledged only Moses, as did the Samaritans at their shrine. The synagogue-teachers such as the Pharisees used the Prophets and Writings too. Some time after the Christian preaching began, and after the fall of Jerusalem in AD 70, the rabbis established a list or 'canon' (that is a 'rule' or 'delimitation') of the books now regularly seen as the core of the Christian Old Testament canon. This list excluded a number of books and chapters widely used in synagogues before, such books as Ecclesiasticus and the books of Maccabees, and chapters like Susanna and Bel and the dragon attached to Daniel, a number of which survive as the Christian Apocrypha or Deuterocanonical books. In some cases, as in the long additions to Esther, the additions existed only in Greek and not in the Hebrew original. But this raises a further question of biblical language.

In Palestine, Syria and Babylonia Christians moved among people who spoke some dialect of Aramaic (later Syriac), and in synagogues the Hebrew Scriptures were explained or read in a free translation called *Targum*. But everywhere else, and to some extent in those places too, Greek was the language of preaching. In many parts a translation of the Law into Greek was in use. It was in existence before 200 BC. Because of a legend that it was miraculously translated at Alexandria by seventy elders it was called 'The seventy' or *Septuagint*, and is represented by the Latin number LXX (*septuaginta*). Other books existed in Greek versions; Christians came to regard a complete set of these as *Septuagint*, though the original legend affected only the books of Moses. These versions varied greatly in closeness to the Hebrew original: Moses and the Psalms were closest; some books like Proverbs, Job and Esther were in part freely rewritten; in some places they were based on Hebrew readings superseded by the official Massoretic text of later Judaism. Even the closer versions reflected sophisticated Greek religious ideas in places. Where God states his name to Moses in somewhat obscure Hebrew as 'I am who I am' (Exod. 3.14) the Greek translator rendered, 'I am he who is' (*ho on*), reflecting the philosophical concept of 'What is' (*to on*), that which truly and permanently exists as distinct from the becoming and changeable. Where human beings are said to 'see' God, the Greek makes them 'appear before him' (Exod. 24.10 and elsewhere).

These Greek versions had become the foundation of religion in the synagogues, and had inspired a considerable literature. Notably the Alexandrian scholar Philo (*c.*20 BC–AD 50) had written detailed expositions of the books of the Law, in which he made Moses the teacher of an ultimate philosophic way of life. Ideas, especially ideas about God, unacceptable to Greek philosophy, inaccurate histories and impossible laws, were all explained in terms of spiritual allegories (in the same way as Stoic philosophers had interpreted unworthy activities of gods in Homer). The rabbis however laid the foundations of modern Judaism on the Hebrew text after the fall of Jerusalem in AD 70, and the old Greek versions were discarded for formal synagogue use. But since most Jews spoke Greek and not Hebrew, some translations were needed; in the early centuries of Christianity three new versions were in circulation, bearing the names of Theodotion, Symmachus and Aquila, which were more accurate. Christians meanwhile stuck to the old text, and sometimes found in it renderings which helped their argument. They were in fact responsible for its preservation, as also of the Jewish Greek writers like Philo and Josephus, whose books were for various reasons useful to Christian scholars and exegetes.

The earliest Christian preaching then usually began in a synagogue with a Greek Bible. If the whole synagogue accepted the message, as may sometimes have happened, it became a church, books and all. Usually individuals would be converted, and would join converts from the state gods to form a new congregation. Such a group might have a problem getting hold of texts to read and teach from. They would probably get copies made from another church. This might be a haphazard process, and the new congregation would be dependent on the authority of the originating church as to what was and was not 'Scripture'; in this way from the start principal churches in great centres like Antioch and Rome exercised enormous influence over their lesser neighbours.

Sooner or later learned men would embark on research to identify the true text and the true canon. The earliest example we know is Melito of Sardis in Asia Minor, who was active about 170. Seeking precise information 'about the ancient books, both as to their number and as to their arrangement', he went back to the East, and 'to the place where it was proclaimed and done', and he got a list of 'the books of the old covenant' (Fragment 4 = Eusebius *HE* 4.26.13-14). The list he gives agrees with the shorter Hebrew canon recently established by the rabbis, a fact which confirms the truth of his claim to have visited Palestine. Approximately the same list (with variations of order) was known to Origen later, who was concerned to use in controversy with Jews only those books which the Jews themselves accept (Eusebius *HE* 6.25.1-2). However, he certainly accepted other works from the Greek Bible as a divine authority, like Wisdom and the additions to Daniel, which seem not to have been doubted in the Church till they were challenged by the Jews. This question continued to divide churchmen. The Eastern fathers generally continued to use the larger canon, but from Athanasius onwards (*Festal letter* 39) made a distinction when discussing canonical questions between those books which strictly belonged and those used in a secondary way; exceptionally the great Antiochenes like John Chrysostom and Theodoret made no such discrimination. The Westerns, dominated by Augustine and councils associated with him (Hippo 393; Carthage 397), generally regarded all the books as of equal authority; it was the scholarly work of Jerome, devoted to the restoration of the Hebrew original as the standard, that established the difference between canonical and deutero-canonical (that is, secondary to the main list), and opened the way for the later Protestant rejection of the Apocrypha.

Interpreting Scripture

Having a copy of the old Scriptures was one thing, using it was another. The initial impact of Christian preaching in the synagogue was to fix on a limited string of texts, and to argue that 'the Scriptures are fulfilled' in Jesus Christ and the events surrounding him: Paul summarizes the original gospel as, 'Christ died for our sins in accordance with the Scriptures and was buried, and rose again the third day in accordance with the Scriptures' (1 Cor. 15.3-4). It is easy to spot from the New Testament itself an original core of passages which provided material for controversial argument, like Psalm 110(109) in Mark 12.35-7 and Heb. 5 and 7. The travelling preacher might have carried a small dossier of such extracts with him; he could not have carried a Bible, which would have been far too bulky. Such collections of proof-texts or *Testimonia* ('evidences') were later written up formally; one collection is attributed to Cyprian, for instance. Scholars got to work trying to enlarge the area of text from which testimonies to Christ could be deduced; this is already happening in Hebrews, and there is much argument of this kind in Justin's *Dialogue with Trypho the Jew* from the middle of the second century. But though this was the characteristically Christian use, there was plenty more to be got from the text, of a kind the Jews already found there. The Bible stories provided examples of good life; the warnings and pleas to serve God and not follow idols, to be faithful and moral, were constantly emphasized. 1 Clement is full of this sort of thing, urging obedience to the precepts and law of God; notably in that letter even where words are cited as of Jesus Christ, the source is usually the Old Testament (e.g. 1 Clem. 22).

Biblical interpretation starts and continues in controversy. It starts in dispute with Jews about the meaning of the prophecies, and whether the OT text means that Jesus is the Christ ('Messiah'). Such was the disputation of Apollos at Ephesus (Acts 18.27–8) and the whole pattern of Justin's *Dialogue with Trypho the Jew*. To see Christ in the Scriptures is itself a gift of the Holy Spirit; when someone turns to the Lord the Spirit removes the 'veil' which prevents Jews from understanding Moses correctly (2 Cor. 3.12–18). It therefore requires both learning and inspiration, beyond the ability of ordinary believers, to understand and expound God's words. Those so blessed emerged as leaders. To understand how doctrine developed from the Bible, this process must be understood too.

Church leaders: Didache

The first leaders were the apostles (rarely called 'evangelists', bringers of good news) who brought the message from God to each place. The original sense of 'apostle' (Gk *apostolos*) is uncertain, but it apparently means 'one sent', that is a 'commissioner' or 'missionary'; the first apostles were sent by Christ personally, but the word could be used more loosely of agents sent by churches to each other or to new places. The gifts of the Spirit which came upon those who believed produced other leaders and officers with different functions. We meet especially prophets and teachers. The early handbook of church order called *Didache* has important guidance about apostles, prophets and teachers (*Did.* 11–13 [*NE* 11–12]). In this one church at least, these were the traditional chief officers, as they seem to have been in St Paul's Corinth (1 Cor. 12.28). *Didache* tries to distinguish true apostles, prophets and teachers from false, and it is clear that the true have a right to be helped with money and food. The apostle is a travelling agent: if he stays more than two nights he is discredited, as he is if he asks for money (11.4–6); the name 'false prophet' in this context merely means 'fraud'. The prophet speaks in the Spirit, and is not to be judged: yet there are false prophets, especially those who do not live according to their own teaching. A prophet may order a 'table' (that is, a meal) while in the Spirit, but if he eats what is produced in response to his inspired message, he is a false prophet; similarly if he asks for money (11.7-12). Prophets are not mere visitors (as apostles are), but settled permanent leaders, entitled to 'first fruits' (probably a tenth part) of all produce, 'for they are your high priests' (13.3). In addition to moral leadership, ordering charitable meals and so forth, the prophet was the inspired leader of prayer: at the eucharistic meal, 'suffer the prophets to give thanks as [*or*, as much as] they will' (10.7). Similar provision is made for teachers (13.2), who were perhaps entrusted with the tradition, and were rather repetiteurs and catechists, teaching converts the kind of thing they needed to know before baptism, rather than speaking from inspiration and originally; they taught the sort of things which *Didache, The Teaching of the Twelve Apostles*, is about. The tests in this book are chiefly to protect the church and its treasury from frauds like the Peregrinus colourfully depicted by the pagan satirist Lucian (*Peregr.* 11-16 [*NE* 128-30]). Elsewhere the activities of prophets are subjected to doctrinal control: in 1 John 4.1-3 the prophet who affirms that Jesus Christ came in the flesh is of God, the one who denies it is antichrist. Such passages indicate why prophecy lost its place, even while some of its functions remained in other church officers. The last book of the Bible, the Revelation to John, is perhaps a typical New Testament prophecy (for the terminology, see Rev. 22.6-10). While fundamentally an orthodox exercise interpreting many Old Testament prophecies in the light of Christ crucified, it is a difficult but powerful work which could easily be misunderstood; and soon persons were claiming inspiration for all sorts of tracts and secret books similar in kind but different in doctrine. Hence as the travelling apostles disappeared and the directly inspired prophets lost their authority, other figures emerged to take command of the churches.

The text of *Didache* already indicates this. It is a compilation, altered and adapted at various periods. Although the main part envisages a church in which apostles, prophets and teachers lead, towards the end we read a direction of another kind. The readers are directed to break bread with thanksgiving every Sunday, after reconciliation of disputes, and 'elect therefore for yourselves bishops and deacons worthy of the Lord, men meek and not covetous, and true and approved; for they also minister unto you the ministry of the prophets and teachers' (14–15.1 [*NE* 12]). Regular gatherings (not just when the prophet commands) demand a more regular ministry, not chosen by a prophetic gift but by approved behaviour, and known to be honest with money ('not covetous'). *Didache* thus represents a transition to a form of government we meet elsewhere: 'bishops and deacons' figure in one epistle of Paul (Phil. 1.1), are implied by 1 Tim. 3.1–13, and are claimed to be a scriptural institution and appointed by God in 1 Clem. 42.4–5 (*NE* 8). These texts are usually taken to imply that in a church governed in this way there was a board of elders (presbyters), who could also be called bishops, and one or more deacons, who helped the presbyter/bishops chiefly in practical ways. But before discussing that, the terminology should be explained.

The word 'elder' or 'presbyter' represents the Greek *presbyteros*, 'an older man'. It can be used of any senior person, but already denoted in Jewish synagogues the older males who formed a governing body. This use is already present in the NT: elders are said to share with apostles the government of the Jerusalem church (Acts 15.6) and to be appointed by Paul in gentile churches (Acts 14.23). But the term seems to be used interchangeably with 'bishop', as at Acts 20.17,28 and Titus 1.5,7. This is so also in 1 Clement, where the deposed 'elders' are apparently bishops (or bishops and deacons). The term 'elder' goes on being used of bishops even when they have taken on a more important and distinct role (so Irenaeus of the bishops of Rome in Eusebius *HE* 5.24.14–16 [*NE* 140]). Later the title 'presbyter' is reserved for the subordinate ministers who assist the bishop, and later still turned into the English word 'priest'.

'Bishop' is the English form of *episkopos*, which seems to mean 'overseer' or perhaps 'inspector'. We do not know how it came to be used of a Christian ministry, but it is natural enough either for a member of a team entrusted with care of others, or of the one in charge by himself of the whole congregation. The possible meaning 'inspector' should not be overlooked. Clement emphasizes inspecting sacrifice as a biblical function of ministry: the good bishop has 'in blameless and holy wise offered the gifts' (1 Clem.

41.2; 44.4 [*NE* 8–9]). One might think of this as meaning simply that he is liturgically sound, or personally pure. But if the sacrifice of the Christian were thought of in terms of giving one's goods into the central pool, to be offered with the thanksgiving of Christ, the bishop is the 'inspector' who makes sure that the sacrifice offered is acceptable to God. In other words, he decides who is qualified to take part in the eucharistic offering and receiving. Beginning as an activity of a presbyter, prophet, apostle or teacher, this role was so important that only the best existing officer could be appointed to it. The power to decide who was fit to offer and receive involved ultimate control over all the congregation's possessions as well as the admission and discipline of members. He determined who should pray and who should preach; as doctrinal disputes increased he might alone do both. Since he would decide whether a visitor was to be admitted, correspondence with other churches was also his responsibility. None of this is incompatible with the other likely meaning of *episkopos*, 'overseer'.

'Deacon' (Gk *diakonos*) means 'minister' or 'servant'. The story of Acts 6.1–6 was told to explain the origin of the office, though in the early days it may have indicated anyone working as an assistant to one of the other ministries. The deacon is soon associated particularly with the bishop as his assistant both in liturgical matters, and particularly in such tasks as distributing the eucharistic gifts and carrying portions to the sick and others unable to be present (Justin *1 Apol.* 65 [*NE* 63–64]). Though in principle serving a secondary, even menial, role, the deacon was close to the bishop, and shared the rise in importance of the bishop. The model of Acts 6 suggests that their administration of charity was intended to free the bishops (here represented by the Twelve) for their preaching and teaching role. But such a diaconate would itself be a powerful position, since the day-to-day letter-writing and administration of money might fall to him; and it seems not at all odd to the writer of Acts that two of his 'deacons' (Stephen and Philip) become very active as preachers too.

Church leaders: Clement of Rome, Ignatius and Irenaeus

In addition to *Didache* we have important evidence, though still slight and fragmentary, from Clement of Rome and Ignatius of Antioch. Clement, probably writing at the end of the first century, deals with a dispute at Corinth, where 'the young' have rebelled against 'the elders' and deposed them. His argument is that the Church functions by mutual charity as a single body, the members submitting to the will of God and to each other. He produces arguments from Scripture to show both that the offices of bishop and deacon were predicted in the OT, and that the principle of a divinely ordered ministry, where functions are divided, was established in the law of Moses and by Jesus Christ through the apostles: his conclusion is that to depose well-behaved bishops is a grave sin (see especially 1 Clem. 40-4 [*NE* 7-9]). He clearly enunciates a doctrine of apostolic succession: the apostles, commanded by Christ, both appointed the first bishops and gave rules for the succession to be carried on. This is a principle which became the norm in Catholic Christianity; but whatever truth it has in it, it seems to have begun as a history discovered from Scripture to fit the known spiritual authority of a traditional ministry. One should note that there is no indication that either in Rome or in Corinth there was a single presiding bishop rather than a board of elders.

The idea of a single bishop in a church is clearly advocated by Ignatius of Antioch in the seven authentic letters which survive from not later than AD 115. His own position appears to have been that of the only or principal bishop in Syrian Antioch, the great centre of the mission to the Gentiles in the Acts of the Apostles. The only earlier figure we know of who might qualify as such a bishop is James, the brother of the Lord, who plays a leading role in the Jerusalem church, even though not an apostle in the sense that Peter or Paul was (Acts 12.17 etc.; 1 Cor. 15.7; Gal. 2.9 etc.). Ignatius writes to various churches in the province of Asia (that is, western Asia Minor), and to Rome, as he is being taken to Rome for trial and execution. He has met various leaders of the churches concerned, and urges them each to overcome their pressing divisions and doctrinal disputes by gathering round the bishop. The errors he opposes are judaizing practices (*Magn.* 8-10 [*NE* 13-14]), and denying the fleshly reality of Jesus Christ (like the false prophets of 1 John 4.1-6; *Trall.* 9-10 [*NE* 14-15]). He pictures each church gathered round its bishop, who is one like God himself, honouring its presbyters who are like the apostolic band, and reverencing the deacons 'as the commandment of God' (that is, as appointed by God; *Smyrn.* 8 [*NE* 15]). Without the bishop, or at least the bishop's authority, no Eucharist, baptism or other spiritual act is valid. It is noticeable that when Ignatius writes to a church he either mentions or addresses its bishop, in every case except Rome. There may be a special reason for this; but the attitude of Clement, and the evidence of the book called *The Shepherd* of Hermas, suggest that the congregations there were governed by boards of elders, who included prophets and teachers, and might be called bishops. Ignatius in fact seems to be writing at a time when divisions in the churches, and especially conflicts over doctrine, make the need for a single bishop as the focus of unity apparent. We shall consider some of these in the next chapter.

Meanwhile it is worth noticing that the principles enunciated by Ignatius and Clement seem rapidly to have prevailed. Whatever we may think of the list of early bishops in Rome, first given by Irenaeus, *Adv. Haer.* 3.3.1–2 (*NE* 114–15), there can be little doubt it is correct from the 'sixth' bishop Sixtus; on another occasion, writing to Victor the Bishop of Rome about 190, Irenaeus listed Victor's predecessors, but went no further back than Sixtus (using the Greek form of his name, Xystus; Eusebius *HE* 5.24.14 [*NE* 140]). We do not know Sixtus' dates, but he could well have followed the martyrdom of Ignatius in Rome, an act which would have profoundly affected the attitude of Christians to the cause which he advocated. Irenaeus about 180 was to argue that everywhere bishops were appointed by apostles, and that the pedigree of the bishops of his time could be traced back to the apostolic founders of churches (see ch. 6). This is a strong form of Clement's doctrine, presupposing with Ignatius that there is one bishop in each church. Irenaeus would also suppose that in each bishop resided a special gift which preserved in him the apostolic truth, and that the succession guaranteed this tradition. An important figure in this process was undoubtedly Polycarp, Bishop of Smyrna, who received personally one of the letters of Ignatius, and was responsible for collecting them and transmitting them to at least one other church (Polycarp, *Ep.* 13 [*NE* 16–17]). He also died a martyr, probably in 156, and Irenaeus claimed that he had learned from him as a boy, and that Polycarp was himself trained by apostles (*Adv. Haer.* 3.3.4 [*NE* 115–16]). So it is reasonable to suppose that the idea of each church gathered round its bishop, who could be easily recognized by his own people and by other bishops, was promoted by such persons as Ignatius, Polycarp and Irenaeus, and proved its worth. We shall see that it was such action which pulled the Catholic Church into a recognizable shape. It meant that each church had a leading figure responsible for the doctrine as well as the discipline of the community, since he would judge between claims to interpret the Bible correctly. Irenaeus in fact elaborated a theory of the unanimity of bishops in a 'Rule of Faith' derived from the apostles, which enabled the whole truth of God's Word to be correctly perceived.

4

PROLIFERATION AND EXCESS

Heresy and schism

In the second century parties and splits in the Church multiplied. As formal orthodoxy became clearer and established by a world-wide organization, it became customary to regard any party as false: there was the Catholic Church, and there were parties, 'heresies' (Gk *hairesis*, 'party'). So heresy becomes the label for false doctrine. Other divisions in the churches, usually due to disputes over possession of office or over discipline, were called 'schisms' (from *schisma*, a 'split'). Catholic theory, beginning with Irenaeus and Tertullian, regards heresy as due to the introduction of novelty. The original gospel was pure and complete as Jesus gave it to his apostles. Error results from changing things. This view still has its defenders. But modern students of the history of doctrine are more impressed by the fact that doctrine develops, as does so much else about the Church: fourth-century orthodoxy is not the same as what Peter and Paul believed, any more than modern Roman Catholicism or Anglicanism is. The modern believer may wish to claim that he or she believes the same as Christ's first disciples, or tries to; but what makes it the same will not be the explicit words and formulae used to express the faith. This is not a new truth, but one which great theological minds have tried to deal with in the past: two very different examples from a large number one could name are John Henry Newman and Adolf Harnack in the nineteenth century. But the importance of the question for the earliest period was brought out by the work of Walter Bauer.

Bauer argued that heresy precedes orthodoxy, in the sense that from the beginning we meet a great many different kinds of Christianity, with different and often competing organizations and doctrines. In some places like Edessa on the eastern frontier, or Alexandria, Antioch and Ephesus, the original Christianity was of a form later labelled heretical by the great Church, as it began to clarify its belief and to impose norms of orthodoxy. Bauer (who was a Protestant) also held that it was the church in Rome which gradually imposed its own principles on the more numerous and miscellaneous churches of the East, thus producing what came to be recognized as orthodoxy. His view has been criticized in detail on various grounds, especially that he underestimates the strength of features later judged orthodox, and that he ignored Judaeo-Christianity. It could be added that Rome itself was afflicted with just as much doctrinal dispute and schism as any other great church, and it emerged to a more coherent and unified view at the same time as others did, in the period between 180 and 250. But to understand the process which Bauer is trying to interpret, one must look at some of the 'heresies'.

Marcion

Marcion of Pontus (see generally *NE* 92–8) was active in Rome about 140, where story had it that the church there rejected him (Tertullian, *Prescription* 30 [*NE* 93]). But the time of his chief activity is not certain, nor is his relation to the 'gnostic' groups to be discussed later. He had a considerable following by 150, and his church lasted for some centuries. Marcion did not, as commonly said, reject the Old Testament. On the contrary, he accepts it as a divine revelation, and insists it be taken literally. It is the work of the God who created the physical world and gave the Law to Moses and sent the prophets, who did and predicted the various things there attributed to him, and who intended to send his Christ (Messiah) to destroy the wicked and set up his kingdom on earth. But for Marcion such a God cannot be the God and Father of Jesus Christ, who is absolutely good. Jesus says that a good tree cannot produce evil fruit (Luke 6.43–4), and that people are not to judge, but to be merciful as their Father is merciful (Luke 6.36). The behaviour of the Creator is incompatible with these principles, since he does evil to those he hates, and condemns and judges those who break his laws and displease him. Besides, his creation is imperfect, including harmful insects, fierce beasts, and sex; his behaviour is erratic, since he sometimes changes his mind (in a manner incompatible with the Greek ideal of the unchanging deity); and he falsely believes himself to be the only God, when there is in fact another. Marcion held that this other God, the

Unknown, who is pure goodness and love, took pity on the unfortunate victims of their unpleasant Creator, and sent (or came as) Jesus to put matters right. At first stupidly mistaking Jesus for his own Christ, the Creator finally learned his error and came to terms with him, exchanging the souls of all those he had condemned by the Law for the death of Jesus. Thus began the original gospel of free forgiveness of all the sins done against the Law, and the abolition of the limitations of the Law; the Gentiles rallied to the good news. Jesus could not be held by the Creator in death; rather he used his death to release all the dead prisoners in Hades. But, said Marcion, the Creator had not finished. Frustrated in other ways, he managed to deceive the apostles of Jesus, so that they confused his message with the message of the Creator's Messiah (part of the history of this process is described in Paul's criticisms of Peter and James in Galatians 2.11–14). Hence the books of our New Testament are a false amalgam of Jesus' gospel with the principles of the Creator. Marcion held that only the original letters of Paul and a short version of the Gospel of Luke genuinely represented the gospel. Even these had to be 'corrected' so as to eliminate corruptions introduced by judaizing enemies. So Marcion's Gospel has no narrative of the birth of Jesus (which would implicate him in the processes of sex and creation), but starts with the year's date (Luke 3.1) and Jesus appearing fully adult in the synagogue (Luke 4.31), when he 'came down to Capernaum'.

This system had strong pathetic appeal: an absolutely loving and infinitely forgiving God who saves creatures to whom he has no responsibility; a simple and complete escape from the rigours of the Law and the undoubted moral, literary and historical difficulties of the Old Testament; and a message of release from the hardships of this present life into a serene one above for those who believe. It might also appeal to those whose Platonic philosophy committed them to the absolute goodness of God, and who saw this world as needing an inferior Demiurge as its creator, limited by the material he had to work with. Many chose to follow Marcion's challenging message, adopting sexual continence, sparse diet, and commitment to martyrdom in the face of persecution, as they did battle against the Law and the Flesh in the name of pure Spirit. But Marcion was repudiated by other Christians on various grounds. The concept of two gods was flawed: Marcionites could give no coherent account of the providence holding the universe together (see the attack on Apelles in Eusebius *HE* 5.13.2–7 [*NE* 96–7]); two gods amounted to no God, since one cannot be good *and* indiscriminate (Irenaeus, *Adv. Haer.* 3.25.3; Tertullian, *Against Marcion* 1.27 [*NE* 94–5]); and just as the Marcionites cannot live in this world without constantly using the Creator's materials, so they had to deny that the flesh or the world would be saved. As a consequence Marcion is generally held also to have been a docetist in Christology: he is alleged to have held that Christ had a body only in appearance (Gk *to dokein* or *dokesei*; similarly Tertullian, *Against Marcion* 3.8 [*NE* 95–6]). But no actual text of Marcion says this, and it may be a mere inference (though perhaps a reasonable one) from what he did say. If his was the first system to set a superior God above the Creator, it is possible that he had simply not thought out the precise implications. Like the connection between the Creator and the Unknown, the nature of Christ was something which later Gnostics filled in while adopting the main features of his system. If this is correct, Marcion may have been active already while the NT books were still unfinished and Ignatius was writing against docetism. Alternatively Marcion could have worked later, responding to gnostic systems as well as to the more 'orthodox' tradition. If so, he was producing what he felt to be a simple, straightforward interpretation of the OT Scriptures and of Christian history in the face of the enormities of gnostic speculation and the fudging and uncertainty of those who clung to the Creator while rejecting Judaism. Where he fits in is still debated.

Gnosticism

Many teachers and groups are usually classed under the umbrella-term 'gnostic' (see *NE* 68–91). In the second century this term was used of one particular group, also known as Ophites; but Irenaeus used it more widely to include two other schools, Valentinians and Carpocratians, as well. The word *gnostikos* means 'having or claiming knowledge', the Greek for 'knowledge' being *gnosis*. It should be said that there is nothing obviously wrong with claiming to know spiritual things, or in aspiring to know God. It is a biblical idea (as in Jer. 31.34 = Heb. 8.11; John 17.3), and some great writers in the early Church used the word freely of their spiritual ideal (Clement of Alexandria, *Stromateis* 4.22.135–138; 6.13.105–106; 6.14.114 [*NE* 184–6]; similarly Origen, Evagrius Ponticus). But in modern times it was first extended to label together a wider group of 'heresies', including with those named the early followers of men like Simon Magus, Saturninus, and Cerinthus, and major schools like the Sethians and the followers of Basilides. It was still thought of as a form of deviant Christianity, both by traditionalists who thought it a heresy, and by modernists who thought of it as a radical development: Harnack about the turn of the twentieth century saw it quite sympathetically as 'the acute hellenization of Christianity', a sort of primitive modernism. But in our century a wholly new development occurred, when the German 'Religious-history School' led by Richard Reitzenstein and Wilhelm Bousset claimed that important elements common to Gnosticism and Christianity were older than Christianity. These features derived from the dualistic ('two-god') Zoroastrian religion of Iran; its shape was powerfully expressed in the doctrine of Mani (Manichaeus; some information is in *NE* 264–8), who was active AD 242–77 in Persia, but already clearly expressed in various New Testament documents. Many modern exponents of the New Testament, notably Rudolf Bultmann, therefore found Gnosticism there, particularly in Paul and John. On this showing Gnosis or Gnosticism is a religious movement embracing pre-christian sects, early Christianity, the various gnostic sects (in varying degrees Christian) of the second century, Manicheism, and various later movements of dualism like medieval Catharism and some modern cults. While this view still has strong support in some quarters, other scholars reject it firmly, denying that Gnosticism existed early enough to affect Christian origins. Statements about Gnosticism or Gnosis must be read with a clear idea of the sense in which the word is being used, and with an awareness that many things about it are controversial, especially whether it existed early enough to influence the earliest New Testament writings such as Paul's letters and 'Q'. Here we are setting that controversy aside, and concerning ourselves with the impact of heresies, whether labelled 'gnostic' or not, which afflicted the churches in the second century.

There are many different gnostic groups. Irenaeus compared Gnosticism to the mythological Hydra: cut off one head and two new ones grow. The library of books from Nag Hammadi in

Egypt, first discovered in 1945 and published slowly over the next decades, shows that serious Gnostics could use various different forms of teaching as spiritual resources; they are syncretists, blending elements of philosophy and pagan religions with Christianity (and perhaps also Judaism). But despite the many differences, Gnosticism usually exhibits certain family features:

1. There is an ultimate spiritual being, variously named Father, or Man (father of the Son of Man), or Great Invisible Spirit, or Abyss (so for instance Irenaeus, *Adv. Haer.* 1.1.1 [*NE* 79–80]). In Basilides he is the nameless and non-existent God; non-existent in the sense that to say he exists is to say more than one can know (Hippolytus, *Refutation* 7.21–22 [*NE* 73]). This being is superior to the physical universe and its creator, who is often called the Craftsman (*Demiurge*), (Great) Ruler, or God, and may have a Hebrew-sounding name like Ialdabaoth or Saklas. The creator is ignorant of the superior world, until enlightenment comes, usually as part of the process of salvation, when he may learn and repent. The physical world and the god and angels associated with it are at best inferior to the spiritual, if not absolutely evil. Flesh also is evil.

2. Human beings, or some of them, have an element in them derived from the higher realm of spirit, which needs to be aroused by knowledge (*gnosis*). The elect person is essentially spiritual, and by knowing that escapes from the oppression of the flesh. He knows 'who we were, what we have become, where we were, where we were placed, whither we hasten, from what we are redeemed, what birth is, what rebirth' (Clement, *Excerpts from Theodotus* 78.2 [*NE* 68]; compare *Book of Thomas the contender, NHLE* 188–9 = *NE* 69). This means living a new kind of life now, usually one of sexual and dietary abstinence, and it promises a destiny of returning to the realm of spirit after the body is discarded.

3. The doctrines of Gnosticism are chiefly attempts to explain how things came to be as they are. Hence the mythologies. In various versions Sophia or Achamoth (both names mean 'Wisdom') is one of the pure spiritual beings (*aeons*, 'worlds' or 'eternities') who constitute the Fulness or Entirety (*Pleroma*). She desires too much knowledge of the ultimate Spirit, and

from her passion conceives a shapeless abortion, which is excluded from the Pleroma as mere passion, and this becomes the material basis of the creation; exegetically it is the formless void of Gen. 1.2, which awaits the Spirit to give it shape. Sophia and the other aeons appeal to the Father. From her abortion she is enabled to generate one who becomes the creator, and he receives enough spirit to give form to the abortion (so in the *Apocryphon of John, NHLE* 103–4, and Valentinus in Irenaeus, *Adv. Haer.* 1.2.2–3; *NE* 68–9, 80–2). Somehow Sophia manages to endow his human creatures with some wisdom. Basilides has a triple sonship emerging from a seed of the Non-existent God, and the god of this world is produced at the lowest level, ignorant of all above him (Hippolytus, *Refutation* 7.22.3–27.12 [*NE* 73–6]).

4. Christian Gnosticism (or Jewish, if it ever existed independently) expresses itself in terms of the Scriptures, and bases its doctrine on them. Usually fundamental is an exposition of the early part of Genesis, but in one case (*The Apocalypse of Adam*) it sweeps on through substantial parts of Old Testament history, seen as the history of a secret remnant constantly persecuted by the Creator. There are often complicated exegetical theories: different names for God may be taken to indicate distinct beings, almost invariably including the principal deity of the Old Testament. This God is ignorant or malevolent, and especially in the Ophite or Naassene teaching which centres on the snake, the serpent who tempts Eve is her rescuer, imparting knowledge (*gnosis*) which the creator tries to prevent. The schools of Valentinus and Basilides use very careful exegesis of a whole range of Scripture and New Testament writings, and we have a good schematic account of one method in a pamphlet called *The Letter of Ptolemy to Flora* (*NE* 85–9). Ptolemy argues that the Law is threefold, part compiled by the elders, part by Moses, and part by God; but that God is the God of Justice or Craftsman (*Demiurge*), not the Father of Jesus Christ, who is superior to all law. They are therefore operating in a context where the authority of the Old Testament and much of the New is taken for granted, and the text interpreted with care. In fact the earliest known commentary on a New Testament

book is that on John's Gospel by the Valentinian Heracleon, who constantly finds in it spiritual rather than historical meanings.

5. Salvation is knowledge, which comes from the great Spirit. The first to hear may be Ialdabaoth or the Archon. In Basilides' system the gospel first reaches the Great Ruler of the heavenly spheres, then the lesser Ruler who governs this realm below the moon, and only after these gods have been illuminated does the message reach the Sonship still imprisoned in the seed and waiting to be formed, in other words the true Gnostics. In Basilides, as in Valentinus and others, the one who brings the Good News is Jesus Christ, who awakens spiritual persons to their true nature, and sets them on the way to perfect knowledge; though at the same time he initiates a distinction of kinds, so that the lower orders of being accept their ignorant places contentedly. Other saviour/illuminator figures also occur: Seth (the third son of Adam who is also an angelic being) in the many Sethian documents, who may also be the one who comes in Jesus; or Hermes in some non-Christian gnostic documents, which are called Hermetic texts for this reason.

6. There were differences about the destiny of mankind. A common formula resembled that used by the Valentinians, which classed men in three categories (see *The Treatise on the three natures*, cited *NE* 72; Irenaeus, *Adv. Haer.* 1.6.1 [*NE* 83]). The spiritual will certainly be saved; they are the elect, the Gnostics. The carnal or fleshly being material will certainly perish. The 'psychic' or 'soulish' (Gk *psychikos*, sometimes translated 'animal' in the sense of 'having life or soul', but 'natural' in older versions of 1 Cor. 15.44–6, the text from which Valentinus got the idea) may be trained through life in the flesh and ultimately attain salvation, though of a modified kind and not like the spirituals. Ordinary Christians were usually regarded as in this twilight category. The three categories corresponded to features of the mythology: the creator (Ialdabaoth or the Demiurge) was usually *psychic*, and attained the same modified salvation as those like him, outside the Pleroma. The idea of three kinds of people repeated itself in the early Church outside gnostic circles, for example in Origen,

Tertullian, and various aspects of the monastic movement; and to this day many try to distinguish 'real' or 'born-again' Christians from others. Some of the Gnostics took a sharper view of the fate of those who did not share their beliefs, especially when they suffered any kind of correction or persecution from the main body of the Church.

7. The Gnostics made serious efforts to account for the person and work of Christ. Often they distinguished between a created man, miraculously produced and virtuous, and a heavenly Christ who descends upon him or is joined with him. Earlier doctrines make the baptism of Jesus the occasion of this. The spiritual Saviour suffers no fleshly birth and no mortality: he leaves Jesus at the crucifixion (interpreting 'My God, my God, why hast thou forsaken me?' as the man Jesus addressing the spiritual Saviour). Irenaeus attributes one version of this story to Basilides, perhaps falsely (*Adv. Haer.* 1.24.3–7 [*NE* 76–8]). Among the Valentinians a very complicated theory of the person of Christ involves various stages and beings, and indeed occurs with important variations in different Valentinian schools. The human Jesus formed in the Virgin is the son both of the Creator and of Holy Spirit (who operates outside the purely spiritual realm in gnostic systems); he is thus both 'psychic' and spiritual. To this human Jesus is joined the Word (Logos) descending at the Father's behest from the Pleroma, who becomes man by identifying with these two elements, a process which does not require enfleshment or incarnation in the strict sense. The incarnation is merely putting on a robe of flesh, which is discarded once the sacrifice of the cross has been made. Spiritual men are saved through the spirit of Jesus and the psychics through his psychic nature. The flesh is not saved, and matter needs no salvation: the goal is eternal life in the spiritual realm, the life of true knowledge.

While in retrospect it is easy to dismiss gnostic meditations as mythic fancies, they arose from attempts to sort out the New Testament Scriptures in the light of the dualistic framework. Their interpretation allowed the Old Testament to stand, while pointing to a purer intellectual or spiritual realm more compatible with current philosophy. There is no doubt that much serious devotion and theology went into the theory and practice of such

Gnosis, and won a wide following which persisted even after the Catholic Church had been established as the religion of the Empire. The response of writers like Irenaeus and Tertullian was to insist upon one God, who is both Supreme and Creator, and one Jesus Christ, who is both flesh and spirit. They also insisted upon the unity of the Church which holds that faith, and tried to give it concrete identification. Origen was to find a spirituality which attached the best features of Gnosticism to the One God and his One Word.

Eastern Christianity

The teachings of Marcion, and of Valentinus, Basilides and the other Gnostics spread widely in Egypt and the East, and were known in Rome and Gaul. How far their adherents were separated from or included within congregations of Christians who did not share their ideas probably varied greatly. So did reactions to them. In the Syriac-speaking East a powerful movement of ascetic Christianity was present, often associated with the name of the apostle Thomas (or Judas Thomas). Here it was common for baptism to be administered only to those committed to sexual abstinence: the unmarried would stay unmarried, the married would live together in continence, and the majority of Christians remained unbaptized catechumens. It came to be called the 'Encratite' heresy (from Gk *enkrateia*, 'continence'). Some expressions of this movement embody ideas which are apparently gnostic: such are the *Acts of Thomas* and the *Book of Thomas the contender* and the *Gospel of Thomas* (cf. *NE* 69, 99–100). But the work of Tatian (poorly reported by Irenaeus, *Adv. Haer.* 1.28.1 [*NE* 100–1]) was based squarely on the four Gospels. He compiled his famous *Diatessaron* (Eusebius *HE* 4.29.6–7 [*NE* 125–6]), a harmonized version of all four, which became the standard Gospel-book for nearly three centuries in eastern Syria. Tatian wrote theology similar to that of Justin Martyr (whom we shall discuss later), whose pupil he apparently was. While the Greek and Latin churches about 200 were sorting out the theological issues raised by Marcion and Gnosticism in their own way, a notable figure in eastern Syria called Bardaisan (Bardesanes) refuted Marcion and developed accounts of the origin of the world and of human religion independently; inevitably he was regarded as a heretic further west (extracts in *NE* 154–6). The same area would produce in the third century a most powerful amalgam of Christian, gnostic-dualist and ascetic ideas in the missionary theology of Mani (Manichaeus) (cf. *NE* 265–8), which was to influence Augustine. This all illustrates the startling variety of Christianity in the second century, and the context in which theology was to develop.

Syriac Christianity grew in ways which the main Church in the Empire eventually rejected, and later theology in these oriental regions is overlaid with ideas and principles from the Greek-speaking churches. It nevertheless survived with rich and illuminating ideas of its own, which we are unable to deal with adequately in this book. Western and Greek theologians ought to take more account of these traditions than we do. See Robert Murray, *Symbols of Church and Kingdom* (Cambridge 1975), and *The Syriac Fathers on prayer and the spiritual life*, edited by Sebastian Brock (Kalamazoo, and Oxford, Mowbrays, 1987).

Montanism

Besides Gnosticism and Marcion, another vigorous movement caused turmoil and trouble in the churches. The most strongly Christian area of the Empire in the second century was Asia Minor, and there the churches were split in the 170s by Montanism, known to the Greeks as the Phrygian or Kataphrygian heresy because it arose and prospered in Phrygia. The accounts in Eusebius (*HE* 5.16–18 [*NE* 102–8]) were based on hostile sources recounting hearsay. These portray a revival of ecstatic prophecy, particularly among women in which jibberish accompanies strange actions and miraculous signs, all attributed by its opponents to a demon, and condemned as such by meetings of bishops (called 'presbyters' *HE* 7.16.5 [*NE* 106]). The Montanists in fact imposed a more rigorous standard of conduct than others, as even their scurrilous critic recognizes (*HE* 5.16.9 [*NE* 102], 'shrewd and plausible rebukes'), were able to boast martyrs among their number (*HE* 5.16–22 [*NE* 104]), and were stricter than others about fasting, second marriages of widows and widowers, forgiveness for grave sin after baptism, and flight from persecution. They believed that in these ways the Paraclete, promised in such verses as John 14.26, had now come to bring in a stricter discipline than that allowed by Jesus; this was their chief unorthodoxy.

Prophecy was still recognized, though the practice was declining, among the main body of Christians; and their apocalyptic expectation that the end was imminent, and might come in Pepuza in Phrygia, was little different from what many Christians believed (both Justin and Irenaeus expected an earthly reign of Christ to come soon). The nub of the matter was their sharper discipline, as is apparent from comparing the writings of Tertullian before and after he attached himself to the 'new prophecy' about 200 in Africa. He became much stricter about second marriages, flight in persecution, fasting, and the forgiveness of grave sins committed by the baptized. The movement was therefore one of strict discipline based upon prophetic revelations. It may have had social roots in the local loyalty of the Phrygian population, engaging in a kind of mass movement of ardent Christianity. It may reflect resentment about the compromises of city churches growing more worldly, or with the intellectual presumptions of church teachers like the gnostic leaders and Justin; we do not know. It certainly led to formal decisions by councils of neighbouring bishops to denounce the whole movement as demonic, and to refuse to recognize Montanist baptisms. It therefore raised large problems for the rest of the Church.

5
DEFENCE AND DEFINITION: EARLY APOLOGISTS

Apologists and apologetic

From the inner turmoil and outer perils of second-century Christianity some documents survive which are usually called 'apologies'; they are classed as 'apologetic literature', and their authors are known as 'apologists'. The modern use of the words 'apology' and 'apologize' gives a wrong impression of the meaning. In this and later theological literature the idea of an apology is not to admit you are wrong and ask for pardon; on the contrary, it is a defence of yourself and your actions against accusations. An apology is an argument to show that you are right. The earliest example is Plato's *Apology*, which he wrote after the execution of Socrates; it takes the form of a speech by Socrates at his trial, in which he defends his teaching and conduct against charges of introducing strange gods and corrupting the young. Similarly the Christian apologist argues the case for Christianity, negatively by rebutting false charges, positively by arguing its truth and refuting other beliefs. In the case of Plato, the defence is partly fictitious: it is not a real record of what Socrates said, but Plato's argument for Socrates presented in this literary form. Similarly the Christian apologetic of the second century is in the form of an open letter to an inquirer (so *Letter To Diognetus* and Theophilus' *To Autolycus*), or an address to an emperor (Justin, Athenagoras and Melito). It is very unlikely that those addressed to emperors ever reached them, and they may not have been sent; the form is a literary convention.

Most Christian literature of the second century is lost. By the time the last papyrus and parchment copies were wearing out, the theology in them was at best out of date, and usually looked heretical to contemporary readers. No one thought them worth copying. The most important apologist, Justin Martyr, has left us three works, two *Apologies* addressed to the emperors, and the *Dialogue with Trypho the Jew*; we owe them to one manuscript, itself destroyed by war in modern times. He wrote between 140

and 163. Of Athenagoras (about 170) and the anonymous author
of the *Letter To Diognetus* (date uncertain) we possess one ancient
copy each. The earliest apologist, Quadratus, is known only from
Eusebius' report and fragment (*HE* 4.3 [*NE* 58]). Aristides,
somewhat later and writing about 140, is lost in the original
Greek, and survives in an expanded Syriac translation, though
parts of the Greek were copied into the seventh-century legend of
Barlaam and Joasaph (for a sample see *NE* 52–5). The apology of
Melito of Sardis (*NE* 65–6), written about 175, is lost apart from
Eusebius' quotation, though what we have may be most of it.
Besides these, the chief apologies are three books of Theophilus of
Antioch *To Autolycus* and Tatian's *Against the Greeks*, both
written about 180. All these writers together are known as 'the
Greek apologists of the second century'. About the end of the
century, and into the next, works in Latin began to appear. The
most notable are Tertullian (*NE* 157–64) and Minucius Felix (*NE*
177–8; 131). In Greek were written the great introductory book of
Clement of Alexandria (*Protreptikos; NE* 180–2), and the
accomplished polemic of Origen *Against Celsus* (*NE* 208–12;
compare 131–5). These are not included here, though they picked
up many of the arguments of their predecessors.

Charge and counter-charge

One regular theme is protest about the unfair persecution of
Christians. They are good and loyal subjects, it is said. Melito
protests about 'new decrees' which have exposed Christians to
barbaric looting; there is a political background to these measures
under Marcus Aurelius which we do not fully understand (*NE* 65).
A common complaint is against persecution merely 'for the name'
of 'Christian'; the whole burden of the story of Ptolemy and Lucius
in Justin's *Apology* 2.2 (*NE* 30–1) is summed up in Lucius'
protest:

> Why have you punished this man, not as an adulterer, nor
> fornicator, nor murderer, nor thief, nor robber, nor convicted of
> any crime at all, but who has only confessed that he is called by
> the name of Christian? This judgment of yours, O Urbicus, does
> not become the Emperor Pius [i.e. Marcus Aurelius], nor the
> philosopher, the son of Caesar [the co-emperor and heir-apparent
> Commodus], nor the sacred Senate.

Consequently the apologists write a good deal about Christian moral principles. Theophilus writes on the ten commandments. Aristides (14–15 [*NE* 52–5]) and the anonymous *Letter to Diognetus* (5–7 [*NE* 55–7]) give eloquent descriptions of Christian practical morality and community life, the virtuous 'soul of the world'. Apologists specifically repudiate charges of abominations such as cannibalism ('Thyestean feasts') and incestuous orgies ('Oedipodean intercourse'), which they point out are the stuff of Greek fable, not Christian belief. Here in Justin, as in Athenagoras and Melito, there is an appeal to the justice and (moral) philosophy of the ruling powers: let Christians be lawfully and honestly examined, and their innocence will appear (see Athenagoras, *Embassy* 1–3 [*NE* 66–7]). Justin goes so far as to describe in some detail the practices of Christians at baptism and the Eucharist, chiefly in order to repudiate false notions of what goes on in their meetings. The secrecy which normally surrounded these ceremonies had clearly contributed to suspicions about their behaviour.

The apologists began to claim that Greek culture pointed to and was consummated in the Christian message, just as the Old Testament was. This process was done most thoroughly in the synthesis of Clement of Alexandria. It can be done in several ways. You can rake through Greek literature, and find (especially in the oldest seers and poets) references to 'God' which are more compatible with monotheism than with polytheism (so at length Athenagoras). You can work out a common chronology between the legends of prehistoric (Homeric) Greece and the biblical record (so Theophilus). You can adapt a piece of pre-Christian Jewish apologetic, which claimed that Plato and other Greek philosophers got their best ideas indirectly from the teaching of Moses in the Bible, which was much earlier. This theory combines the advantage of making out the Greeks to be plagiarists (and therefore second-rate or criminal), while claiming that they support Christianity by their arguments at least some of the time. Especially this applied to the question of God.

Much apologetic consists of a critique of non-Christian religion, sometimes savagely attacking Greek literature (a good example is Tatian). The attack is especially directed against the myths and religious cults of polytheism. In Homer's poetry and the classical dramas of Athens the gods were often involved in the actions of human history. Their stories were the principal reading in the schools. Long ago Socrates (as reported by Plato in the *Republic*) had attacked the reading of immoral stories, especially those which implied that gods could do things unworthy of the changeless, perfect and transcendent being of God. Before Socrates, first Xenophanes of Colophon (about 530 BC) and others had argued that ultimate Being must be unique, simple, self-moved and omnipresent, and Theagenes of Megara shortly afterwards had tried to justify the Homeric literature by finding that the stories of many gods were allegories, hiding deep philosophical and moral truths in story form. Both historic views had numerous followers down the centuries, and provided plenty of material for Christian philosophers like Justin, who finds in Socrates a natural ally (*Apology* 1.46 [*NE* 61]). Where contemporary cult was concerned, it was not denied that gods appear and perform miracles, as they were generally thought to do, especially at their shrines and oracles; Justin and others attribute this to evil demons, deceiving people and feeding on their gifts (*Apology* 1.6 [*NE* 60]).

At this point we reach the most serious of the charges against Christians, that of atheism, or godlessness. Christians were not Jews, following their ancestral custom of worshipping the one God of the Bible. The great majority were converted from Greco-Roman religion: they had rejected the gods, and they knew it. As we have seen, repudiating the demons was central to the baptismal commitment. The defence is predictable: The gods we repudiate are false gods and demons, and we do it in the name of the one true God. A good example is Justin, *Apology* 1.5-6 (*NE* 60), where he claims that persecution comes from the evil *daimones*, who deceive people into thinking they are gods. Socrates died as a result of their manipulations, and so do Christians. The same *logos* which led Socrates to criticize these false gods was manifest in Jesus Christ and his followers, who are punished as atheists for repudiating them. Justin now falls back on something not unlike a baptismal confession:

> We confess that we are atheists, as far as gods of this sort are concerned, but not with respect to the most true God, the Father of righteousness and temperance and the other virtues, who is free from all impurity. But both him, and the Son who came forth from him and taught us these things, and the host of the

other good angels who follow and are made like to him, and the prophetic Spirit we worship and adore, knowing them in reason and truth.

The virtues connected with the Father contrast him with the malignant demons (gods). The angels associated with the Son reflect the desire of Justin to make it plain that Christians have their 'pantheon' too, and it reflects the strong sense of being surrounded with spiritual agents, good and bad, which early Christianity manifested. Its doctrinal import is discussed later.

God and his Word

Justin's 'creed', as we saw, spoke of a transcendent God and Father, of his Son (with the angels), and of the Spirit of prophecy. This triple confession is in line with what we know of the baptismal confession. But when we look at the theology of the apologists, we find that generally their thought is 'binitarian' rather than 'trinitarian': it speaks of God and his Word, rather than of Father, Son and Holy Spirit. The term 'Trinity' was not yet in use in the Church. Theophilus is the first to use the Greek word for Trinity (*trias, triad*), when he takes the first three days of creation as signifying the trinity of 'God and his Word and his Wisdom' (*To Autolycus* 2.15), and Tertullian soon after 200 was using the Latin *trinitas* of God.

If we suppose that the baptismal confession and central Christian belief was in a threefold form, we have to account for the binitarian thought of Justin and those like him. The most obvious explanation is that their apologetic is directed towards Greek thought. They began from what appeared to be common ground.

Among the Greeks a familiar notion was the thought of an utterly transcendent, perfect, unmoving God, and of a second, mediating, active being responsible for the created order, whether as its superior governor or as its immanent soul. Such a theology was being propounded, for instance, by the Platonist Albinos in Asia Minor at the same time that Justin was himself there, before he moved to Rome. If Jesus Christ was the Word of God, in addition to the scriptural backgrounds, the idea supplied a pattern for philosophy. God is, as Justin likes to say, superior to any name, immoveable, indescribable, not to be confined to any place, and absolutely good (*Apol.* 1.10, 1.61 [*NE* 63], 2.6); This echoes Plato's *Timaeus* 28–9, a very popular passage with later philosophers. God is 'that which is in all respects always the same as itself' (*Dial.* 3, echoing Plato, *Phaedo* 78d). Yet he is also depicted in Scripture as active in the world, and particularly in its creation and enlightenment. He therefore identifies the Word as an intervening, active principle, who can appear on earth, for instance as the God who confronted Moses at the burning bush, but who is the whole source of order in creation, who is the Reason or Wisdom enlightening all the great men of the past, Socrates as well as Abraham, and who himself took shape and became a man in Jesus Christ, to make known the whole truth perfectly.

The apologists knew well that *logos* had various meanings. Elementary Stoic logic distinguished the *word immanent* (Gk *logos endiathetos*) from the *word expressed* (Gk *logos prophorikos*). When *logos* refers to the inner faculty of thought or reason (as when you think of a word before you say it), that is the immanent word. Once spoken, it is expressed; but it remains rational, articulate, otherwise it would not be *logos*, but the kind of noise made by *irrational beasts* (Gk *aloga zoa*). Once the idea had occurred that Christ or the Son of God could be called God's Word, *logos*, this distinction could be very useful. Justin implies it, and Theophilus states it plainly. God always has *logos*, because he is always wise and rational. At the creation he speaks, saying 'Let there be light', and his *logos* becomes Word, 'another beside himself with whom the Father could converse' (Justin, *Dial.* 62.4). This uttering of the *logos* also reflects Platonic thought, since things consist of form and matter, and it is the form which the mind grasps in understanding them. Creation is therefore seen in Platonism as the imposing of rational form on shapeless pre-existent matter; it is precisely what the Demiurge does in *Timaeus*. Justin is happy to regard the opening verses of Genesis as making the same point: The earth is 'without form and void' until God speaks and his *logos* shapes it. He goes so far as to claim that Plato plagiarized the thought from Moses (*Apol.* 1.10, 1.59; Plato, *Timaeus* 51a). When God says, 'Let us [plural] make man in our own image', it is to his *logos* that he speaks (*Dial.* 61.4). This Word is also the ordering principle of creation. At the burning bush, it is 'another god', and not the Father (who has neither name nor location), who appears to Moses (*Dial.* 60). Justin uses a Stoic expression, 'generative [or, seminal] reason' (Gk *spermatikos logos*) to account for the truth in non-Christian philosophy. The universe was controlled and ordered by its own rational principle, and so were people when they were wise; but the philosophers had only part of the truth. To Christians the Word 'who is from the unbegotten and ineffable God' was given in his fulness, because 'he became man for our sakes, that, becoming partaker of our sufferings, he might also bring us healing'; he is therefore worshipped and loved, 'next to God' (*Apol.* 2.13 [*NE* 62]). So they understand the creative principle of the universe in its completeness, and that includes being rescued from ignorance and suffering by his presence in Jesus Christ. The same 'rational power' or 'glory of the Lord', begotten by God before all things, appears repeatedly in the Old Testament Scripture under various names and guises: 'sometimes he calls himself Son, sometimes Wisdom, sometimes Angel, sometimes God, sometimes Lord and Word, sometimes Captain' (*Dial.* 61.1).

Holy Spirit and Trinity

We have noted that the worshipping tradition of the church to which Justin belongs has a threefold idea of God and his actions. Unlike some other writers, Justin boldly describes what Christians do at their meetings, and the formulae show through. His purpose is to prove that Christians are innocent of the abominations attributed to them, and at certain points to draw comparisons with non-Christian religious practices which were regarded as acceptable among non-Christians. He describes baptism, and twice refers to the threefold name:

> In the name of God, the Father and Lord of the universe, and of our Saviour Jesus Christ, and of the Holy Spirit, they then receive the washing with water . . . there is pronounced in the water over him the name of God the Father and Lord of the universe; . . . and in the name of Jesus Christ, who was crucified under Pontius Pilate, and in the name of the Holy Ghost, who through the prophets foretold all things about Jesus, he who is illuminated is washed. (*Apol.* 1.61 [*NE* 63])

When the president at the Eucharist takes the bread and cup, he 'offers up praise and glory to the Father of the universe, through

the name of the Son and of the Holy Ghost' (*Apol.* 1.65 [*NE* 64]).
With these descriptions goes the declaration we cited about the
objects of Christian worship: 'the most true God, the Father of
righteousness and temperance and the other virtues, who is free
from all impurity . . . and the Son who came forth from him and
taught us these things, and the host of the other good angels who
follow and are made like to him, and the prophetic Spirit' (*Apol.*
1.5 [*NE* 60]).

In these passages Christ is described in biblical language, not in
terms of the *logos* which Justin uses to explain the faith to the
outsiders. The reference to the angels is intriguing, but angelology
is not an exact science, and it should be noted:

1. Often in the stories of Scripture angels are not, as depicted in
art, quasi-human creatures separate from God, but actual
manifestations of God himself (so for example Gen. 22.11–12);
sacrifice to the angel of the Lord is therefore in order (Judg.
13.15–23).

2. Jesus Christ may be regarded as himself the angel in such
manifestations, as Justin understood the God who spoke to
Moses in the bush to be the Word (*logos*) and not the
transcendent Father. He is often represented as one of the
angels – though vastly their superior – in early Christian texts
associated with Jewish traditions (see Daniélou, *The Theology
of Jewish Christianity*, ch. 4).

3. Jesus Christ's own self-manifestation to a prophet may be
called an angel (Rev. 1.1).

4. The idea of Christ coming with a host of angels is certainly
scriptural (Matt. 16.27; 2 Thess. 1.7). In the second century it
was developed in Christian speculation. Valentinus associated a
host of angels with the heavenly Christ at his coming, each
angel being the heavenly bridegroom of an elect soul. The idea
that one angel belongs to each of the elect is also present in the
New Testament (Matt. 18.10).

It is nevertheless true that the Holy Spirit is here apparently
subordinated to the Son as a kind of special angel, and that may
reflect Justin's particular views. In two of the passages just cited
he names the work of the Spirit as prophetic, inspiring the

prophecies which point to Jesus. Even that is a work which elsewhere is that of the *logos*, who makes wise the antecedents of Christ in the Old Testament. So we look in vain for a deeper doctrine of the Trinity or the Spirit.

It is also notable that when Justin expounds the passage in Luke (1.35) where the angel promises that the Holy Spirit will come upon Mary, and the Power of the Most High will overshadow her, he takes the Holy Spirit to be the Word who became incarnate in her (*Apol.* 1.33.6). This became the customary interpretation in the West, figuring even in the influential *Tome* of Leo in 449. The credal statements, that Christ was born 'of Holy Spirit and the Virgin Mary' and the like, are to be taken as referring to the Son or Word as a divine Being or Spirit, not to Holy Spirit as a distinct person of the Trinity.

On the life of Christ generally, it should be noted that the apologists are generally reticent. Theophilus and Atenagoras never refer to Jesus Christ, but defend Christian beliefs about God and the world, and Christian behaviour. Their reticence is consistent with the practice of initiating Christian catechumens in the Old Testament, and only reading the Gospel to them in the weeks just before baptism. God's deeper purposes are not to be bandied about. Justin is more forthcoming than others, as he is about Christian worship. It was possibly in response to Justin that the pagan Celsus launched his devastating critique of Christian superstition, and ridiculed faith in Jesus as the Word enfleshed (*NE* 131–5).

6

TRADITION AND TRUTH:
IRENAEUS OF LYONS

Lyons and Irenaeus

In AD 177 or soon after, the churches in Vienne and Lyons in southern Gaul wrote a triumphant letter 'to the brethren in Asia and Phrygia', reporting a short but savage persecution. Eusebius preserves much of this letter (*HE* 5.1–2; see *NE* 34–44 and 46). There had first been disorderly harassment of Christians, then arrests and public hearings at which some Christians apostatized. The authorities tried especially to get evidence that Christians were guilty of cannibalism, and the terrified testimony of some slaves seemed to confirm it. The final judgement was deferred to the national festival of the 'three Gauls' at the beginning of August, so that the Emperor's judgement could be given on whether those who renounced Christianity were still to be punished as cannibals, and on those with the privilege of Roman citizenship. In the interim, most of those who had denied the faith at the first hearing were won back to the faith, and at the later hearing refused to renounce or take advantage of the emperor's proffered clemency. Altogether more than forty Christians died, some after atrocious tortures. Some of these died in the arena, others in prison, among them the aged bishops of Lyons, Pothinus (or Photinus), who had been beaten up by the police at his trial.

After the persecution the new bishop was Irenaeus. He had played a significant part in what happened, and a letter is preserved in which the martyrs commend Irenaeus to Eleutherus, Bishop of Rome, as a worthy presbyter (Eusebius, *HE* 5.3–4). Eusebius' report is however confused and unreliable – he even says that the letter included a list of the martyrs and the way they had died. But he does include it in a discussion of Montanism (see pp. 46–7). It is possible that Irenaeus was an envoy of the church in Lyons, which was sustaining its judgement on the Montanism of Phrygia and Asia with the authority of the martyrs; or perhaps 'presbyter' is used in its old meaning of 'bishop', a usage we find in Irenaeus' own writings, and the letter was meant to commend him – and his views on Montanism – to Eleutherus. The other letter, which recounts the story of the martyrs of 177, contained doctrinal or polemical passages which Eusebius omitted. These may have been about the Montanist dispute; certainly the idea that those who first renounced the faith were reconciled on the authority of those who had stood firm, and went on themselves to become martyrs, is hostile to Montanism as we see it in Tertullian (see pp. 67–8). Some writers have taken the opposite view, and have seen the references in it to the Paraclete and the impending judgement of God as indicating support for Montanist ideas; but these were commonplace Christian notions in the second century, and this view is probably wrong.

Whatever the case, Irenaeus became bishop of the most important city of Roman Gaul when the persecution subsided. He is the most important theologian of the second century who has remained in the orthodox tradition (otherwise Marcion and Valentinus might be thought to rival him). Even Irenaeus' original works have been lost, apart from a few fragments and extracts. One reason was probably that he adopted the view that Christ would return to reign for a thousand years on earth (the millennium), a doctrine rejected by most Eastern theologians from Origen onwards: Eusebius makes excuses for Irenaeus' error at *HE* 3.39.11–13 (*NE* 48), saying that he was misled by a primitive writer called Papias. For whatever reason, the original Greek of Irenaeus' two surviving books is largely lost. They are the five books *Against Heresies* (usually known by their Latin title, *Adversus Haereses*, or *Adv. Haer.* for short, or Greek *Elenchos, Refutation*) and a short handbook or catechism, *The Demonstration of the apostolic preaching* (known as *Demonstration* or *Epideixis*). Both books survive in late Armenian versions, and *Against Heresies* in an early Latin translation; on the latter it should be noted that Latin theologians retained their faith in the millennium for some centuries after the Greeks largely dropped it, and were never as doubtful as the Greeks were about the apostolic authority of John's *Revelation* (from which the doctrine comes: Rev. 20.1–8).

There is no reason to doubt that Irenaeus originated in Asia, nor his claim that as a boy he heard the old bishop there, Polycarp (*Adv. Haer.* 3.3.4; Eusebius, *HE* 5.20.4–8 [*NE* 115–16, 121]).

Like most Western Christians he spoke and wrote in Greek, and like him most of the Christians in the Lyons persecutions had connections with Asia and Phrygia. Irenaeus was clearly an active bishop. He had read some Greek philosophy as well as Christian writers, and he claims that he had learned to speak to the Gallic barbarians in their own language.

Irenaeus is important to us, first because of the way he tried to identify and stabilize true Christianity and to distinguish it from heresy, and because of the rich theology he developed in the process.

Apostolic succession

Irenaeus' longer surviving work was provoked by the success of a Valentinian movement in Gaul, led by one Markos (Marcus). His followers are called 'Marcosians' (a brief fragment about their baptism is *NE* 91). The movement seems to have had some success in drawing away some members of Irenaeus' own church. He therefore wrote his five books, outlining the beliefs of the Valentinians and 'other Gnostics'; this remains a valuable source of information to us (there are ten pieces of Irenaeus on gnostic and Marcionite teaching in *NE* 76–96). To him these doctrines are the 'knowledge falsely so called' of 1 Tim. 6.20. They have come about through defection from the original truth received by the apostles from Jesus Christ himself.

Marcion, Valentinus and Basilides, and all the gnostic sects who saw themselves as Christian, claimed to present the apostolic doctrine, that is the truth as Jesus Christ gave it to his apostles. Marcion claimed that he had restored again the truth specially revealed to Paul, after the Twelve had defected. Valentinus was said by his disciples to have been taught by Theudas, a disciple of Paul; Basilides was claimed as a disciple of Glaucias, amanuensis of Peter; and the *Apocryphon of John* makes John the recipient of special revelations of the great Barbelo. With this went the claim to report a higher, more spiritual, truth than that held by ordinary Christians, the secret knowledge of the elect. A principal feature of Irenaeus' doctrine is worked out in refutation of those claims. It is worth studying closely, *Adv. Haer.* 3.3–4 (*NE* 114–17).

Irenaeus argues that, if the apostles had any such secret knowledge to impart, they would certainly have entrusted it to those they left in charge of the churches, who were the bishops. So it is very important to Irenaeus that the 'ancestry' of existing bishops can be traced back to apostolic times. He may not have originated this argument, since the idea of succession-lists appears also in the fragments of the anti-gnostic writer Hegesippus some years before (Eusebius, *HE* 4.22.2–3 [*NE* 109]). But he elaborates it for us most fully, giving the Roman church, and Polycarp of Smyrna, as his two specific examples. In order to refute all those who meet in 'unauthorized meetings' it is enough (1) to indicate the traditions derived from the apostles of one great church, that of Rome. That church, he says, was founded by Peter and Paul (this is actually false, since there were organized Christians there before either of the apostles). And (2) one may consult the faith preached there in succession to the apostles by means of the succession of bishops.

There follows an expression of the representative authority of the Roman church, which is exceedingly difficult to interpret, and has been highly controversial: 'It is necessary that every church, that is, the faithful everywhere, should resort to [? agree with] this Church, on account of its pre-eminent authority, in which the apostolical tradition has been preserved continuously by those who exist everywhere' (3.3.1). This does not mean that the Roman church dictates doctrine to others. Rather Irenaeus is keen to suggest that the same apostolic faith exists throughout the entire world (see the opening sentence of *Adv. Haer.* 3.3.1), and the very ancient Roman church, with its assured succession from pre-eminent apostles, and with its constant contacts with other churches ('those who exist everywhere') is a sure place to find that faith.

Irenaeus then gives the Roman succession list (*Adv. Haer.* 3.3.2–3). This has become the foundation of all other such lists. The list is probably valid from Sixtus (also called Xystos) onwards. When he wrote to Victor of Rome about 190, Irenaeus would start his list with Sixtus, naming none earlier. Sixtus could have been the first 'monarchical' bishop appointed after Ignatius sealed his testimony to that system with his martyrdom (see pp. 33–5). To satisfy his own theory of succession, Irenaeus needed some more names, and worked out the list (or perhaps borrowed it from someone else before him, like Hegesippus). Since 'Sixtus' means 'sixth' it was obvious that he had five predecessors; he was 'sixth from the apostles'. Linus was the last named male person in Paul's last martyr-letter (2 Tim. 4.21, a reference Irenaeus was aware of), and a few verses down the same page of the New Testament are the words, 'the bishop must be irreproachable' (Gk *anenkletos* = Anacletus; Titus 1.7). The apostles' successors were thus easily deduced, and Clement, who had exercised clear episcopal functions (so Irenaeus thinks) in writing his famous letter, was regarded as the Clement of Phil. 4.3. Where the fourth and fifth names came from, we cannot tell. Such inventive manipulation, if it happened, would be regarded as spiritual and prophetic, rather than as dishonest: compare the arguments used by Irenaeus to prove that there must be four and only four Gospels (*Adv. Haer.* 3.11.8 = *NE* 117-18); they have nothing to do with historical information.

Besides this Roman succession list, Irenaeus had a special link with apostolic times. Polycarp of Smyrna provided Irenaeus not only with evidence of a champion of orthodoxy and martyr, who had ostensibly consorted with John and Philip and other apostles of Jesus, but with one who had been heard by Irenaeus himself. Inasmuch therefore as Irenaeus claims a succession of true teachers in the Church, entrusted with the churches in their appointment as bishops. Polycarp provides him personally with a direct, and almost immediate, link with the apostles. Irenaeus' own gospel, and the idea of episcopal tradition which goes with it, is thus especially verified within his own theory (see *Adv. Haer.* 3.3.4; *HE* 5.20.4-8 [*NE* 115-16; 121]).

In all this Irenaeus is concerned with the succession of true doctrine, and its transmission in the public teaching of the bishops. 'Apostolic succession' may have included for him some idea of a sacramental grace exclusively passed to bishops from apostles; but if so, he never refers to it. That is in fact a later idea.

The Rule of Truth

Three times Irenaeus summarizes the universal teaching of the churches, derived from the apostles. It is often called 'The Rule of Faith', an expression used by Tertullian (*regula fidei*). Irenaeus' own word for it is 'Rule of Truth', but he can use other words, like 'The preaching' or 'The faith' (see *Adv. Haer.* 1.2-3 [*NE* 111-12]). It contains broadly the same ideas as most creeds: One God the Creator, Jesus Christ and his coming, the Holy Spirit, the Church, and the future judgement. Irenaeus and other writers who mention such a Rule (Tertullian, Hippolytus, Origen) invariably word it differently every time, which suggests that each is a summary of a known set of ideas and not a fixed form of words.

Irenaeus asserts that the whole meaning of the gospel is summed up in this Rule. Barbarians who cannot yet read or hear the Scriptures are saved by it (*Adv. Haer.* 3.15.1; cf. 3.4.1). In the face of heretical interpretations, it tests the true meaning of Scripture. Heretics use the Bible to produce grotesque ideas, like someone taking apart a mosaic picture of the emperor and using the bits to make the picture of a dog or fox (*Adv. Haer.* 1.1.15). This Rule is not a supplement to the biblical truth derived from the apostles and prophets, nor a tradition of independent material, but a key to interpret the Scriptures which is compatible with the Scriptures as a whole. It is fair therefore to call Irenaeus' work a 'biblical theology', in the sense that it aims to interpret Scripture by Scripture itself.

This is a good idea, but needs qualification or comment. First, the limits of Scripture were not yet clearly fixed. We have already said (pp. 23–8) that the list of Old Testament books was not agreed. The same is even more true of the New Testament. Marcion relied on a shortened Luke and corrected Paul; Sethians, Valentinians, Thomas Christians, Basilideans, multiplied texts. Various spurious documents were popular among orthodox Christians (the *Gospel of Peter*; the *Letter of Barnabas*). The writings of John (Gospel and Revelation) were favoured by heretics, but suspect in the churches. Irenaeus stood firmly by something like our New Testament, with four and only four Gospels as its foundation (*Adv. Haer.* 3.11.8 [*NE* 117–18]). Although he believed these to be the genuine apostolic documents, his reasons, as can be seen, were not historical ones. He argued from the four winds (in Greek 'spirits'), which inspire and vivify the Church on every hand, and the four symbolic cherubim of Ezekiel and Revelation. Irenaeus' Rule works only if there is an agreed set of Scriptures.

Secondly, later Fathers from Origen onwards were to pursue the principle of interpreting Scripture by Scripture. They would assiduously collect uses of a word, and apply their discoveries to the text under discussion. This was often illuminating, but more often made it impossible to determine the historic meaning and nature of each particular biblical document. Irenaeus, like his distinguished successors, in fact brings other ideas, religious and philosophical, to his understanding of the text. We all do.

God and Christ

In opposition to the heresies, Irenaeus lays weight on the unity of God. The first and most important point, he writes (*Adv. Haer.* 2.1.1), is that the Creator is the one and only God, maker of heaven and earth, and those who postulate a higher god are blaspheming him. Prophets, apostles, and the words of Christ himself attest this. But Irenaeus follows the threefold Rule, and confesses the Son and the Spirit as God's Word and Wisdom, the 'hands' by which he created and adorned the universe. God is never without his Word (Logos, Reason) and Wisdom. The origin of the Word is mysterious; 'His generation who can tell?' (Isaiah 53.8) is applied to this question.

How precisely the one God relates to his Son and Word, Jesus Christ, is also obscure. The Word created the universe, and the Spirit adorned it. But Irenaeus specifically rejects some of the notions favoured by his predecessors the apologists; he had certainly read Justin and Theophilus. He rejects the idea of the Word as first immanent, then expressed, on the ground that God is always complete in self-expression. He rejects the idea of 'another god', which had been used by the apologists of the Word appearing to Moses and others (*Adv. Haer.* 2.28.4–5). He rejects the idea of the Word as one light kindled from another, 'light from light', which had been begun by the apologists and retained popularity later, even in the Nicene Creed (*Adv. Haer.* 2.17.4). He plainly feels that such Logos-speculation, like the two gods of Marcion and the junior Demiurge of the Gnostics, undermines the absolute unity of God.

In the case of Jesus Christ, he also emphasizes unity: he repeatedly used the expression, 'one and the same'. Christ is both God as Word of God, and Man. The gnostic myths often comprise a dualistic or adoptionist element: the human Jesus is distinct from the heavenly Christ-spirit, who descends on the man at baptism. Alternatively, other ideas are used to evade the contamination of the divine Spirit with flesh, usually saying that

Christ was a purely spiritual being who merely appeared as a man (examples in *NE* 76–7; 85; 95–6). For Irenaeus it is vital that Jesus Christ was both God and Man. As one and the same person, both Son of God and Son of Man, he lived, suffered and died: the suggestion that the divine Word remained impassible (untouched by suffering), while the humanity suffered death, an idea which commended itself to Antiochene theologians later, was rejected as divisive heresy. If he were not Man, humanity would not be saved in him; if he were not God, he would not have power to save. To understand this, one needs to understand Irenaeus' thought about man (in the sense of 'human' not 'male') and his destiny.

Irenaeus developed the thought that God created man in his own image and likeness (Gen. 1.26–7). The earthiness of his argument, especially in *Adv. Haer.* 5.6.1, is often overlooked. God shaped man in his image and likeness (Gen. 2.7), conforming what he shaped to the image of his Son (Rom. 8.29). What he made was not part of man, so not just soul or spirit, but body and soul. So the complete man, and the true image and likeness of God is 'the mingling and union of the soul which receives the Spirit of the Father, and which is mixed with that flesh which was moulded in the image of God'. All three elements, body, soul and Spirit, are needed for the perfect man in the likeness of God. Since the sin of Adam, the Spirit was lost, and the image incomplete, imperfect. It could not be restored, as long as the Word remained invisible. 'But when the Word of God was made flesh, he affirmed both [image and likeness]: he revealed the true image, becoming himself what was in his image; and he established firmly the likeness, making man like the invisible Father through the visible Word' (*Adv. Haer.* 5.16.2). It is thus precisely in his incarnate state that the Word makes plain the image of God, and in the flesh that man is complete.

The heretics of Irenaeus' day, and most Christian thinkers from Origen onwards, have rejected the idea that the human body is in the likeness of God (Augustine himself could not accept Christianity till he had rejected it). Some modern theological books evade it, even while commending Irenaeus' ideas in general. But the cutting edge of Irenaeus' thought was precisely to defeat the view that mankind is saved spiritually by escape from the body. To him that was false. For the same reason, he was deeply committed to the view that at the second coming of Christ the dead would rise physically from their graves, and the righteous would reign on earth in a rich kingdom centring on a restored earthly Jerusalem. When God is all in all, some of the elect live in heaven, others on earth enjoying the lush fruits, others in the new Jerusalem; but it will be a new world, where death is no more. That hope flowed directly from Irenaeus' vision of God the Creator of this world, who would be vindicated in it – and his reading of the prophets and the Revelation to John. But between the creation and the glorious end there is another process.

Mankind and redemption

In contrast to the gnostic doctrines of the fall, illumination and restoration of the fallen spirits, Irenaeus teaches the biblical story of mankind: creation, transgression, redemption, judgement and final glory. Unfortunately we must piece together his total system from bits of argument aimed usually to explain particular biblical texts which the Gnostics misinterpret. God created man to be in his own image and likeness, a copy of his Son the Word. He was made a living soul, and remains such until spiritual death. But he was not endowed with Spirit unless he kept free of fleshly lusts, that is, used the absolute freedom he received to seek the vision of God; for to see God and to be like him are the same. But from the start man was juvenile, easily deceived. His disobedience over the tree in Eden was little more than an accident, unlike the deliberate, compounded crimes of his son Cain; but it lost him his childlike innocence. Adam immediately feared God, and put on the fig-leaf as a sign of repentance, saying: 'Since I have lost by disobedience the robe of holiness which I got from the Spirit, I now acknowledge that I deserve such a garment as gives no pleasure, but chafes and pricks the body' (*Adv. Haer.* 5.12.2). The likeness to God had been lost.

Although Irenaeus believes the story of Adam and Eve to be historical, he also writes of Adam as a cosmic person: his disobedience is that of all mankind. Of all human beings it is true that 'the first Adam was made by the Lord into a living soul, the second Adam into a lifegiving spirit' (Adv. Haer. 5.12.2, quoting 1 Cor. 15.45): 'So just as the one made into a living soul turned to the worse and lost life, so the same one will himself return to the better, receive the lifegiving Spirit, and find life.' This cannot happen however without a new initiative from God. While the Word remained invisible, he provided ways to train and prepare mankind, but there could be no complete fulfilment of the divine design. The Word, who had always existed with the Spirit as the agent of creation, also appeared enfleshed in Jesus Christ.

Using a term borrowed from Paul (*anakephalaiosasthai*, Eph. 1.10), Irenaeus says repeatedly that Jesus Christ recapitulated ('summed up afresh') the career of Adam (see *Dem.* 32–4 [*NE* 120]). He did this by coming in the flesh like Adam, and living through the years of a human life, triumphant always over the temptations of Satan. So he goes over the ground again, does well what was badly done before, and sums up the whole purpose of mankind's existence. Those who now believe in him receive his Spirit. Individually and corporately they are thus restored to the completeness for which they were designed, in the image and likeness of the Word, body, soul and spirit. In him and like him, they can now see God and live for ever.

If Irenaeus leaves many questions unanswered and even unasked, he left a powerful, thorough and reasonably complete picture of the world under God, which many moderns still find compelling. In the last chapter of *Against Heresies* he writes of 'the same God the Father, who formed man . . . one Son, who completed the will of the Father, and one human race, in which the mysteries of God are fulfilled'. All things in heaven and earth are united in the salvation of mankind.

7

LATIN THEOLOGY LAUNCHED:
TERTULLIAN

Tertullian the Christian

By the end of the second century the gospel had established itself in Roman North Africa, chiefly in the area of the city of Carthage. Some Greek was spoken among the commercial and educated classes, and probably more among Christians than most, since their connections were, like those of Lyons, with Asia Minor and Greek-speaking Rome. There were relics of the old Carthaginian or Punic tongue, and of the native Numidian dialects. But the prevailing culture was Latin. The first translations into Latin of the Scriptures and the liturgy probably originated in Africa, and it seems to have happened before Tertullian started writing around 190. Apart from the Old Latin Bible, only the account of the martyrs of Scilli (*NE* 44–5) is Christian Latin earlier than Tertullian.

Tertullian (*c.* 160–*c.* 220) was well educated in Latin rhetoric, well read, and deeply imbued both with Stoic philosophy and Christian Scripture. He has a powerful argumentative style, and ever since Jerome in the fourth century it has been asserted that he was a professional lawyer. But there is no sure evidence. He seems to have been an adult convert to Christianity. From the start he was concerned about the behaviour of Christians, and constantly wrote on practical subjects such as repentance, prayer, baptism, fasting, behaviour in persecution, and advice to his wife about what to do after his own death. He strongly urged absolute obedience to the revealed will of God, a continual, penitent striving after holiness. Like many Latins after him, he referred to the gospel message, the Christian Scriptures, or Christian belief as a whole, as 'the law' or 'our law'. It was conduct that marked out those who belonged to Christ from the evil world.

In keeping with this character he became a Montanist. That he broke from the main church in Carthage and joined or led a

schism is now disputed. But his later works show an increasing
tendency to support the 'new prophecy' (see pp. 46-7) against the
main church, the 'spirituals' against the 'natural men' (*psychici* =
'soulish' or unspiritual; see 1 Cor. 2.14). And it is difficult to
interpret a statement like this without assuming a split amounting
to schism: 'I for my part was subsequently separated from the
natural men by my acknowledgement and defence of the Paraclete'
(*Prax.* 1 [*NE* 168]). He understood the prophetic claims of the
Montanists perfectly well. He wanted difficult disciplinary
questions to be resolved by a board of prophets, and seriously put
forward the vision of a prophetess to resolve a metaphysical
question (*On the soul* 9 [*NE* 175-6]). But he chiefly saw the
difference as one of strict obedience to God in a holy church,
which the 'natural men' compromised, both by breaking with
tradition (on adultery) and by failing to innovate with the new
prophecy on whether little girls needed veils in church. In a
pamphlet *On modesty* he attacks as outrageous some bishop's
announcement that he would grant remission of sin to those guilty
of adultery and fornication (see *NE* 176-7). The bishop may have
been a Roman one, extending his jurisdiction to Africa in a
remarkable fashion; more likely it was a bishop of Carthage, who
is given the secular title 'sovereign pontiff' as a sarcastic joke. But
whoever it was, Tertullian is clearly departing, as a narrow-
minded Montanist, from the position he had urged upon erring
Christians in his earlier *On repentance*; there repentance and
reconciliation were available for any sin, however grave (see
Repent. 7, 9 [*NE* 174-5]).

Besides practical works, Tertullian wrote notable apologies, in
which persecution is criticized with powerful sarcasm as immoral,
unlawful, and futile (see *NE* 157-63). The number of Christians
in Africa is said, no doubt with exaggeration, to be enormous
(*Apol.* 37 [*NE* 162-3]). He includes a fascinating account of
Christians at prayer and their finances (*Apol.* 30-3, 39 [*NE* 161-2,
163-4]).

Tertullian the churchman

Before he defected to the New Prophecy, Tertullian had already
become a vigorous defender of Catholic truth against heresy. The

position he adopted was a version of that of Irenaeus (see pp. 59–63). Apostolic churches are dispersed throughout the world: not only Rome, 'from which the authority of the apostles is at hand for us [Africans]', but Corinth, Philippi, and Ephesus in the leading Greek areas; and by now the potency of Rome has been further strengthened by the legend that the apostle John was tortured there, as well as the executions of Peter and Paul (*Praescr.* 36 [*NE* 164]). He also knows well the 'Rule of faith'. This summarizes faith in God the creator, who sent the Word his Son to be the God who appears in the Old Testament, and with the Holy Spirit brought down the Word to be enfleshed in Mary. After his mission and passion Jesus Christ ascended and sent the Spirit on believers, and will return to raise the dead, to take the saints to glory and condemn the wicked to everlasting fire. 'This rule . . . was taught by Christ, and raises among ourselves no question except those which heresies introduce, and which make men heretics' (*Praescr.* 13 [*NE* 165]). Like Irenaeus and Hippolytus, he blames heresy on philosophy. Like philosophy, heresy asks questions, and argues about fundamental things. This leads him to a famous denunciation of philosophy: 'What indeed has Athens to do with Jerusalem? What has the Academy to do with the Church? What have heretics to do with Christians?' (*Praescr.* 7 [*NE* 166–7]). But it would be a mistake to think that Tertullian has no philosophy. His work is shot through with philosophical arguments, mostly of Stoic origin, and some creative and acute. Like most bigots, however, he pretends successfully to himself that he just gives the simple original gospel.

Tertullian's argumentative posturing is nowhere more apparent than when he denies the heretics any right to appeal to the Scriptures for arguments. They are not Christians, and to use the church books is trespassing on other people's land, inherited by sure title-deeds from the apostles (*Praescr.* 37 [*NE* 169]). He has not the slightest awareness that the debate was about the nature of the original revelation. To him, what he had received was the one and only truth, and everything else was a diabolic perversion of it. Innovation was heresy, and the whole faith and practice of the Church had been delivered to the apostles, and by them to the churches they founded (*Praescr.* 21 [*NE* 166]). It is a paradox that one who could defend even the last details of church practice as apostolic, even when not written in Scripture (*Cor.* 3–4 [*NE* 171–2]), could also fervently support the New Prophecy when it arose. He always argued the case intensely from where he stood, and must be treated with appropriate caution.

Tertullian the theologian

A most conspicuous case of philosophical influence is the concept of God's nature as material (*corpus*). To the Stoics both God (the world–soul) and the human soul were spirit, but spirit itself was a fine fluid or gaseous element, not (as in Platonism) intangible and independent of space and time. So the words 'God is spirit' mean to Tertullian that God is material, and he argues the same for the soul (cf. *De Anima* 9 = *NE* 175–6). Tertullian's most elaborate doctrine of God and Christ is stated in response to Praxeas, a heretic otherwise unknown to us; since his name means 'fixer' or 'fraud', it may be a nickname Tertullian invented; it is not even out of the question that Irenaeus is the person concerned, since Tertullian is in his book *Against Praxeas* trying to attach heresy to a known opponent of Montanism. 'Praxeas at Rome managed two pieces of the Devil's business: he drove out prophecy and introduced heresy; he put to flight the Paraclete and crucified the Father' (*Prax.* 1 = *NE* 168). Tertullian alleges that Praxeas dissuaded a bishop of Rome some time ago from recognizing Montanus and Prisca (= Priscilla) as prophets and receiving their churches into communion, and that he went on to teach a pernicious doctrine, which amounted to crucifying the Father.

The rest of his book is about the heresy. Praxeas asserts the 'monarchy' of God: God is single, and so Father, Son and Spirit are 'one and the same', but he rejects the 'economy' or 'dispensation'. The term 'economy' (Gk *oikonomia*, Lat. *dispensatio*) sums up Tertullian's idea. The term needs care. Originally referring to household administration or 'stewardship', it came to be used in ancient theology to refer to God's dispensations for creating and saving the world; among the Greeks in particular 'the *oikonomia*' by itself often meant the saving work of Christ in the flesh – what moderns often refer to broadly as 'the incarnation'. In modern theology 'economic trinitarianism' is a doctrine of the Trinity in which God is three in his works, but one in his being; it means that to us he operates in a threefold way, but may in himself be one and simple. It contrasts with 'immanent' or 'essential' trinitarianism, where the being of God in himself has a threefold quality. That is not what Tertullian, or any ancient writer means by *oikonomia*, though it can be debated whether Justin, Irenaeus or Tertullian is an economic trinitarian in the modern sense.

Justin probably is: in eternity the Father is one, and his *logos* becomes another beside him for and in creation. Irenaeus is not (though sometimes said to be), because he repudiates the 'economic' models used by Justin, even though he regards the inner being of God as beyond our knowledge and is not strictly an essentialist either. Origen we shall find (p. 106) to be an essentialist: God, his Son and his Spirit are co-eternal and eternally distinct. Tertullian uses the figure of the Word being put forth at creation just as the apologists do: the immanent reason (*ratio*) of God is always with him, and that already meant that God was not alone, but had as it were another beside himself even before the creation of the world (*Prax.* 5); still the 'complete birth of the Word' was when he 'came forth from God' with the sound, 'Let there be light' (*Prax.* 7). He is perhaps an 'economic trinitarian' trying to be an 'essentialist'. But when he actually uses the word *oikonomia* against Praxeas it has a special and different meaning.

Tertullian has two chief models of this 'economy': imperial administration, and biological or natural organism. The emperor is a monarch whose sole rule is not impaired when he bestows part of his functions on his son: the 'economy' is an administrative arrangement of his own sole rule, which is not thereby disrupted. Again, the Greeks used the word of the arrangement of parts in a plant or animal body, and Tertullian appears to exploit that meaning. Father, Son and Spirit are one in the same way that a tree has a stem and a fruit, but they are not separated from the root. Two other images work similarly: the sun, the ray of light, and the point where the light falls; or the spring, the river from it and the irrigation canal which the river feeds (a familiar picture in Roman Africa). In each case there is only one tree, one light, one water, determined by the single source, which is the root, the sun or the spring. So God and his Word (*sermo*) and his Spirit are three stages of one Being. Two things about this are noteworthy: the Stoic idea of God as material makes these organic models for

God easier to understand; and Tertullian resembles Irenaeus rather than Justin in the steady place he gives to the Holy Spirit in his scheme.

Tertullian invented the customary Latin terms for God as Trinity. 'Trinity' (*trinitas*) means 'threeness', and is defended against those monarchians who insist on 'simple unity' (*simplex unitas*). The threeness consists of the Father, the Son and the Spirit, each of whom is a 'person' (*persona*). These three are distinct, but not divided. They share, or rather are, a single 'substance' or 'being' (*substantia*). At one time Harnack's idea had some currency, that 'person' and 'substance' were being used in a technical legal sense, meaning 'one with legal rights' and 'property'. But this is to be rejected: Tertullian is using logical or philosophical terminology. 'Substance' can mean 'existence', or it can mean 'substance' in the regular English sense of the stuff or material which things are made of; but in this context Tertullian seems to use it to mean '*a* being'. It is what makes God one, though distributed in three persons.

An important consequence of Tertullian's language is that it fixed Western terminology in referring to God as 'one being', while in the East, following Origen, the idea of 'three beings' (Gk *ousiai, hypostaseis*) prevailed. This led to confusion and dispute later, even though both Origen and Tertullian were arguing against the same kind of monarchianism.

Tertullian is consciously trinitarian and gives the Spirit full weight (as a Montanist should). But much of his argument concerns the personal distinctness of Father and Son. The crime of Praxeas is that he 'crucified the Father' by denying the personal distinction: texts like, 'I am God and beside me there is none' (Isa. 45.5), and 'I and the Father are one' (John 10.30) were taken to prove that Father and Son were one person, so that in Christ the Father suffered, or at least 'co-suffered' (*compatitur*) as the invisible or spiritual part of Christ. Tertullian deploys many Scripture texts to prove that the two or three persons are distinct from each other, with simultaneous roles, and he insists that the divine suffers only in the Son. The Father remains untouched by the Son's experiences, as the fountain-spring is not clouded when the stream from it is polluted; the Spirit also remains in his own person untouched, just as he inspires Christian martyrs and enables them to make the good confession, without himself suffering in them (*Prax.* 29).

This idea is important, since the passion of Christ could be used to prove that the Son is inferior to the unchanging, impassible Father.

Tertullian's opponents had tried to argue that Christ was twofold, the Son, flesh, man, Jesus, and the Father, Spirit, God, Christ. Such duality he repudiates as Valentinian, and offers an alternative (see *Prax.* 27). Using technical Stoic vocabulary, he rejects the idea that the Word was changed into flesh, and particularly the idea that there was a sort of alloy of God and man as electrum is an alloy of gold and silver. Jesus Christ has both 'substances', Word (also called Spirit) and flesh, God and man, but they are combined, not fused together. In his one person there is a double quality (*status*). The consequence is important for later Christology:

> To such a degree did there remain unimpaired the proper being of each substance, that in him the Spirit carried out its own acts, that is powers and works and signs, while the flesh accomplished its own passions, hungering in company of the devil, thirsting in company of the Samaritan woman, weeping for Lazarus, sore troubled unto death – and at length it also died.

It is not easy to like Tertullian. But he has much powerful and ingenious theology to offer. He left his mark, particularly on the ethos of African Christianity.

8

SECTARIAN RELIGION AND
EPISCOPAL AUTHORITY

As the second century closed and the third began, there are signs that leading bishops tried to strengthen the organization and administration of the churches. The chief officer of a large city congregation was likely to be abler and better served administratively than his counterpart in a small village. Since large cities had considerable areas dependent upon them for civil and economic purposes, the church in that city was looked up to by those in the surrounding areas. So the bishop of a large city exercised leadership and (perhaps more important) jurisdiction over the adjacent churches. This probably begins as appellate jurisdiction, in other words, when a dispute occurred the weaker party might appeal to the senior church and its bishop.

Dionysius of Corinth, Serapion, and Demetrius

Some such situation lies behind the correspondence of Dionysius of Corinth recorded by Eusebius; but since the texts are not preserved, we are obliged to guess at what was going on. As bishop of the metropolis of Achaea (southern Greece) it is no surprise to find Dionysius about 170 writing pacifying letters to Lacedaemon (Sparta) and Athens (*HE* 4.23.2–3), which are in the same civil jurisdiction. Persecution had hit Greece under Marcus Aurelius (161–80), and the Bishop of Athens, one Publius, was martyred; this led the Athenians to 'apostatize from the Word' until the new bishop Quadratus pulled them together. Whatever that crisis was at Athens, in Crete Dionysius apparently supports one bishop, Philip of Gortyna, against another, Pinytus of Cnossus, with whom he has a difference of view about the necessity for sexual chastity (4.23.5/7–8). The same topics occur when he writes to churches even further away: Nicomedia (4.23.4) and Amastris (4.23.6); in the last case he writes to the church about its bishop Palmas, perhaps supporting Palmas' critics. Pierre Nautin

is probably right to assume that in each case the powerful bishop
Dionysius had been approached and asked to intervene in other
churches. If so, his letter to Soter of Rome (4.23.9–12), in which
he praises Soter and complains that his letters have been textually
misused, is his own defence against appeal to an even stronger
bishop by those he had rebuked. This illustrates the exercise of
leadership over more immediately adjacent churches, but also the
building up of a pattern of a universal Church of the kind which
Irenaeus interpreted theologically.

Serapion was Bishop of Antioch about 190–209. He knew
enough to write against Montanism. But he is chiefly interesting
for advising the Christians of nearby Rhossus that he had changed
his mind about the propriety of using the *Gospel of Peter* since his
visit to them; and for appointing Palut as Bishop of Edessa, which
became a great centre of Syrian Christianity. Christianity at Edessa
had been developed on unusual lines by followers of Marcion and
Bardaisan (Bardesanes) and Tatian. None of these used the
conventional four-Gospel canon, all were notable for their ascetic
(encratite) principles, and all were reckoned heretical by more
Westerly Christians. Serapion's action can be seen as an attempt
to impose Catholic faith and order where they had not previously
existed (*NE* 126–7, 154).

Demetrius, Bishop of Alexandria 189–232, is alleged to have
been the first bishop of that place to appoint bishops in other
cities; presumably some more casual organization prevailed before.
With his successors Heraclas and Dionysius the old system
whereby the new bishop was appointed by the presbyters of
Alexandria ceased, other bishops now being responsible (Jerome,
Ep. 146.1). Demetrius shepherded his flock through the Severan
persecutions, and tried to suppress the 'heresy' of Origen.

The church in Rome under Victor

In the same decades a series of active bishops began to bring
uniformity to the churches in Rome: Victor (about 189–99),
Zephyrinus (about 199–217), and Callistus (about 217–22). The
church seems to have been pluriform in the same way that,
according to Bauer, the main Eastern centres were. The first
congregations arose from an already divided Jewish community.
Hermas shows that the organization was loose, and the first sole

bishop was probably Sixtus I (Xystos), about 120. Victor tried to impose uniform practice about keeping Easter. Jews observed the Passover as the yearly spring festival, even after the fall of the temple made it impossible to keep the sacrifice as prescribed in the law of Moses. Christians in the main stream carried on the observance of the Passover as a commemoration of the passion and resurrection of Jesus, which happened at Passover time. The Christians of the Roman province of Asia (i.e. western Asia Minor) traditionally observed the *Pascha* (Passover) by breaking their Paschal fast on the day when the Jews 'put away the leaven', that is the fourteenth of the Jewish month Nisan. They were later nicknamed 'Quartodecimans' ('Fourteenthers'). Rome and most of the churches kept the fast till the Sunday following, a practice which perhaps originated in the desire of Jerusalem Christians to distinguish themselves from the Jews. Victor came into conflict with Polycrates of Ephesus on this issue (Eusebius, *HE* 5.23–4 [*NE* 138–9]), but it seems to have started with an attempt to correct the Asian immigrants in Rome itself; otherwise it is impossible to understand how the past bishops 'sent the Eucharist to members of those communities who observed [the fourteenth day]' (5.24.15 [*NE* 140]). The narratives of Eusebius may be based entirely on a letter of Irenaeus, of which he quotes puzzling fragments. Irenaeus, torn between his respect for the Asiatic tradition, including the pillar of orthodoxy Polycarp, and Rome which he held to be the great example of apostolic tradition, was plainly embarrassed (see pp. 59–61). He claims that 'the difference about the fast enhances the unity of our faith' (5.24.13 [*NE* 140]), which is very hard to believe. The Sunday Easter and Victor prevailed; but a local Roman Quartodeciman group led by Blastus continued for a time.

Victor's standing is indicated by the story that he was able through the emperor Commodus' mistress Marcia to get Christian prisoners released from the Sardinian mines, one of them the rising young Callistus, whom he sent with a pension to Antium, no doubt in some ministerial capacity (Hippolytus, *Adv. Haer.* 9.12.10–13 [*NE* 148]).

Victor is said to have taken first steps against a heresy from Asia Minor attributed to Theodotus the Cobbler (leatherworker), which we know only from fragmentary and hostile accounts (especially in Eusebius, *HE* 5.28 [*NE* 143–5]). Modern writers call his doctrine 'dynamic monarchian', on the ground that it saved the unity (Gk *monarchia*) of God by making the divinity of Christ an impersonal power (Gk *dynamis*). This name was not given it in ancient times, where 'monarchian' referred to the modalist position described below. The Theodotian teachers were also called 'psilanthropists', because they were alleged to teach that Christ was a 'mere man' (Gk *psilos anthropos*), and their doctrine 'Artemonite' after a later third-century exponent Artemon. The Theodotians were sophisticated; they are reproached for using Aristotle and the medical writer Galen, for practising textual criticism on the Bible, and for arguing that their own doctrine was traditional in the Church before Victor's day. There were certainly other leaders: another Theodotus, called 'the Banker' (to whom a speculative doctrine based on the Melchizedek model for Christ is attributed: *NE* 145), Asclepiodotus, and notably one Natalius, a confessor who joined the group and became its bishop in Rome.

Doctrinal disputes: Hippolytus

The christological problems became more serious under Victor's successor Zephyrinus. In his time a Roman presbyter called Caius (Gaius) wrote against the Montanist theologian Proclus, who also worked in Rome. In the process Caius challenged the apostolic authenticity of John's Gospel and Revelation (Hippolytus in *NE* 153). The fourfold Gospel canon was already defended by Irenaeus, and presupposed earlier by Tatian in his *Diatessaron*. Caius appears to have been in other respects orthodox, though we know little about him; he used philological arguments, and especially pointed to the discrepancies between the Synoptics and John, which he attributed to the Judaeo-gnostic Cerinthus. Caius in turn was attacked, and the Gospel and Revelation defended, by another Roman presbyter called Hippolytus, the leading Roman theologian of the day.

To Hippolytus are attributed various works. He wrote a pungent pamphlet *Against Noetus* (see *NE* 145–6). Noetus was the earliest serious representative of those called 'Monarchians', one of whom, nicknamed Praxeas, stimulated Tertullian's important work, *Against Praxeas* (*NE* 167–9). These identified Jesus Christ as God, denying any personal distinction. Because they see the Father and the Son (and the Spirit if he is mentioned) as different modes of operation of the one person who is God, some moderns class them as 'modalist' or 'modalist Monarchian', and the term 'Sabellian' is used in the same sense (see below). To outsiders Christians looked like a group who worshipped Christ as a cult-god (Pliny, *Ep.* 10.96.7 [*NE* 19]), and many felt like it to themselves; in the popular *Acts of John* (early third century?) Christ is repeatedly spoken of as the (only) God and worshipped accordingly. The chief point of the gospel was monotheism, belief in one God, creator, lawgiver and judge. Since Christ performed all these functions, one feels no need to look further.

Melito of Sardis, who is among those praised by the critic of Theodotus (Eusebius *HE* 5.28.5 [*NE* 144]), in his *On Pascha* attributes to Jesus Christ all the works of God from creation to judgement, who is also the object of doxologies. The concerns leading to monarchianism are various: Gnostics and Marcionites divided the Creator and Lawgiver from an alleged superior God; Theodotians denied Christ's personal deity; the apologists asserted that Christ was a 'second God' beside the Father, an intermediate Logos who did not share the Father's utter transcendence, and they had been rebuked for it even by Irenaeus. 'What evil am I doing in glorifying Christ?', asks Noetus. But the 'presbyters' (probably Asian bishops) who condemned him stuck to assertions of one God and the suffering Son: 'We too know in truth one God; we know Christ; we know that the Son suffered even as he suffered, and died even as he died, and rose again on the third day, and is at the right hand of the Father, and comes to judge the living and the dead', they said (Hippolytus, *Noet.* 1 [*NE* 145–6]). Tertullian's heretic Praxeas also visited Rome at an unknown time, and so probably did Noetus; Hippolytus names the successors in his 'school' – a separate church organization – as Epigonus and Cleomenes, and alleges that the latter bribed Zephyrinus to tolerate him. This brings us to the fiercest dispute in Rome of the period.

We know the career of Zephyrinus' successor Callistus (Calixtus I) through the fierce onslaught in the long *Refutation of all heresies*. If, as is usually held, its author is Hippolytus, then on the death of Zephyrinus that learned presbyter reckoned himself bishop, and himself alleges that the heretic Callistus 'established a school against the Church', that is, he set himself up as bishop against Hippolytus with a congregation which claimed to be the 'Catholic Church' (*Ref.* 9.12.20, 25 [*NE* 151–2]). The *Refutation* was written after Callistus died. It surveys heresies past and present, with long quotations proving (perversely) that each derives from a pagan philosophy; Callistus is its climax, and his heresy compounds the faults of all. After a damning account of Callistus' fraudulent and disorderly early career, and the trick by which he got the name of 'martyr' (he spent time in the mines of Sardinia with other Christian prisoners), Victor sent him to the sea-port Antium (9.12.1–13 [*NE* 146–9]). He was recalled by Zephyrinus and put in charge of the Roman cemetery, an important piece of property with underground galleries where the increasing Christian cult of the dead was performed. Callistus led the stupid Zephyrinus to make contradictory pronouncements: 'I know one God, Jesus Christ, nor except him do I know any other that is begotten and susceptible to suffering'; 'The Father did not die, but the Son.' Callistus' own view was held to be compounded from the contradictions of Heraclitus and the heresies of Noetus and Theodotus. He had condemned Hippolytus as a ditheist, and held that Logos and Spirit were not distinct from the Father; the Spirit incarnate in Jesus was the Father, the visible flesh was the Son, so Father and Son are one Person (Gk *prosopon*) and the Father suffered with (Gk *sympeponthenai*) the Son (9.12.15–19 [*NE* 150--1]). The doctrine is like that which Tertullian attacks: 'The Son is flesh, that is, Man, that is, Jesus; the Father is Spirit, that is, God, that is, Christ', 'The Son suffers, the Father co-suffers (Lat. *compatitur*)' (*Prax.* 27, 29). Reading between the lines of the malicious report, Callistus was cautiously and conservatively steering a course, resembling that of Irenaeus, between Hippolytus and Sabellius.

We know little of Sabellius, who came from Libya (where doctrinal enthusiasms were always strong) and must have worked in Rome. His teaching is impossible to isolate from better-known heretics of the next century with whom he was constantly compared (especially Marcellus of Ancyra), but it was a sophisticated form of Modalism. God was *huiopator* (a coinage meaning 'Sonfather' or 'Sonfathering'), and the Son and the Spirit are projected for redemption and sanctification at the appropriate time like rays of warmth and light projected from the sun. There is no reason to doubt that Callistus excommunicated Sabellius, though Hippolytus tries to blame him for Sabellius' heresy and says he was thus inconsistent. The name 'Sabellian' came to be used conventionally for any doctrine which speaks of Father and

Son, or of Father, Son and Spirit, as one person in different guises.

Hippolytus outlines true doctrine in the last book of the *Refutation* (10.32–4) in terms not identical with those in *Against Noetus*. One God in foreknowledge of all things formed the elements and every being first in thought. This inner thought or deliberation was Logos, his firstborn Son. This Logos when spoken gave the thought substance, and the created world came into existence; so he is mediator of creation. In the incarnation he recapitulated the stages of human life, to the point of suffering and death, and became the firstfruits of redemption by his resurrection. Man as the lord of creation must learn to know himself (a classic Platonic thought) as God's image. Despite Hippolytus' onslaughts on philosophy, this scheme uses ideas typical of middle Platonism. In *Against Noetus* 10–11 Hippolytus presents a God who 'while single was many', having within him Word, Wisdom, Power and Counsel. Thus God's being is complex even before creation. There are not however two Gods: Power issues from the All like light from light, water from a spring, a ray from the sun. When made visible in the 'sent one', i.e. Jesus Christ, the Logos becomes Son. While the Word forms the universe, Wisdom adorns it, and is thus apparently identified (as by Irenaeus) with Holy Spirit. The Holy Spirit is formally named, but not in this context. Similarly in *Ref.* 10.32–4 the Spirit is not named, but appears to be identified with the Truth of the prophetic Scriptures. While Hippolytus' two accounts are not wholly reconcilable, there is enough similarity to perceive a coherent picture, and to leave the impression of a serious and learned theology.

Discipline and order: Callistus

As 'bishop' Hippolytus compiled a liturgical handbook called *The Apostolic Tradition*. Unfortunately lost in its original Greek, it has to be reconstructed from a close Latin version of part of it, from expanded editions in Coptic and Ethiopic, and from extracts incorporated in later documents in Greek. Though the reconstruction is at times uncertain, it provides precious information about the ordination of the clergy, baptismal preparation and practice, and the daily discipline and worship of individuals. Purporting to record ancient practice, it may provide evidence of second-century life in the Roman church. The bishop is thought of as a 'high priest' whose main function is to offer prayer and sacrifice. Hippolytus' liturgy for the bishop's Eucharist is the oldest eucharistic anaphora (thanksgiving prayer) to survive apart from those in *Didache*, and has been used as a model for various twentieth-century liturgical rites. His baptismal rite (*NE* 141–3) is discussed elsewhere (see pp. 18–22).

Hippolytus' attack on Callistus did not stop at the charges of mean birth, fraud and heresy: the upstart had also wrecked church discipline (*Ref.* 9.12.20–6 [*NE* 151–3]). He had said that bishops should remain in office, even if guilty of mortal sin (21). He had permitted men who had married more than once to be ordained as bishops, presbyters and deacons, and did not treat it as a sin when one already ordained got married (22). He connived at unions between women of senatorial rank and low-born men, which Hippolytus calls 'adultery' (as in Roman law it was), and claims that it leads also to murderous abortions (24–5). The incidental value of this information is considerable: the Bishop of Rome's influence over other bishops (perhaps only in Italy, we do not know), disputes over clerical morals and clerical marriage, and the problem of a church in which there were more high-born women than high-born men for them to marry. But the first and most significant charge is that Callistus 'first invented the device of conniving with men as to their pleasures, saying that sins were forgiven to everyone by himself' (20). This particularly affected those called Christians who belonged to other congregations, including various heresies and Hippolytus' own group ('the Church'). If they were expelled by others for sins, Callistus allowed them in, and his 'school' was thronged and claimed the name of 'Catholic Church' (20–1; 25). This admixture of sinners was justified by misused Scripture texts like, 'Let tares grow up along with the wheat' (Matt. 13.30), and led to the enormity of second baptism (22;26). It should be noted however that even Hippolytus cannot say that Callistus practised second baptism, only that it happened in his time; it was associated with the movement of the Judeo-Christian Elxai, whose agents reached Rome at this period; they perhaps practised repeated ritual washings. It is best to see Callistus' policy, like Stephen's later, as one of admitting baptized members of all sects by a rite for reconciling penitents (presumably the laying-on of hands). It was a policy, apparently successful, of unifying as many Christians as possible under his authority by acknowledging their existing baptismal commitment. The Church was not so tightly defined as to exclude those of other congregations, and perhaps even the clerical status of their leaders could be acknowledged. This was all hateful to Hippolytus, the vindicator of orthodoxy, who saw all heresies, including Callistus' own, as founded upon non-Christian philosophy and utterly false.

It should be said that Callistus' acts are often interpreted differently. He is identified with the bishop attacked by Tertullian in *On modesty* 1 (*NE* 176), who had decreed that baptized persons who had fallen into adultery and fornication might be reconciled after due penance. If this identification were right, it is a remarkable case of a Roman bishop laying down a rule and trying to impose it in another province (North Africa). But such 'papal' activity is probably an anachronism; there is nothing in Tertullian's book to prove that he is attacking a Roman bishop (certainly not the title *papa* ('pope'), which is used at this period of bishops of Carthage, not of Rome); and above all the allegations are quite different from those made by Hippolytus.

Hippolytus is probably the 'presbyter' who was condemned with Bishop Pontianus of Rome (230–5) to labour in the Sardinian mines in 235, where both died. Hippolytus wrote his *Refutation* after Callistus' death, and cannot have been reconciled immediately with Bishop Urban (222–30). Perhaps the joint martyrdom led to the reconciliation of their two congregations; we do not know. Someone, perhaps a wealthy admirer, put a new male head on a statue of a female figure, still preserved, and carved on its base a list of Hippolytus' books. One must assume that his *Refutation* was preserved because of its curious and damning account of so many heresies, and that its readers did not know that Callistus was among the honourably recorded bishops of Rome. Both he and Hippolytus were involved in disputes touching vital matters of Faith and Church. Callistus would not allow the distinction which Hippolytus drew between the Father and his Word or Son, and was pilloried as a heretic for it. Hippolytus followed the apologists and resembled Tertullian, while Callistus was closer to Irenaeus. At the same time Callistus used generous rules to enlarge his communion, while Hippolytus pursued the rigorous line one comes to expect of able theologians (like Tertullian and Origen). Some of the same issues were to emerge again as the third century reached its crisis.

Reconciliation and renewed persecution

The persecution of 235-8 was singular in that it was clearly political. Alexander Severus, emperor 222-35, allowed Christianity to be tolerated; his successor Maximin Thrax (235-8) destroyed leading persons associated with Alexander, and that included Christian leaders like Pontianus and Hippolytus. After 238 the churches enjoyed some peace, especially under Philip the Arabian (244-9). Rome had an able bishop, Fabian (236-50), to whom tradition attributed a division of his church between seven congregations, led by deacons and presbyters. It also produced a theologian, who was to come to the fore in the crisis of 250, the presbyter Novatian. We know little of Novatian's earlier career, but at some time he wrote a book *On the Trinity*, which by a quirk of later history survives: it proved useful in some debates a century later. It is a skilful work of polemic against the heresies which divided the Roman church: he demonstrates that the Son is distinct from the Father, and at the same time strongly argues that this does not imply a doctrine of two gods. His response thus embodies principles enunciated by both Hippolytus and Callistus. The Father spoke his Word, not as a mere sound, but as a real being (*in substantia*). Following Tertullian, he speaks of a community of substance between Father and Son, and calls him 'a second person (*persona*) after the Father'. Novatian extends the traditional use of Old Testament theophanies to prove that there is a duality: wherever God is said to intervene on earth in a visible or local manner, the divine person is the Son. So the God who descends to confound the tongues at the tower of Babel is neither the Father (who is never spatially limited) nor an angel (because in Deuteronomy it is God who allocates nations to angels), but the Son (*Trin.* 17). Novatian envisages a Son who existed as an individual being (*in substantia*) before time; even if the Father in a sense 'precedes' him, he was *in* the Father before he was *with* the Father. This approaches Origen's doctrine of 'eternal generation': God is in himself a Father with a Son, and the Son is not simply a function of God's actions in time ('economic trinitarianism'), but belongs to his own being. Though the book is known as *On the Trinity*, the status of the Spirit is not discussed, only his function as the inspiring and sanctifying power of prophets and Church: he must be presumed to be one of the creatures of the Son; in this respect Novatian resembles Hippolytus rather than Tertullian. This accomplished theology, rooted in careful and learned exegesis of Scripture, must have been persuasive in its time. When the disaster of 250 hit the churches, there is no trace of the theological disputes which divided Hippolytus from Callistus. The resolution of issues may have been due to Novatian.

ONE CHURCH, ONE BAPTISM: CYPRIAN

Persecution and the problem of the lapsed

After 235 the Empire was afflicted with repeated barbarian invasions and plagues, the economy was in poor shape, and legions on the frontier repeatedly installed their commanders as emperors. This is what happened in 248 in Pannonia, where the victorious troops proclaimed Decius, and he led them back to Italy to overthrow his friend Philip the Arabian in 249. Decius took over, and strove to consolidate his power; this process included bargains with various power-brokers, including some in Egypt who were decidedly anti-Christian. The expansion of the Church, its progress among the educated classes, the economic collapse which affected pagan religion as well as everything else, had led some to blame Christianity for the evils. In Egypt Christians were already in 248 subjected to informal harassment and lynching. Decius publicly declared himself a restorer of ancient values and morality; he may have sincerely believed he had such a mission. Beginning with his own offering to Jupiter in Rome on 3 January 250, he required the same to be done throughout the Empire. So began the first systematic, and the most successful, imperial attack on the churches. Leaders were cut down: Fabian of Rome and Babylas, Bishop of Antioch, died among the first in January 250. Then all persons were required to sacrifice, and a commission was set up in each city to supervise the sacrifice, and to give countersigned certificates (for examples see *NE* 214–15). Euctemon of Smyrna was probably not the only bishop to lead all his congregation to the pagan altars. Dionysius of Alexandria was rescued from his captors (unwillingly, he says) by some revellers; Cyprian of Carthage went into hiding. To these two bishops we owe our firsthand records of the effects. In the great cities where the imperial edict first took effect, people flocked to fulfil the command. Dionysius and Cyprian describe the urgency with which Christian populations, unused to persecution and anxious to be

safe, crowded round to make their sacrifice and get their piece of
paper (Eusebius *HE* 6.41.9–13 [*NE* 213]; Cyprian, *Laps.* 8–9 [*NE*
216–17]). A few fled, a few suffered imprisonment and torture
before yielding, a very few died.

Within a year the persecution itself collapsed, Decius had
embarked on a rash northern campaign in which he was killed in
251, and exiles like Cyprian were free to return. But the churches
had suffered a stunning blow. Most of the lapsed still saw
themselves as Christians. Perhaps they relied upon the system of
restoration already known to the young Tertullian. By this grave
sin could be forgiven and a Christian could be formally reconciled
after a period of good behaviour under supervision in which some
of the catechumen's restrictions were reimposed. But now the
numbers, and the lapse and decimation of the clergy, made such
process seem impossible to implement. Standards dropped, and
new forces intervened. They might turn to any remaining clergy.
Some of these simply restored on their own authority those who
had committed idolatry. This happened in Carthage. But their
hand was greatly strengthened by the confessors. The term
'confessor' refers to confessing the faith before the world, especially
in court or by suffering torture and imprisonment. Originally the
meaning is the same as 'martyr' (Gk *martys*, 'witness'), but the
terms came to be used differently: the martyr had died for his
confession, the confessor had survived. But special qualities still
attach to the confessor. He has received the inspiration promised
by Jesus to confessors (Matt. 10.19–20). Hippolytus (*Ap. Trad.*
10.1–2) allows a confessor who has been imprisoned to become a
deacon or presbyter without further ordination; it was normal for
confessors to sit with the presbyters, even if not exercising the
office. More significant, during the persecution at Lyons in 177,
those held in prison exercised the right to reconcile lapsed persons
held in prison with them and God had vindicated their judgement
when both confessors and reconciled achieved martyrdom in the
arena (Eusebius, *HE* 5.1, especially 1.45–9 [*NE* 40–1]). In
Carthage in 251 the confessors began to play a large part in
authorizing the reconciliation of the lapsed. Beginning with
individuals they knew, some of those who had been imprisoned
began signing documents (*libelli pacis*, 'certificates of reconciliation') giving the clergy authority to restore sinners to
communion, and even demanding this. Cyprian was particularly

shocked by a letter informing him that 'we have granted peace to all with whose behaviour, since the commission of the crime, you are satisfied', and inviting him to notify his fellow-bishops (*Ep.* 23, 27 [*NE* 217–18]). To understand Cyprian's reaction, we must appreciate the kind of man he was.

Cyprian was not brought up a Christian. He was typical of those well-to-do and well-informed persons who were joining the churches in the West as well as the East. He was trained in the literary skills needed for official work, but grew to despise and hate the self-seeking of the world he lived in. Sickened by his own sinfulness, he rejoiced to learn the gospel and felt great relief as he was spiritually renewed in baptism about 246. It is typical of him that on his election to the bishopric two years later he sold his property to give alms – even though some of it was bought back for him by friends – and that he forsook every trace of secular literature in his Christian writings, where no other writer is alluded to but only the Scripture. His thinking was modelled on the sharp distinctions characteristic of Tertullian, who was to him 'the Master'. Such a man took the office of bishop with utter seriousness, and though he did not see it as his duty to expose himself to arrest and death (as he did afterwards in 258), he was appalled at the mass apostasy. The persecution was God's judgement on a slack and worldly church (*Laps.* 5–6 [*NE* 215–16]), the act of sacrifice was a fatal betrayal of God and his law. From hiding Cyprian tried to build up a team of loyal clergy, and urged there should be no restoration till the bishops were in a position to take decisions (*Ep.* 17.1 [*NE* 219]). Once returned he set about repairing the disaster. He vigorously opposed lax restoration to communion, whether or not it had confessors' support. He wrote a book *On the lapsed* in which the horror of apostasy is described, with cautionary tales of God's judgements on those who presumed on his mercy while still unclean. Even an infant who had been fed sacrificial meat unknown to its parents became ill and vomited when fed the eucharistic elements (*Laps.* 25). The tone is so stern that some interpreters think that he considered no remission to be possible, as Tertullian held in his later years. But in the last chapter it becomes clear that God can and will forgive; where there is true repentance, demonstrated in devotion and good works, God can note what the confessors recommend and the bishops judge to be right. That illustrates a

significant feature of Cyprian's view: the only proper earthly judge
of such matters is the bishop. It took effect insofar as the book *On
the lapsed* was probably presented at a council in Carthage in 251.
The bishops there assembled agreed a moderate policy: penitents
were to be individually examined, and subjected to different grades
of penalty according to the gravity of the offence. In the first place
this merely distinguished those who had obtained certificates,
presumably by bribery or influence, without sacrificing (who were
to be readmitted to the Church) and those who had sacrificed
(who were to be restored to communion only on the point of
death). Soon a more detailed agreement would be reached with
Rome, and later councils were to make more subtle distinctions;
when persecution once more threatened, the opportunity for
reconciliation was extended to all. Thus at Carthage Cyprian's
view prevailed at his council. But the dissidents, who could claim
to have stayed on when the bishop fled, and to have the charismatic
authority of confessors on their side, continued as a separate
congregation led by a deacon; in the face of Cyprian's steady
campaign against them they later appointed as bishop one
Fortunatus (Cyprian, *Ep.* 59 [*NE* 226–8]). As respect for Cyprian
grew, so did his policy of moderate discipline in the hands of the
bishops prevail.

The Roman church meanwhile was also gravely split. There
mass apostasy had followed the death of Fabian. No meeting to
elect a new bishop was possible. Some church business continued,
and from exchanges of letters with Cyprian we know that the
presbyter Novatian took a leading role. What divided the Roman
church in 251 was the rigour of Novatian towards the lapsed. His
high-minded repudiation of those who had broken their baptismal
seal during the persecution led the church to prefer the indifferent
Cornelius to the brilliant Novatian when it finally dared appoint a
new bishop. Novatian's supporters included bishops and confessors,
and these behaved as though Cornelius were not ordained, and
made Novatian bishop. The leaders of churches everywhere
received letters or deputations from both claimants to the office.
Dionysius in Alexandria preferred Cornelius (see Eusebius *HE*
6.45; 7.8 [*NE* 232–3]); Fabius of Antioch sided with Novatian,
though he died soon after. Cyprian wavered, having been close to
Novatian, but being satisfied that Cornelius was ordained first,
supported him firmly but without enthusiasm (*Ep.* 55.8 commends

him for mediocrity; see *NE* 225). Cyprian was to have difficulty bringing all the churches of Africa round to his position. Cornelius' letter against Novatian was crude and abusive, but it did include an impressive list of the clergy and pensioners whom the Roman church supported (Eusebius *HE* 6.43.7–12 [*NE* 230–2]), and who must be supposed to support Cornelius. The Roman confessors soon forsook Novatian, but his dissident church grew and prospered, and he himself outlived Cornelius and several of his successors. The influx of half-converted multitudes in the imperial church of the next century was to favour the growth of a puritan group which came to withdraw all the penitential machinery for lapsed Christians, whom it left exclusively to the judgement of God. Novatian's church preserved purity of doctrine as its founder had defined it, and the threefold washing of baptism was unchanged. But it instituted one thing previously unheard of in Rome: it refused to recognize any baptisms other than its own. Lapsed and heretical Christians of all denominations were treated no differently from pagans, and were exorcized and baptized accordingly. The consequences were to be fateful.

Schism and unity

The schisms (splits) in the churches drew from Cyprian an important tract *On the unity of the catholic Church*; the word 'unity' means 'uniqueness' and not merely 'undividedness'. He does not specify whether his assault on schismatics is directed at his dissidents in Carthage or at the Novatianists in Rome and Africa; they would apply to both. Those who forsake the one true Church, he argued, are like the biblical rebels Korah, Dathan and Abiram, who took the priesthood unlawfully and were burned and swallowed up by the earth. Nothing can excuse or make up for this sin of division: even one who gives his body to be burnt is no martyr; since he lacks love his sacrifice is worthless. But where is unity found? In the single universal Church throughout the world (see *Un.* 4–6 [*NE* 228–30]). It has many members, but it is one, just as the sun is one but has many rays, the tree has many branches but one root, many irrigation channels are fed by a single spring (5). Cut off from source or root, the ray disappears, the branch dies, the channel dries up. Such are the schismatics. The believer knows he is part of the Church because his bishop is part of the unity which forms the whole. The crucial part of Cyprian's understanding of unity is the role of the bishops world-wide. They are the glue which holds the universal Church together. In this conception the insights of Clement of Rome and Irenaeus about apostolic succession and unanimity of bishops in the doctrine of the apostles are strengthened by several new features:

1. The world-wide ('catholic') Church identifies itself by the mutual recognition of the bishops. The rule that three bishops are needed to make a new one is already established at this time (Eusebius *HE* 6.43.8 [*NE* 231]); and a new bishop in a major see would make himself known to the others, and would know and guarantee those in his area with whom he was in communion. Thus a bureaucracy parallel to that by which the Empire was run, managing dossiers of letters and documents, had grown up, and for Cyprian only those recognized in the system belonged to it. His own training in public affairs made him take this for granted.

2. The privileges of confessors were now firmly set aside, though not without protest. It is notable that the chief dissident body both in Carthage and Rome is based upon a group of confessors; this perhaps accounts for the otherwise inexplicable career of Novatus (not to be confused with Novatian), who was involved both in the group which promoted indulgence to the lapsed in Carthage, and with the appointment of the rigorist Novatian at Rome. For Cyprian the inspired recommendations of confessors could only be effective on the bishop's decision.

3. The charismatic prophets had already lost their liturgical role to the bishops. Preaching and teaching were shared by bishops, presbyters and (increasingly uneasily) lay teachers with outstanding gifts. Now the priestly function came to the fore. Already Hippolytus had identified the episcopate as a high priesthood, evoking the sacrificial and liturgical role of the biblical (Aaronic) model. To Cyprian this biblical authorization is vital; the schismatics are like those who rebelled against the Moses who had selected exclusively the family of Aaron. The bishop was an authorized priest offering prayer and sacrifice acceptable to God. His usual word for a bishop is *sacerdos*, 'priest', which is not yet generally used to designate a presbyter. One result was that the eucharistic offering of gifts with

thanksgiving and intercession is increasingly seen as a sacrificial cult, the lawful fulfilment of the Old Testament prescriptions, but also the Christian equivalent of current pagan rites. Another result was that Cyprian felt obliged to insist that bishops carried in them a spiritual status; it was like that formerly associated with prophets. Just as in earlier times the test of a true prophet was whether he lived up to his words, so now Cyprian held that a bishop must be pure in every way, or God would not hear his prayer and accept the sacrifice he offered. A sinful bishop had ceased to be one, as Hippolytus had implied in his criticism of Callistus.

The tract *On the unity of the catholic Church* contains a contested passage which has never been wholly and finally explained (see *NE* 228–30). The manuscripts of chapters 4 and 5 have various versions, which on analysis reduce to two, usually called the 'Received text' (or 'Hartel text') and the 'Primacy text'. Both present reasons from Scripture why the Church is only one, and both begin with Matt. 16.18–19, where Christ calls Simon the Rock (Peter) on which the Church is built, and gives him the keys of the kingdom of heaven. The Received text uses the uniqueness of Peter to exemplify the one Church, whereas the Primacy text speaks of his primacy (*primatus*), and of the danger of forsaking the 'chair of Peter on whom the Church is built'. It is easy to see why later writers, concerned with disputes over papal primacy, have claimed one or other of these as original. An attractive explanation is that of M. Bévenot, who argued that both versions originated with Cyprian, but at different stages in the debate: originally he wrote the Primacy words, but these were later used against him when he fell out with Rome, and he then revised his work to produce the Received text. Bévenot holds however that the primacy had in Cyprian's original meaning no reference to Rome; if anything, the chair of Peter is the bishop in each place, whose unity figures forth the unity of the whole Church. But it is one hypothesis among others.

Cyprian on defaulting bishops and on baptism

Cyprian began to disagree with Rome after Cornelius died in exile and his successor Lucius died a few months later in 254. Stephen (254–7) was to cause Cyprian difficulties on two issues, both of which were related to basic questions of the nature of the Church and its bishops: sinful bishops, and the baptisms of heretics.

Cyprian's letters reveal the first issue, provoked by an important bishop in Gaul who sided with Novatian, Marcian of Arles. His fellow-bishops wanted to depose him, but they got no support from Stephen, and they could not securely act without him. Cyprian wrote to urge him to support Marcian's removal and the election of a replacement (*Ep.* 68 [*NE* 233–4]). In Spain two bishops were accused of various offences involving (fairly minor) matters of pagan religion. Their opponents removed them, but they were able to rally some local support, and importantly that of Stephen of Rome. The replacement bishops and their supporters appealed to Cyprian, who held a council and vindicated them against those they had deposed (*Ep.* 67 [*NE* 235–7]). Both these cases show how Cyprian saw the bishopric as a spiritual gift, so that any vice or defect disqualified a person from the office, even if validly appointed. Christ's Spirit could not be where Christ's law was broken, and God would not hear the prayer of a guilty priest. Stephen, like Callistus before him, upholds the bishop's lawful role even where there is doubt about his correct behaviour; Augustine would later clarify the distinction between office and person, validity and effectiveness, when the same issues were raised more sharply by the Donatists.

The second question, often misunderstood and misstated in modern times, was about baptism. Cyprian inherited a tradition, apparently settled by councils in Carthage and Asia Minor, that those baptized by schismatics and heretics were not treated as Christians at all, but were prepared for baptism and baptized like other candidates (Cyprian, *Ep.* 73.3 [*NE* 240]; Eusebius *HE* 7.5.5; 7.7.5). It was not rebaptism, and had nothing directly to do with lapse or post-baptismal sin. Everyone believed there was only one baptism. But Cyprian and those like him, notably Firmilian the Bishop of Caesarea in Cappadocia, held that to mean that there was no baptism except in the one Catholic Church. Their opponents saw the one baptism as what the individual undertook, no matter who officiated in whatever church, and regarded Cyprian's practice as rebaptism. The matter was precipitated by a statement of Stephen, the meaning of which is in part obscure, quoted indignantly by Cyprian: 'If any come to you from any heresy whatsoever, let there be no innovation beyond what has been handed down, namely that hands be laid on such to repentance, since those who are properly heretics do not baptize such as come to them from one another, but only admit them to communion' (Cyprian *Ep.* 74.1 [*NE* 238]).

From this three points are clear: Stephen argues for a traditional position against innovation; the subject is heretical, not (or not only) schismatical baptism; and he appeals to general Christian practice extending to heresies outside his own communion. We know that other issues did arise. Some clergy distinguished baptisms done in the name of the Trinity (the threefold washing) from other formulae, like that simply in the name of Jesus Christ: the anonymous tract *On rebaptism* argues that all are valid; Cyprian argues that even Novatianist baptisms are invalid, in spite of the names of the Trinity (*Ep.* 69.7 [*NE* 237]). It is not certain how the dispute arose. But it is known that Novatian had adopted the policy, perhaps learned from associates in Africa, of recognizing no baptisms but those of his own church. The tradition which Stephen affirms against him appears already in what Hippolytus alleged about Callistus, that he accepted renegades from all kinds of Christian denominations. Even Stephen's astonishing appeal to heretical practice relates to the long-standing Christian conviction, older than the formal system of Catholic episcopacy, that baptism above all else registers the individual's rejection of the world and commitment to God in Jesus Christ, and cannot be repeated. The dispute led Stephen to excommunicate his opponents in Asia Minor and Africa, or at least to threaten excommunication. That in turn struck at the heart of Cyprian's cherished doctrine of the unanimity of bishops, whose harmony holds the whole Church together. We therefore find, at the same time as Cyprian consolidated support for his own position among the churches of North Africa, attempts to salvage the position. At a council in Carthage in 256, for instance, he asserted that each bishop was free to decide for himself, and renounced any claim to dictate to others, as by implication Stephen was doing (Seventh Council of Carthage, CSEL III.1 435–6 [*NE* 243–4]). The rift between Rome and Cappadocia seems not to have lasted, as the Eastern churches went their own way on the question of heretical baptism. But that between Rome and nearby Africa remained, and it became a major cause of division in the next century.

Cyprian was arrested in 257, as the emperor Valerian came

under the influence of the same Egyptian pagan leaders as had Decius, and began persecuting church leaders. His dignity at his public execution the following year could only strengthen the resolve of his partisans.

The crisis of the 250s left the churches considerably changed. The idea that all individual baptized Christians were holy could hardly be sustained. The penitential system had to be developed to deal with unprecedented numbers of lapsed. Some able and dedicated Christians would not tolerate this, and in the Novatianist schism they defected; that in turn precipitated divisions over baptism which were to persist. The dispute about the lapsed first strengthened the hand of the bishops against alternative sources of authority, then other disputes called in question assumptions about their holiness and unanimity, by which Irenaeus had sought to stabilize doctrine and by which Cyprian set such store. These problems may have deflected the churches from further disputes over doctrine. Whether that is so or not, we find that argument over Sabellianism and its contraries flared up about 260 between Dionysius the bishop of Alexandria and some of his flock, and that the bishop of Rome, also called Dionysius, was in a strong enough position to reprove or question the position taken by his powerful and able colleague. The writings of the Dionysii show that Rome had reached a clear idea of the divine Trinity, but with a strong sense of the unity of Word and Spirit in the supreme God, sharply distinguishing the Son from the creation. Dionysius of Alexandria had been accused of denying that Christ is of one substance (*homoousios*) with the Father, and had been rather anxious to assert (as Origen had) the distinction of the Son from the Father (as vine from vinedresser). He clarifies his view to Dionysius of Rome, where a firm moderate view prevails (Athanasius, *Decr.* 26; *Sent. Dionysii* 18 [*NE* 252–5]). So while authority and unity were under threat, fundamental doctrine was stable in the West. Men like Cyprian, when not involved in controversies of the kind described, could devote themselves earnestly to matters of true applied divinity like writing small books *On the benefit of patience* and *On the Lord's Prayer*.

10

THE ALEXANDRIAN HERITAGE: CLEMENT

Alexandria and Clement

Alexandria, the greatest city of the East, was a centre of Greek learning with a fine library, and also a centre of Greek-speaking Judaism (see pp. 26-7). Here the Bible was turned into Greek, and Philo presented the Scriptures as containing a hidden mystical philosophy, and Jewish synagogues as schools of this high system. Here also the impact of Christianity was to generate a great ferment of thought, and leaders of the Valentinian and Basilidean schools, as well as other Gnostics, flourished. We know little precisely about the origin of the church there (the story of St Mark founding it is pious legend). But in Clement of Alexandria we meet a fascinating kind of Christian teaching, plainly more like what later orthodoxy held than most Alexandrian Christianity was, yet very different from what we have seen in Tertullian.

Clement was apparently a professional teacher of the kind who in all parts dispensed the ideas of philosophers and the skills of rhetoric, but who from the start played a large part in developing and transmitting Christian ideas, like St Paul in the school of Tyrannus (Acts 19.9). In one of his books Clement describes the sources of his learning, summarizing what he learned from distinguished teachers in Greece, southern Italy, Palestine and finally Egypt. These included an Ionian, and teachers from Coele-Syria, Egypt and Assyria, one of Hebrew birth, and finally a 'Sicilian bee' whom he met in Egypt. Following a coy convention, he names none of these (*Str.* 1.1.11.1-3 [*NE* 180]). The last is almost certainly Pantaenus, whom he names as his teacher elsewhere. Eusebius probably got the information about the much-travelled Pantaenus, himself a convert from Stoicism, from what he read in Clement (*HE* 5.10.1-3 [*NE* 179]). Clement taught in Alexandria, and may well have taught Origen (though neither mentions the other). In what capacity he taught is uncertain. It has been claimed that he was a presbyter, and trained catechumens in the church; Eusebius says that he ran the 'catechetical school', but is not to be relied upon. More likely he was, like his own tutors, an independent teacher with a school of his own. Whatever the case, he apparently left the city during the persecutions of 202/203, and spent time in Jerusalem, a friend and counsellor of bishop Alexander, and died there, probably in 215–16 or in 221.

Clement the teacher

Clement wrote a great deal, and much of it survives. His *Protreptikos* is an apologetic work refuting pagan religion and urging conversion to Christianity (specimens in *NE* 180–2). It leads into *Paidagogos*, a 'paraenetic' work exhorting to good behaviour. The Word himself is the true 'pedagogue', which in Greek referred not to the schoolmaster, but to the slave who trains the boy in morals and manners (see 1.12.99–100 [*NE* 182–3]). All sorts of practical questions, about food, drink, entertainment, prayer, are covered: the advice on the kiss of peace (3.11.81.2–3 [*NE* 183]) is typical. The third work, *Stromateis* ('patchwork coverlets'; also called *Stromata*, 'bedding'), is a miscellany, which is difficult to interpret. While *Protreptikos* suggests that further teaching is to come, *Stromateis* seems to be about advanced ethics: there are books or chapters on the relation of philosophy to Christianity, on belief, repentance, eschatology, sexual continence, martyrdom and asceticism. Perhaps more advanced 'spiritual' teaching was in the lost parts of *Stromateis*, which is incomplete, or the entirely lost *Hypotyposeis*. If so it would be entirely in line with the threefold division of spirituality which Origen promoted later. But even as is stands, *Stromateis* points to the superior spirituality of the true 'Gnostic' (see *NE* 184–8, discussed below). Two other works survive. One is a booklet on the salvation of the worldly-rich, usually known by its Latin title *Quis dives salvetur?*; its existence, and its argument, show that Clement wrote for a church with well-to-do and well-educated members (*NE* 188–9). The other, attached to *Stromateis* in one manuscript, is the mysterious *Excerpts from Theodotus*, a collection of passages from a Valentinian writer with comments by Clement, not uniformly hostile to Theodotus.

The ethos of teaching schools at Alexandria may be deduced

from Eusebius' account of the young Origen, orphaned perhaps in the self-same persecution which drove out Clement, earning his living under the patronage of a rich lady. But she also patronized an older, popular teacher called Paul of Antioch, who was apparently a Valentinian (*HE* 6.2.13–14 [*NE* 190]). Origen had to defend himself later against the implication of heresy in himself, and he is the source of Eusebius' information.

A tradition of independent teachers holding authority in the Church alongside the institutional ministry remained strong, in spite of the bad name which many teachers got as heretical leaders. Clement seems firmly set in this tradition. He knew and admired the work of Irenaeus, but his notion of apostolic tradition is quite different. In the passage about his teachers (*Str.* 1.1.11.1–3 [*NE* 180]) he says that the six he named, 'preserving the true tradition of the blessed teaching straight from the holy apostles Peter and James, John and Paul, as son inheriting from father (howbeit few sons are like their fathers), came under God even to our own time, to deposit those seeds of their ancestors the apostles'. He met these men in various parts of the world and they themselves travelled from other places. They thus represent for him all that Irenaeus saw in the apostolic sees: a tradition derived from the apostles and spread throughout the world. But Clement hardly mentions bishops and presbyters anywhere, and certainly not here. For him the catholic and apostolic faith was what his excellent teachers got from their apostolic predecessors. Orthodox Christianity operates like a Greek philosophical school, just as Valentinianism does. The truly spiritual person, the 'Gnostic' who lives according to the gospel, is the true presbyter and deacon, though he lacks ecclesiastical office (*Str.* 6.13.106 [*NE* 186]).

Clement is hostile to heresy, and particularly objects to its being made an excuse for rejecting Christianity itself (*Str.* 7.15.90–1 [*NE* 187–8]). But what exactly he means by the 'rule of the Church' or 'the apostolic tradition' is not easy to determine. Richard Hanson argued that it means ultimately the allegorical interpretation of the Old Testament: if the Scripture is read spiritually, it points to Christ. It is broken up and its authority impugned when mistaken and misused by Marcion and the heretics (see *Origen's doctrine of tradition*, pp. 56ff.). Clement does not summarize the 'rule of faith' as Irenaeus, Tertullian and others do.

But the 'confession' he refers to is also apparently the baptismal creed, which would presumably include the names of Father, Son and Holy Spirit. These three undoubtedly play a significant role in his theology.

The knowledge of God

Clement saw God as the source of all good things, and that included Greek philosophy. It was good for Christians now, though secondary to Scripture, and in the past had prepared the Greeks for Christ 'as the law did the Hebrews' (*Str.* 1.5.28 [*NE* 183–4]). The goal of philosophy, as of the gospel, is knowledge, *gnosis*, and the one who reaches it is the true Gnostic. On this Clement writes a great deal; some of it is indirect, since the knowledge of God is something which cannot be directly described, but only approached by parables and illustrations. Lower forms of virtue, like refraining from evil, or doing good through fear of God or in hope of an earthly or heavenly reward, fall short of knowledge. The Gnostic loves the knowledge of God for its own sake (see *Str.* 4.22.135–8 [*NE* 184–5]).

Clement's account of this knowledge uses concepts from Greek philosophy. A difficulty for Christians arose from the high value they set upon 'faith' (Gk *pistis*), teaching people only to believe, irrationally (see the attacks of Celsus in Origen *Against Celsus* 1.9 and of Galen [*NE* 134 and 136]). Clement certainly regards faith as a first stage, a learning of the essentials which enables one to change from heathen practice to virtue, and knowledge as the developed, rationally sustained expression of that faith (*Str.* 7.10.57.3–5 [*NE* 186–7]). But faith is for him the proper way in which fundamental truths are apprehended. As in Aristotle's epistemology, the fundamentals in the nature of the case cannot be demonstrated; they must be accepted before any proofs and argument can be begun. Faith is thus not irrational belief on someone's say-so, but the true foundation of rational knowledge.

God for Clement is absolute Unity (Gk *monas*). His Son the *Logos* is the means by which he communicates being to all others, and the one who makes known truth in a multitude of ways to mankind. The incarnation in Jesus Christ is real, and final, revelation of the truth. The Holy Spirit plays a definite, but subordinate, part, chiefly as communicating the truths of Scripture and inwardly teaching the believer. But in none of this do we find precision, which would not be compatible with the way Clement thinks about the nature and the knowledge of God.

The same concern for the knowledge of God leads to a spiritualized eschatology: Clement is not interested in the physical resurrection and the restoration of earth, and sayings about that are taken to refer to heavenly events and destinies. He is however interested in angels and demons and their origin.

His ideas were to be developed by Origen.

11

ORIGEN THE THEOLOGIAN

Origen

Origen was born in Alexandria about 185, and became a teacher in Alexandria while still young. Originally a private teacher, he appears to have been entrusted with the catechetical teaching by Bishop Demetrius perhaps as early as 203. The persecution at that time was directed particularly at converts, and the catechetical work was particularly dangerous for teacher and pupil alike. Origen's own father had been executed, and was probably a convert; he had given Origen his pagan name. The promising lad was helped and housed by a wealthy patroness, whose support for a Valentinian teacher was later to embarrass Origen. As instructor of those preparing for baptism Origen is said to have sold his secular books, and to have lived a harshly ascetic life. Eusebius' account of these things is compiled from word-of-mouth stories still circulating among Origen's partisans about a century later, and from snippets from letters in which Origen defended his own career against critics in the Church (HE 6.2–3 [NE 190–1]). The tales included unverifiable accounts of his juvenile precociousness, and of his making himself a eunuch to protect his chastity. He is said to have attended lectures of the Platonist philosopher Ammonius Saccas, who also taught Plotinus, the chief originator of Neoplatonism; certainly Origen's thought resembles that of Plotinus in some respects (see HE 6.19.6 [NE 207]).

Origen fell out with Demetrius, the powerful bishop of Alexandria. Travelling abroad about 215 in order to avoid political turmoil in Alexandria, Origen was welcomed, as Clement had been, by the bishops of Aelia (Jerusalem) and Caesarea, and preached there, though unordained. Demetrius objected, and Origen afterwards (perhaps as a result) resumed his role as a private teacher. Travelling further afield, Origen apparently visited Cappadocia, Athens and Rome. He was finally ordained presbyter in 231–2 by the bishops in Palestine, who used him as a teacher and theological consultant. Demetrius was, however, gravely offended, and had him synodically condemned not only in Alexandria but in most other churches (see Origen's remarks in *Comm. on John* 6.2.8–12 [*NE* 194]). Finally settling at Caesarea in Palestine, Origen was a private teacher, whose methods are perhaps fairly described by Eusebius (*HE* 6.18 [*NE* 192]). But he also continued his scholarly work with the aid of a wealthy public servant called Ambrosius, whom he had converted from Valentinianism, and who supplied him with materials and scribes. As a philosopher of note he was summoned to speak before an empress (Eusebius, *HE* 6.21.3–4 [*NE* 195]). Tortured during Decius' persecution in 250, he died two or three years later.

Origen's works were numerous, and though the greater part is lost, much survives, either in the original or in Latin translation. He composed many commentaries and homilies on Scripture, including important works on Genesis, Psalms, Song of Songs, and the Gospels of Matthew and John. In response to the attack on Christianity by Celsus he wrote *Against Celsus* (*Contra Celsum*). Smaller works of special interest are *On prayer* and *Exhortation to martyrdom*. An Origenist library from the fourth century recovered during the second World War includes the illuminating *Dialogue with Heraclides* and *On Pascha*. But perhaps his most famous work is *On first principles*.

The system and the Scriptures

Quite early in his career Origen wrote his work of systematic theology, *On first principles* (Gk *peri archon*, Lat. *De principiis*). Most of it is known to us only in a controversial Latin translation: in the course of a later dispute (see Chapter 18) Rufinus, believing the texts to have been tampered with to make Origen appear heretical, 'corrected' them accordingly. So we cannot rely upon his Latin version. Some parts survive in Greek in a selection from Origen's works called *Philocalia*, and that helps. The work may have originated as a result of Origen's instructions to the catechumens, whose diet would begin with the reading of Genesis. It would explain why much of his work is concerned with the meaning of the creation story, and with principles of scriptural interpretation. If this is right, Origen was already defending his interpretation and methods when he wrote *On first principles*. But it is certainly as much a constructive as an argumentative work.

In the Preface (2–10 [*NE* 198–201]) Origen lays down clearly the basis of his argument. Others may differ on fundamental doctrines, but he begins from the teaching, 'handed down in unbroken succession from the apostles and existing to this day in the churches . . . that only is to be believed as the truth which in no way conflicts with the tradition of the Church and the apostles' (*pref.* 2). This truth is stated in plainest terms for all to understand. But the apostles left unexplained 'the ground of their statements'. This was quite deliberate, to give room for the exercise of spiritual gifts by the more diligent of those coming after (*pref.* 3). He then sets out a version of the Rule of Faith, which is not in itself unusual. It is trinitarian, and emphasizes the continuity of the God and revelation of the Old Testament with that of the New. But Origen draws attention to points left obscure: whether the Holy Spirit is to be thought of as begotten or unbegotten, and whether he is a son of God or not; whether the soul is transmitted 'with the seed' at conception, or whether it has another origin outside the body; what the devil and his angels are, and how they came to exist; when angels were created, and what their nature is. Anyone seeking to construct 'a connected body of doctrine' has to start with the clear points, and use the holy Scriptures and logical method to deal with the things not made clear (*pref.* 10). Thus in creating his own system, Origen sees himself as beginning from the apostolic tradition, and arriving at other doctrines by exploring their rational (philosophical) basis, and reading the Scriptures in the light of reason. The method differs little from Clement's conception of knowledge. The idea of a system already exists not only among pagan philosophers, but among the Gnostics; it is the orthodox apostolic tradition that distinguishes Origen.

Scripture and allegory

Few theologians have known the Scripture as well as Origen did. He constantly drew in texts from all over the Bible to prove his point, to demonstrate the meaning of another text, or to overcome a difficulty. The whole Scripture of the Greek Bible, every word down to the last dot, came from the Holy Spirit – even variant readings. But it was not to be read simply literally. Just as a human being is body, soul and spirit, so the Scripture is threefold. It has 'flesh', the simple literal meaning, which helps some people; it has 'soul', which when he identifies it is a kind of moral lesson to be drawn from it; and there is the 'spiritual law', where allegory often prevails, and where the meaning is usually quite different from the literal (*Princ.* 4.2.4 [*NE* 205]). He rarely elaborates all three: though the recently-discovered tract '*On Pascha*' has the first two running together, and a separate section of spiritual exegesis of the same text at the end. He is also quite clear that difficulties and impossibilities in the text are there to force us to look for a more spiritual meaning (*Princ.* 4.3.1 [*NE* 205-6]). Most of these passages are in the Old Testament, and even there are outnumbered by those where the simple meaning is historically correct; but it can occur even in the New Testament, as with the impossible mountain where Christ was shown all the nations of earth.

The allegorical method is inherited from Philo and Clement, and from the Stoic interpreters of Homer before them. It emerges however also by a natural progression from the New Testament, where Paul can use a complicated allegory (Gal. 4.21−5.1), and can deny the literal meaning of an ancient law (1 Cor. 9.9-10), and where it is asserted that the whole meaning of the Old Testament is Jesus Christ (e.g. John 5.39). It is in principle implied by Irenaeus' belief that the Rule of Truth applied to every part of the Bible and summarized its meaning. All ancient Christians found types ('models') of Jesus Christ in many parts of the Old Testament. Some however, in ancient times and modern, find the allegorical method wrong, because it cuts off the text from historical reality: the spiritual meaning corresponds not to the historical events or persons the text describes (as in typology), nor to the laws which it originally laid down, but is got merely out of the words. So the allegorical interpretation of the story of the Garden of Eden is the sixth of the heads cited by Jerome against Origen about 396 (*Adv. Joann.* 7 [*CCC* 192]). Origen certainly is rather weak on historical reality: for him it is the universal spiritual truth which counts, and he has no interest in the different circumstances in which the biblical books took their origin. Nowadays we are able to overcome many divergences and contradictions, the legal and theological oddities, with the aid of historical criticism, which was simply not available to Origen. But who shall say that the story of Adam and Eve is meant to be taken literally? Or who would claim that Origen read the Song of Songs wrongly, when he found in it love-poems about the union of the soul with Christ? It was unconventional in his day, when Jewish and Christian interpreters already found in it the union between God and his people, or Christ and his Church. Origen's creative addition has down the centuries been the prevailing interpretation of what were originally love-songs for a wedding, even among Origen's sharpest critics like Jerome. His allegorical readings of the Old Testament have in all kinds of ways affected the liturgy of the churches too.

Origen was an able and careful scholar. With sponsorship from Ambrosius he employed clerks to compile a synopsis of the existing Greek versions of the Old Testament. This work, lost apart from a couple of pages and quotations from individual columns, consisted originally of four translations in parallel:

Aquila, a very literal and unreadable Jewish version;

Symmachus, another Jewish or Judaeo-Christian version;

The Septuagint (see p. 26);

Theodotion, an older Jewish version.

According to Eusebius (*HE* 6.16 [*NE* 197]) this synopsis constituted the *Tetrapla* or 'Fourfold'. In addition, he discovered a fifth and sixth, and seventh for parts of the Bible; but chiefly he added two to the *Tetrapla* and set six versions side by side; this was the *Hexapla* or 'Sixfold'. The six versions were set out in short clauses beside the Hebrew, which was written in Greek letters. Eusebius' account is not altogether clear, but this description of the two synopses fits the odd page of *Hexapla* which survives. Late in the fourth century Epiphanius misread Eusebius and asserted that the *Hexapla* included a column in Hebrew letters, which with the Greek transliteration of the Hebrew and the four versions of the *Tetrapla* made up the six. Jerome popularized this explanation, and it is often held today; but it is probably false. Since the Septuagint came third in the *Tetrapla*, and pride of place went to Aquila, it is likely that Origen based his work on a pre-existing Jewish synopsis. Although what is left of this scholarly activity is of immense interest to textual scholars of the Old Testament, its purpose was probably that to which Origen's successors and disciples put it: he intended the other versions to throw light on the meaning of the one text he regarded as sacrosanct, the Septuagint; it was an interpreter's tool.

God and the Trinity

Origen held God to be transcendent in a manner combining Platonic and Aristotelian notions. God is pure spirit, without body or parts. This contradicts Tertullian's Stoic view, and also the notion of Irenaeus, that God is the ultimate model for human bodily shape as well as soul and spirit. Origen argues that God is pure mind, and any similarity to creatures is in their rationality, their *logos*. In his essential self he is indescribable, unknowable. He is the absolute Unity, in contrast to the multiplicity of creation: 'Altogether solitary (*monas*) and, so to speak, unitary (*henas*)' (*Princ.* 1.1.6). This divine character is sustained even through apparent contradictions in the revealed tradition, as we shall see. Such a transcendent God can be thought of and known only through another, and that other is his Wisdom, Word or Son. All rational beings, all minds, reflect the thought of this primary *Logos*; they derive their being through him, since (being another beside God) he is the principle of multiplicity: 'in him all things consist', as St Paul says (Col. 1.17). The divine Logos is the means whereby God creates and communicates with his creation. Without him God could only remain unique, absolute, motionless, uncommunicated. In generating the Son, the Father in principle generates everything else.

God was however always Father: he could not change from one condition (not-Father) to another (Father). So the Son exists in God's timeless eternity. When popular christological texts speak of the Son being begotten by the Father (as in Ps. 2.7), or of the Word being 'uttered' (Ps. 45.1), it does not as for Justin imply an act or event. For Origen the Father constantly begets the Son by what modern theologians call 'eternal generation'. A favourite text is Heb. 1.3, where the Son is called 'the effulgence of his [God's] glory', with Wisdom 7.26, where Wisdom (= the Word/Son) is 'the effulgence of eternal light'. God cannot be without his glory, and so everlastingly possesses the Son (*Hom. in Jer.* 9.4 and *Princ.* 1.2.2 [*NE* 204]). He asserts against modalists and 'economic trinitarians', that 'there is not when he was not' (*Princ.* 4.4.28).

At the same time the Son exists as a distinct being (*hypostasis*) beside the Father. Father, Son and Spirit are three in *hypostasis* and *hypokeimenon*, all terms for 'being' in the objective sense, that is, each is *a* being. It is no surprise to find him involved in theological debate with a learned bishop who still rested in more traditional 'economic' doctrine (Eusebius, *HE* 6.33.1–3 [*NE* 195–6]). Beryllus of Bostra is reported to have said that 'our Saviour and Lord did not pre-exist in an individual existence of his own before his coming to reside among men, nor had he a divinity of his own, but only the Father's residing in him.' While Eusebius is wrong to assert that Origen's is the original and apostolic view, and that Beryllus had originally held it, the gist of the account is likely to be right. In a recently-recovered book, Origen is called in to persuade a bishop called Heraclides that he should confess that beside the Father 'there was a God, the Son of God, the only begotten of God, the firstborn of all creation, and . . . that in one sense there are two Gods, while in another there is one God' (*Dial. with Heraclides* 122: *Alexandrian Christianity*, p. 438). Just as man and wife are in Scripture one flesh, and the righteous and Christ are one spirit, so the Saviour and his Father are one God (*Dial. with Heraclides* 124–6, p. 439). In a long discussion of the nature of the Son as Word and Wisdom, Origen makes it clear that the Son is God by derivation, not intrinsically and self-sufficiently like the Father: the gospel calls the Father 'God' in an absolute sense (Gk *ho theos, autotheos*), while the Son is merely 'god' as predicate ('the Word was god [*theos*]', not 'God was the Word'). In this and other respects the Son is less than the Father. The Father is superior to everything existing (including the Son), and the source of all other being; the Son is superior to all rational creatures (including the Holy Spirit); the Holy Spirit is superior to the 'saints' (that is, holy beings, including angels and sanctified humans) (*Princ.* 1.3.5 [*NE* 202]). This subordination caused Origen later to be regarded as a precursor of Arianism, and he was attacked for it (see the first of Jerome's cavils, *CCC* 192). But though his subordinationism, and the sharp distinction of the pre-existent Son from the Father, look like what Arius taught, his strong doctrine of eternal generation was exactly what Alexander upheld against Arius.

Like the apologists, Origen says more about the Son than about the Spirit. The Father and Son, he holds, are known by reason even without the aid of Scripture. The Holy Spirit is known from the Scriptures alone, and indeed is especially closely related to the biblical revelation. Not only is he its author, but he also inspires with spiritual gifts its true interpreters.

Creation, flesh and the humanity of Christ

The most remarkable feature of Origen's thought is his account of creation, and the Christology which depends upon it. Before this world existed there was a prior creation of rational spirits or 'minds'. God was never without his creation, and created just so many minds as his providence could manage. They were pure, unembodied intelligences, and remained so as long as they were content with the contemplation of God. But they were free, and they exercised their freedom by turning from him: the devil resisted God, and the others turned with him. Their turning is inexplicable; perhaps they were 'sated'. But this inexplicable choice against God is the cause of the existence of the whole universe we know. Even the archangels sinned, though slightly. The demons sinned gravely, and particularly plot to ruin other creatures. Some spirits sinned less than the demons, but more than the angels, and for them God provided this world, and human bodies, as a punishment (*Princ.* 1.8.1 [*NE* 201]). But punishment for Origen (as for his Alexandrian predecessors) is beneficial, educational, medicine for sick souls. So every person coming into the world has a different spiritual past, which accounts for the inequality of birth and experience. There is only one life in this world; contrary to what his enemies alleged, Origen does not teach the transmigration of souls to other bodies. But the ultimate destiny, after the retraining process in this world and others (*Princ.* 2.8.3 [*NE* 202]), is to become like the Son of God, pure Mind or *Logos*. Free will which wrought the fall (a term which can now be correctly used in Christian theology) can bring about the restoration.

Logically all spirits may be restored in the *apokatastasis*, the 'restoration of all' (Acts 3.21). Origen allowed himself to speculate about the possible salvation of demons and evil human beings (*Princ.* 1.6.3 [*NE* 203–4]). His enemies made much of this, and turned his suggestion into a positive statement (see Jerome, *Adv. Joann.* 7 [*CCC* 192]). They also objected to the pre-existence of souls in eternity. But truly more serious for the Christian tradition was the part which they largely swallowed: that human destiny is to escape the body and to adore God in a purely spiritual or intellectual existence. This was a thought derived from Platonic and Pythagorean philosophy, favoured by the Valentinians and Gnostics, but quite incompatible with the earthy creationism of primitive Christianity, with its hope of bodily resurrection and millennium. The world and the body are to Origen essentially the consequence of sin, and when the souls are cured of sin, they will not be needed.

God's curative effort was disrupted by the intrusion of the demons into the physical creation. Human beings lost the image and likeness of God, and could not find or know him. Hence the incarnation of the Son of God, the *Logos*, in Jesus Christ. At this point Origen scores his greatest theological triumph, drawn from him by the formidable attack of Celsus. Along with various other arguments (specimens in *NE* 131–6) Celsus poured scorn on the notion of the coming of the Son of God to earth; it made nonsense of the concept of divinity. Origen certainly insists that Jesus Christ is both God and man, 'a composite thing' (Gk *syntheton ti chrema*), with a human nature and a divine nature; there is a union or combination, not merely an association of the two. Yet the divine Word 'remains unchanged in being', while descending to take part in human affairs. To account for this Origen postulates a created spirit as the subject of the visible, tangible Jesus, who can grow and suffer. One only of all the originally created minds never turned from perfect adherence to God, and did not fall. This created mind was uniquely united with the Son of God; the union was like that of iron red-hot in fire: it becomes indistinguishable from the fire. In the incarnation,

> We say that this [divine] Logos dwelt in the soul of Jesus and was united with it in a closer union than that of any other soul, because it alone has been able perfectly to receive the highest participation in him who is the very Logos and the very Wisdom, and the very Righteousness himself. (*Against Cels.* 5.39 [*NE* 202])

So it comes about that the Logos, in himself the transcendent creator who cannot be seen or suffer, in Jesus wept like a little child. He is the absolute controlling power, since the created mind had become 'one spirit with him' (a favourite text from 1 Cor.

6.17). Yet the created mind, able to suffer the circumstances, pains and mental distresses of a human being, is sufficiently distinct for the Word to remain unimpaired in divinity.

Origen grasped clearly the problems which the Logos–doctrine caused for Christology, and in his own terms resolved them. Several features were to become normative in orthodox thought: the two natures, and the distinct created soul as subject of the human dealings and sufferings. His work was not accepted as authoritative, however, because it presupposed the pre-existent created spirits, and that doctrine was rejected.

The function of the incarnation is debated. It has been suggested that for Origen it is the heavenly Logos or Wisdom that counts, rather than the fleshly Christ, and that ultimately salvation is a matter of revelation and knowledge, rather than the effect of the historic incarnation and passion of Jesus Christ. One feature of this is the teaching on 'aspects' of his person. The heavenly Word is the principle of multiplicity, and his own being has many aspects (Gk *epinoiai*): Wisdom, Word, Life, Truth, etc. The higher aspects belong to his eternal being, the lower (like Shepherd, Priest) to his incarnation. Human beings apprehend him first in the lower aspects, but may rise ever higher, until as pure spirits they contemplate God purely, and themselves become gods (in the sense implied by John 10.34–5). Such a doctrine might suggest that the human Jesus was merely an illustration, the elementary lesson, which the spiritual person rises above as he ascends the ladder of the *epinoiai*. These 'aspects' also affect the appearance of the human Jesus: the occasions when he is not recognized, or when events are reported differently by different evangelists, are due to different people seeing him differently; his body, though real, had a god-like or ethereal quality, especially after the resurrection. But whatever Origen held about the higher destiny of the soul, the atoning sacrifice of the cross is repeatedly emphasized. Without it human beings cannot be turned from their sinfulness, they remain under the wrath of God and separated from him; the death of Jesus removes sin, and makes peace with God possible. It is not of course God who needs appeasing: he is the one who gives the victim for sacrifice. But there is no higher spirituality until people are brought to repentance, and their sin taken away.

The influence of Origen: Dionysius and Paul

Origen's influence was wide but controversial. His views on biblical interpretation, on the Trinity, on the nature and destiny of the soul, and on the devil, were all attacked. One notable critic was Methodius of Olympus, an ascetic writer who died probably in 311, and asserted against Origenism that the physical body is raised from the dead. Eusebius' teacher, Pamphilus of Caesarea in Palestine, cherished the dead scholar's library and collected material to defend his memory, which Eusebius himself published as a *Defence of Origen* soon after 300.

Two personalities have been especially associated with Origenism, positively or negatively. One is Dionysius, the great Bishop of Alexandria 247–64. Eusebius quotes him especially for his views on the Revelation of John, which he attributed to another besides the Apostle, and which he held should be interpreted allegorically and not literally, thus avoiding the earthly millennium apparently envisaged in Rev. 20.1–6 (*HE* 7.25 [*NE* 255–7]). He was also opposed to 'Sabellianism', and asserted in strong biblical images the distinction of the Son from the Father. This drew criticism from the other Dionysius, Bishop of Rome 259–68, who referred to those who divide the Monarchy of God into 'three powers and separated substances (*hypostaseis*), and who say that 'the Son is a work' created by the Father (Athanasius, *Decr.* 26 [*NE* 252–3]). Dionysius replied that he allowed the Father and Son to be consubstantial (*homoousios*) like the plant with its seed or root, and the river with its source, but that in those cases, and with the generation of human children, that did not destroy the distinctions (Athanasius, *Sent. Dion.* 18 [*NE* 254–5]). These passages came into prominence when 'consubstantial' was in debate a century later. Although Dionysius is not now regarded as generally an Origenist, his views here seem to tally with those of Origen.

Late in life Dionysius declined to attend a synod which tried for heresy the Bishop of Antioch called Paul of Samosata. A colourful personality, he was apparently in favour with queen Zenobia, who set up the rebel kingdom of Palmyra in 261, and could only be removed from his church when the emperor Aurelian overthrew her in 372. Possibly for political reasons, other bishops in the East pinned upon him accusations of heresy, and he was condemned by a synod in 268 (see Eusebius, *HE* 7.30 and extracts from the trial proceedings in *NE* 258–62). The group of bishops who reported the trial were associated with Origen (like Gregory Thaumaturgus and Firmilian of Caesarea in Cappadocia), but it is not clear that it was an Origenistic cabal. Eusebius cites the more scandalous parts of their letter on Paul's arrogant misconduct, and we must divine the heresy from that and from the dubious Syriac record of the trial. Paul apparently asserted that 'Jesus Christ is from below': 'Christ' means 'anointed', and 'a human being is anointed, the Word is not anointed . . . for the Word is greater than the anointed one' (*Acts* S 26, p. 153 [*NE* 261]). The letter Eusebius cites suggests that Paul denied the deity of Christ: 'He is not willing to acknowledge with us that the Son of God came down from heaven' (*HE* 7.30.11 [*NE* 259]). The matter was so serious the Eastern churches regarded the baptisms of his followers as invalid on doctrinal grounds: their faith was not sound. It is sometimes supposed that with this christological denial, dividing the Christ into the 'man from below' and the 'Word from above' rather as in the case of the prophets, went a form of Sabellian or unitarian belief. This arises because in the controversy of the next century opponents of the word 'consubstantial' (*homoousios*) claimed that Paul's critics had synodically condemned that word. Its defenders Athanasius, Hilary and Basil found ingenious explanations as to how this came about (*NE* 263). If Paul used the word, and if his opponents attacked it, it is probably because, like Beryllus and Heraclides, he questioned the permanent distinction between Father and Son, and saw the Word as part of the Father. But we do not know; it is better to assume that the christological heresy was the chief point, in that he asserted Jesus Christ from below and the Word of the Father descending upon him. If that is so, his opponents reveal little explicit Origenism. In fact, they assert that the Word or Wisdom, that is the divine Son from heaven, functioned in Christ's body rather as the soul does with the flesh in a human being (S 36, p. 158 [*NE* 261–2]). If that is so, they not only did not use Origen's most characteristic christological principle, the created human soul of Jesus; they adopted a Christology which left no room for it, but suggested the kind of thought which was to be associated in the next century with Arianism and Apollinaris: in Jesus the only rational soul was the Son of God himself.

12

THE RISE OF CONSTANTINE

The Great Persecution

During most of the third century the Roman Empire was afflicted with difficulties. Foreign enemies, plagues, and economic exhaustion were exacerbated by constant changes of regime, as successful generals overthrew their predecessors every few years. The emperor Decius' attempt to stop the rot included an assault on Christianity in 250. This was repeated under Valerian in 257–8, when Cyprian of Carthage was among those executed (*NE* 247–51). Valerian was disastrously defeated by the Persians in 260, and died in captivity. His son Gallienus restored property and peace to the churches (*NE* 251), and we know of no further formal persecution until 303 (though a few Christians were executed for military insubordination). Renewed persecution came about under what was called the Tetrarchy, the rule of four emperors. This system came about as follows.

Civil war and external pressure continued until the rise of Diocletian in 284. He associated with his rule Maximian in 285, and in 293 enlarged the imperial house by associating two further commanders, so that Constantius as 'Caesar' supported Maximian as 'Augustus' in the West, while Galerius as 'Caesar' supported Diocletian as 'Augustus' in the East. In this Tetrarchy power was decentralized and balanced, and no individual could easily stage a coup; the commanders were already emperors. Other reforms included raising the efficiency of taxation and increasing the solemnity of court ritual, and matters of religion. The syncretistic gnostic religion of the Manichees was spreading, especially in Egypt and Africa; it was attacked vigorously in 302 (a more probable date than 297), ostensibly because it disturbed moral standards, but with reference also to its Persian (and therefore hostile) origins (*NE* 267–8). Similar principles probably caused the launch of a series of persecuting edicts in 303–4 (*NE* 271–3, 275). Christianity was seen as socially and morally disruptive, but had also been made the established religion in the territory of the Armenian kings, who were independent of Rome and Persia. Many Armenians lived inside the Empire, and their loyalty might come into question.

The direct reason for the 'Great Persecution' is obscured by Christian legend. It seemed to have been sponsored in the East chiefly by the Caesar Galerius, whether for military or for personal reasons. But it was also associated with the rise of pagan Neoplatonism, which began in the third century and went on through the fourth. Though this was in origin a learned, spiritual and ascetic philosophy akin to Christianity as practised by those like Origen, its popularizer Porphyry was hostile to Christianity, and promoted a kind of monotheism which left room for pagan observance. His refutation of Christianity was published in the period just before the persecution, and the intellectual assault on Christianity also included the publication of hostile versions of the passion of Jesus (*Acts of Pilate*), and provocative oracles from the shrines of Apollo (*NE* 269–72). There was apparently a systematic attempt to restore public morality and reinforce the reform of government by ridding the Empire of a creed and organization which eroded its religious foundations. The persecution led to the destruction of church buildings and books, and to much torture, forced labour and execution, but it was applied unevenly, and was already petering out when Galerius (now the senior Augustus of the East) ended it in 311 (*NE* 280). A further burst of killing occurred in the dominions of the Eastern Caesar Maximin over the next two years, for political reasons (*NE* 281), but thereafter generally ceased.

As in 250, the assault divided the churches. In Egypt, the principal bishop, Peter of Alexandria, was for a long time imprisoned before his death in 311. Those bishops who were not taken were often suspected of compromise with the pagan authorities, and Peter (even while in prison himself) was blamed for softness towards defaulting clergy. On this and other pretexts a leading Coptic bishop, Melitius (Meletius) of Lycopolis, began ordaining bishops, presbyters and deacons to supply pastoral care where, rightly or wrongly, he deemed it lacking. This provoked other bishops, and Peter himself, to stern rebuke (*NE* 275–8). But Melitius had support among the Coptic churches, and especially among the rapidly increasing numbers of monks. The outcome was mutual excommunication, and the Melitians formed a 'Church of the Martyrs', which kept itself apart from Peter's supporters even in the prisons and mines where they suffered together. After Peter's death the division persisted, and the solution agreed at the Council of Nicaea in 325 was not immediately implemented.

Donatism

More serious still was the division in Africa, usually called the 'Donatist schism' after Donatus, appointed Bishop of Carthage by the dissident majority about 313. The bolder spirits in Africa and Numidia considered it treason for the clergy to hand anything to the authorities. 'One who handed over' was a *traditor*, a word which also means 'betrayer' or 'traitor'. In the East Scriptures seem to have been surrendered without the sense that a grave crime was committed. But in Africa the spirit of Tertullian and Cyprian prevailed, and bishops who compromised in this way were regarded as tainted and no longer lawful priests. The interrogation of bishops at Cirta in 305 (*NE* 297–8) may not be historical, coming from a very hostile source; but it reveals how Secundus of Tigisis, the leading Numidian bishop, regarded the surrender of anything, even medical texts, as disqualifying a bishop from acting spiritually at an ordination. Mensurius, Bishop of Carthage until 312, had surrendered what he claimed were heretical books; since they presumably came from his episcopal library, they may simply have been old-fashioned theology. This act perhaps divided the two chief bishops. Some members of the church in Carthage adopted partisan positions. Caecilian the deacon would not allow support for a group of forty-seven confessors from Abitene, themselves a rigorist collection who had defied their bishop, a *traditor*, as well as the Roman authorities. His objection to unauthorized martyrs also offended a wealthy churchwoman called Lucilla. When Mensurius died, Caecilian sensed the weakness of his position, and got himself rapidly elected and ordained as bishop. The Numidians were affronted, since they and their primate were usually consulted before such elections, and they allied with dissidents in Carthage to appoint Lucilla's chaplain Majorinus instead. Caecilian was no bishop, they said, because he had prevented support for the martyrs, and because one of the three bishops ordaining him was a *traditor*:

Felix of Aptungi was alleged to have handed over Scriptures for burning. It did not matter that in subsequent investigations it became clear that the evidence against Felix had been forged (*NE* 307): the battle had been joined, and the majority of bishops and people were with Majorinus and against Caecilian, and Caecilian's supporters put it about that most of Majorinus' consecrators were themselves *traditores* and villains (see *NE* 297–301). Caecilian found support in Rome, and from the start appears to have adopted the Roman line on baptism, accepting all baptisms as valid no matter who conducted them. His opponents, loyal to Cyprian's principles in this too, denied any baptisms but those of the Catholic communion, which meant their own. They are called 'Donatists' after Donatus, their second Bishop of Carthage, who succeeded on the death of Majorinus. When the rest of the world came to support Rome and Caecilian, they accepted the implication that they were themselves the only Christians. But before that a wholly new factor entered upon the scene: the attitude of the Western emperor Constantine to the churches.

Constantine was the son of that Constantius I, later called Chlorus, who was Caesar of the West under the Tetrarchy. In 305 Diocletian and Maximian retired, under pressure from Galerius. A new Tetrarchy was formed, with Constantius and Galerius promoted to Augustus, and two new Caesars, Severus and Maximin (surnamed Daza), both Galerius' cronies; the sons of Maximian and Constantius, that is Maxentius and Constantine, were passed over. Constantine, who had spent his youth as trainee and hostage in the Eastern court, joined his father, and was with him when he died at York in 306. The troops proclaimed Constantine emperor (in terms of the Tetrarchy an act of rebellion), and he inherited Britain, Gaul and Spain. Maxentius seized Italy and Africa, and was supported by his father. Constantine was reconciled to the Tetrarchs: he allied himself with Maximian by marriage, and watched while Maxentius repulsed attempts by Severus (the nominal Caesar) and Galerius to remove him in 307. By 310, however, Maxentius and his father had quarrelled, and Constantine in the first of his family purges forced Maximian to suicide after a plot. In 312 Constantine invaded Italy, and after some fierce battles in the north defeated a superior enemy force outside Rome, where Maxentius drowned in the Tiber near the Milvian Bridge. The West was in Constantine's hands.

Both Maxentius and Constantine had stopped the persecution of Christianity. Constantine had formed an alliance with Licinius, the Augustus who held the Balkan provinces. At Milan in 313 Licinius married Constantine's sister, and a programme of religious liberty for Christians was agreed. As Licinius defeated the last persecutor Maximin Daza in 313 and took over the Eastern provinces, he published it (see the so-called *Edict of Milan* in Lactantius, *Mort.* 48 [*NE* 284–6]). It gave generous legal basis for restitution of property and civic rights lost under the Tetrarchs. If all men were free to pray in their own way, the Divinity would be favourable to the emperors and those under them. But Constantine went further than Licinius. He began a programme of building and endowing churches in Rome itself. And in North Africa (the only place from which records survive) he gave grants for payments to the clergy and exempted them from the money contributions required of those of curial rank, that is the owners of property who were chiefly responsible for tax payments in cities. He addressed himself to Caecilian of Carthage, with dark hints about 'disturbers of the peace', and to Anulinus the governor, referring to 'the Catholic Church over which Caecilian presides' (Eusebius, *HE* 10.5.15 – 10.7 [*NE* 286–9]). He had the Donatists in mind.

Constantine was apparently guided by the Bishop of Rome, treating the dissidents as unimportant. Anulinus was soon otherwise informed. He received a weighty *Statement of charges against Caecilian, delivered by the party of Majorinus*, which he duly passed on to Constantine (Augustine, *Ep.* 88.2 [*NE* 301–2]). It asked Constantine to order impartial judgement of the issues by bishops from Gaul (Optatus, *On the Schism of the Donatists* 1.22 [*NE* 302]). There was plainly resentment that the state should be subsidizing a condemned minority church (Caecilian's); and from later documents it is clear that in some cities, perhaps many, the local authorities exempted Donatist clergy from taxes while imposing them on Caecilianists. So Constantine found himself not only deciding who should be subsidized, but asked to arrange adjudication of an ecclesiastical dispute. However far the Donatists might later repudiate the Christian Empire, at this stage they were as anxious to use the emperor and exploit his benefits as were their opponents. Constantine first asked Miltiades, Bishop of Rome, to convene a court and settle the matter, with ten bishops of each party present to support Caecilian and Majorinus and three

Gallic bishops (whom Constantine himself commanded to attend); fifteen bishops from Italy were also there (Eusebius, *HE* 10.5.18 [*NE* 302–3 and note]). They found in favour of Caecilian. But his opponents were not satisfied, and pestered Constantine with petitions. The result was the Council of Arles in 314. Thirty-three bishops, their travel publicly funded, there considered the claims of the two parties, and found for Caecilian against the 'troublesome men of undisciplined mind' who accused him (Turner, *Ecclesiae Occidentalis Monumenta Ivris Antiquissima* 1,376–8; 381–95 [*NE* 303–7]). They also produced a series of canons on disciplinary matters in the light of 'the present state of tranquillity' (Hefele-Leclerq, *Histoire des Conciles* 1.1.275–98 [*NE* 293–6]). These included a ruling which made it clear that clergy who had betrayed Scriptures or communion vessels or the names of fellow-Christians were to be deposed, but that their acts of ordination were not invalidated (canon 14[13]). They also ruled on 'the African practice of rebaptizing', that a heretic must be asked about the creed, and that 'if he has been baptized into the Father, the Son and the Holy Spirit, hands shall be laid upon him and no more' (canon 9[8]). The Roman position was thus sustained against that of Cyprian, though heretical baptisms which named only Jesus Christ, or which did not name the members of the Trinity, were now clearly excluded; this agreed broadly with the practice of the East, where the validity of baptisms came to depend on whether the doctrine affirmed was orthodox.

In the century ahead the division was to harden. Constantine personally heard a further appeal by the Donatists, in the midst of other grave administrative and military preoccupations, and condemned them (*NE* 308–9). For a time he was out of patience and tried to force them into submission. But they were passionately serious Christians, with a majority following in many parts of Africa. Not relishing the role of persecutor of the martyrs' God, Constantine decided to leave them to the judgement of God (see *NE* 309, 311). Subsequent emperors had no more success, and it remained for the colleagues of Augustine of Hippo to get Donatism proscribed by law and to deal theologically with the issues which Cyprian had raised about the purity of the church's ministers. Even so, though reduced, Donatism survived until all the Christianity of North Africa was swept away by Islam.

Church and Empire

In the short run it was not the questions of ministry and sacrament that were most important, but the place of the emperor in the Church. Earlier emperors may have taken some note of church affairs, and in 272 Aurelian appears to have removed Paul of Samosata from his church in Antioch at the behest of the Italian bishops (Eusebius, *HE* 7.30.19 [*NE* 263–4]). But Constantine encouraged the idea at least among Christians that he served their God, and was his agent not only for ending persecution, but for liberating and converting the Empire. How far Constantine is rightly called a Christian (and some scholars defend the traditional view of him as a saint and quasi-apostle), and how far he was a cunning autocrat cynically manipulating the rising religious enthusiasm to improve the cohesion and strength of his dominion, has been long disputed among scholars; the truth is likely to lie between these extremes. His letters, now generally regarded as genuine, reveal a Roman deeply concerned that God should be appeased by right worship and true religion. In principle this was also the public policy of the persecutors, but with different gods. Constantine was moved by the Christian argument that the way to peace and prosperity was through friendship with the one true God, and that polytheism led to wrath and disaster; the miserable deaths of one persecutor after another, with their friends and associates, served to confirm this opinion. So did his own invariable good fortune in battle. Not long after the victory at the Milvian bridge in 312, the story was put about by Lactantius, a Christian scholar close to Constantine, that the Emperor had been directed in a dream to put a form of cross or *chi-rho* on his soldiers' shields (*Mort.* 44.3–6 [*NE* 283]). Many years later a similar tale was told to Eusebius at Constantinople, with the addition of a cross of light seen in the sky about noon as the model of a new military standard (Eusebius, *Vit. Const.* 1.26–9 [*NE* 283–4]). It is probable that the emblem originally represented something different, the cult of *Sol Invictus*, the Unconquered Sun, a god who figured large in the propaganda and coinage of Constantine from the time of Maximian's death in 310 (see *NE* 282). From the point of view of Lactantius and Eusebius, however, and of subsequent emperors and bishops, the army now fought under the emblem of the cross of Christ.

Constantine's personal theology reveals a sense of vocation: God had called him from the western fringe to liberate and restore the Empire, and prospered his way. Victory in new wars with Licinius led to the conquest of the Eastern empire by Constantine in 324. He celebrated his success by marking the foundations of his 'New Rome', the Byzantium or Constantinople which would for long become the centre of the Christian Empire; it was dedicated in 330. Statues plundered from pagan shrines were used to adorn its squares and buildings, thus being secularized or even given a Christian interpretation. Constantine would have here a new court and senate, without the ancient paganism still prevailing in Rome. Here he would harangue his courtiers on moral and religious themes, and require his garrison to parade for Sunday worship of the (conveniently unnamed) God of Victory. Meanwhile his programme of christianization went on apace. A letter to the Eastern provinces in 324 made it plain that he wanted all men to worship the one true God, and only forbade compulsory conversion; he denies the rumour that he was forbidding sacrifice in the temples, but admits that he would like to. At the same time he offered public funds to be used for repairing, extending and building new churches to house the inflow of converts, and splendid buildings arose at Tyre, Nicomedia and Jerusalem, as well as Antioch, Constantinople and Rome. Christ was funded as the gods of the old pantheon had been. But the Empire was thus drawn into the Church as well as the Church into the Empire.

The Church was a ready instrument. In its struggle to identify itself against schismatics and heretics, the Body of Christ had come to recognize itself in terms of the communion of individual Christians with their local bishop. The bishops in turn communicated with each other in a bureaucratic system parallel to that of the Empire. Each province had its principal bishop, who presided at meetings and ordinations of other bishops, and who corresponded both with them and with all the other principal bishops. These recognized each other, and formed a universal 'Catholic' communion. Thinkers like Irenaeus and Cyprian had contributed a theological dimension: the bishops were God's appointed means of ensuring truth and lawful validity. Followers of Novatian or Paul of Samosata claimed to have the truth, as did older sects such as Marcionites and Valentinians; but none could match the Catholic organization. So Constantine made his grants to and through bishops of the 'Catholic' Church such as Caecilian of Carthage and Eusebius of Caesarea. But their organization provided ready means to adjudicate. Locally Christians accepted conciliation by bishops: conciliation and judgement of claims to Christian status were precisely their task. Constantine gave to episcopal judgements secular legal status. But Donatism obliged him to set up courts of bishops to consider ecclesiastical disputes. There was precedent in the Church for councils (also called 'synods'); after a few mentions in earlier times, many councils were held after the Decian persecution. Cyprian repeatedly assembled bishops to consider problems, and the meetings of such holy men were regarded as divinely guided. Constantine now summoned bishops, first to Rome and then to Arles, with instructions to judge between Caecilian and his accusers. Like the Donatists themselves, he seems to have expected a spiritual decision which all spiritual persons would accept. When the conciliar decisions failed, he heard the matter himself: the emperor was the final court of appeal in spiritual as in secular matters. Thereafter he tried enforcing the decision, which was both episcopal and imperial, but gave up, hoping that the numerically superior Eastern churches would resolve the issue; but he was to find the Easterns themselves still worse divided, and in need of a yet greater council.

13

ARIUS AND THE COUNCIL OF NICAEA

Arius

The widest dispute and the most important single council in the ancient Church were precipitated because of Arius. He was a Libyan, probably from one of the five cities of Cyrenaica. The notion that he studied in Antioch is based on the fact that he calls Eusebius of Nicomedia a 'fellow-Lucianist', Lucian being an Antiochene scholar; nothing else confirms this interpretation of a literary whimsy. Some ancient sources connect his early ecclesiastical career in Alexandria with the Melitian troubles (e.g. Sozomen, *HE* 1.15.2 [*NE* 321–2]), but the best opinion is now that these are confusions, due partly to the desire to malign the heretic's whole career. He certainly became the presbyter in charge of the Baukalis church, one of the district churches of Alexandria, of which nine were listed later in the century. That was an important and influential position, because the Alexandrian presbyters were like bishops in their own congregations, and indeed played a major role in electing the bishop of Alexandria when there was a vacancy. Such was his status when he quarrelled with Alexander his bishop. It is not certain whether Arius' audacious theology provoked the bishop finally to move against him, as in the account of Sozomen (*HE* 1.15.3 [*NE* 322]), or whether it was Alexander's apparently 'Sabellian' propositions which provoked Arius to protest, as Socrates implies (*HE* 1.5 [*NE* 321]). The latter looks more probable, especially in the light of Constantine's letter, which attributes a rash question first to Alexander (Eusebius, *Vit. Const.* 2.69 [*NE* 333]). The complications of Alexander's relations with other presbyters such as the dissident and anti-Arian Colluthos may also have played a part (see Theodoret, *HE* 1.4.3 [*NE* 328], probably to be dated 321 or 322).

The true nature of the original issue is clouded. Modern theologians have read into Arianism whatever views they themselves particularly abominate. Our ancient sources reveal other problems. First, what we have of Arius' own writing is meagre, and even these documents are preserved by his critics, and selected to be damaging, if not actually misquoted or misconstrued. Secondly, his critics often attribute to him views which he never stated: the most famous is, 'There was once when he [the Son] was not.' There can be no doubt that if he had ever written that, he would have been quoted direct. Thirdly, the dispute about Arius led to divisions between churchmen over many other issues, both ecclesiastical (such as the alleged episcopal tyranny of Athanasius) and theological (such as whether the Son is like the Father or unlike him), and much of this is called the 'Arian controversy', even though Arius had nothing directly to do with the issues. Arius is not Arianism as generally understood.

His surviving letters, and the poem called *Thalia*, show that he thought of himself as a conservative, treading in the footsteps of pious teachers, and following the doctrine of his bishop. He held that there is 'one God, alone unbegotten, alone everlasting, alone unbegun . . .' (*Letter to Alexander, NE* 326), and that the Son of God makes his Father known by being different: 'We call him Unbegotten because of the one in nature begotten; we raise hymns to him as Unbegun because of him who has beginning; we adore him as Eternal because of the one born in time' (*Thalia* II.3–5 [*NE* 330]). It is precisely because the Son is limited in these respects that he can communicate to men, who share his limitations, about God who is absolutely ineffable; it is impossible for the Son or anyone else to describe the Father comprehensively, for he is unutterable even to himself (*Thalia* II.33–4 [*NE* 331]). This unlimited and indescribable God is, he claims, the God of Scripture, and he fathered (begot, or gave birth to) 'an Onlybegotten Son before eternal times, through whom he has made the ages and the universe; and he begot him not in semblance, but in truth' (*Letter to Alexander*). Here Arius uses the old device, familiar since the apologists, of guarding the transcendent divinity of the Father by attributing creative activity to the Son, who makes time and worlds. But other features of the Son are striking. A favourite term used by Arius is 'Only-begotten' (Gk *monogenes*), and his teaching leans heavily on John 1.18: 'No one has seen God at any time; the only-begotten Son who is in the bosom of the Father, he explained him' (some New Testament texts read 'only-begotten God' instead of 'only-begotten Son', a formula also used by Arius

(*Thalia* II.23 [*NE* 331]). The term 'Only-begotten' makes it clear that the Son does not share the Father's essential nature as Unbegotten, but at the same time is vastly superior to all others: 'Only-begotten' also means 'unique': 'perfect creature of God, but not as one of the creatures; offspring (Gk *gennetos*), but not as one of the generated things (Gk *gegennemena*) (*Letter to Alexander* [*NE* 326]). The same kind of formula applies to the Son's beginning and eternity. Two things are asserted: he has a 'beginning' or 'source' (Gk *arche*), in the Father himself; and he himself is the creator of the ages, so there is no time before. Thus he is not eternal in the same sense that the Father is 'alone everlasting'; he was 'born in time', probably referring to his generation before creation. Further features of Arius' programme follow: the Son is different, separate and distinct from the Father, inasmuch as he does not share the Father's essential character as Unbegotten and Eternal. He must also be called a 'creature' (a 'created thing'), inasmuch as he was generated from non-existence; in any case Scripture clearly states (in the Greek Bible) that the Lord created Wisdom as the beginning of his way, the first of his works (Prov. 8.22). At the same time he is wholly superior to all other beings, as their creator: 'a creature, but not as one of the creatures'. This means that he alone is directly produced from the Father in the sense that he exists solely by the Father's will; all else (including presumably the Spirit) exists through the Son. The Father has by this simple act of will showered glories upon him, and in begetting him has gone to the limit of his powers: 'One equal to the Son the Father is able to beget; but more excellent, superior or greater he cannot' (*Thalia* II.28–9 [*NE* 331]). The two names for Christ favoured by Arius are 'Son' and 'God'. He seems to avoid 'Logos', 'Wisdom' and 'Power', except as titles bestowed upon him, because they might confuse the begotten Son with the eternal attributes of the Father: 'Wise is God, since he is himself Wisdom's teacher' (*Thalia* II.10 [*NE* 331]); God is already wise, and the standing of the Son as creative and revelatory Wisdom is derived from the Father's prior wisdom. Some of Arius' friends said that it was an imprecise use to give these titles to the Son. His critics were to claim that the titles Word, Wisdom and Power imply that the Son shares the Father's being and eternity, since God was always rational, wise and powerful. Arius might have qualified 'God' in the same way as he qualifies Logos and Wisdom, but in fact he does so differently: the Son is truly God, but as Son is 'Only-begotten God'.

The key formulae betray important ambiguities. If the Son comes from the Father, he cannot be *anarchos*, 'without beginning, unbegun'. That may mean that he derives from the Father as source, a doctrine which Origen and Arius' opponents held while at the same time asserting that he was eternally generated; or it may mean that one must envisage an eternal existence of God alone without the Son, before the Son existed. Arius' enemies attributed to him the belief that, 'There was once when he was not' (Gk *en pote hote ouk en*), and some lines of *Thalia* (II.20–3 [*NE* 331]) appear to justify this: '. . . the Unity was, but the Duality was not, before he existed. So straight away, when there is no Son, the Father is God. Thus the Son who was not, but existed at the paternal will, is only-begotten God.' If time did not exist, what can that 'before' mean? Arius seems merely to assert the paradox: 'God being the cause of all things, is unbegun and altogether sole, but the Son being begotten apart from time by the Father, and being created and found before ages, was not before his generation' (*Letter to Alexander* [*NE* 327]). Alexander's formal letter of condemnation (dated by Williams 325) fixes on this as the first item of heresy: 'God was not always a father, but there was when he was not a father; the Word of God was not from eternity, but was made out of nothing; for the ever-existing God has made him who did not previously exist, out of the non-existent' (Socrates, *HE* 1.6.9 [*NE* 323]). The most sensitive issue was thus the eternity of the Son.

The views of Arius and his opponents were all partly shaped by continuing debates among philosophers, whose writings were known to some of the Christian theologians, about the eternity of the world and the relation between form and matter. Does the world have a beginning? Did God exist without a created universe? Can intelligible form exist apart from the material which embodies it? Origen had envisaged a world of created rational spirits coeternal with God (which corresponded to the Platonic realm of ideas or forms), and transient physical worlds in which they are embodied. So for him the eternity of the Son, as Logos, went with an eternal created universe of pure intelligence which could inform matter. Like Origen's Christian critic Methodius, Arius cannot accept a created order sharing God's eternity. The universe and its time-spans exist only in the Son, who is brought into being absolutely as God wills: 'Wisdom existed as Wisdom at the will of a wise God' (*Thalia* II.24 [*NE* 331]); 'He made him to subsist at his own will' (*Letter to Alexander* [*NE* 326]). So for Arius what subsists before the Son and the creation is only the timeless God, whose will produces the Son, and with him all time and creation.

Alexander made much of the error of the Arians in saying Christ is 'changeable' or 'mutable' (Socrates, *HE* 1.6.10–12 *NE* 323]). Arius' own letters flatly contradict this (*To Eusebius*, in Theodoret, *HE* 1.5.3 [*NE* 325]; *Letter to Alexander* [*NE* 326]). Mutability implied the possibility of change for the worse, which in Platonic terms is by definition impossible for God. The truth is that Arius held the Son to be changeless in a less absolute sense: it is at the Father's will he is unchangeable, and so could have been changeable. The anti-Arian Council of Antioch in 325 anathematized 'those who say he is immutable by his own act of will, . . . and deny he is immutable in the way the Father is' (*NE* 336). Some modern writers (especially Gregg and Groh) regard the freedom of the Son to change by improvement, or to resist temptation by moral effort, as essential characteristics of Arian spirituality. This does not seem to match Arius' efforts to assert that the Son is unchangeable and vastly superior to all his creatures.

Constantine intervenes

When Constantine defeated Licinius and was establishing his authority in the East in 324–5, he found the churches divided. Scholars disagree about the date of the formal condemnation by the Alexandrian synod of six presbyters, six deacons and two Libyan bishops, which may not have been till early 325 (*NE* 322–4). But there is no doubt that an earlier attempt had been made to get rid of Arius and his supporters, and that they had set up a sort of church in exile in Palestine. Both Arius and Alexander had corresponded with bishops in other provinces. The most influential Eastern bishop was Eusebius, Bishop of the Eastern capital Nicomedia, and he was supporting Arius. So were several bishops in Palestine and Syria, the most important being Eusebius of Caesarea, the great scholar and historian, who is also called Eusebius Pamphili because of his tutor the Origenist Pamphilus.

Constantine tried to resolve the crisis by addressing a joint letter to the principal persons, Alexander and Arius, probably late in 324 (Eusebius, *Vit. Const.* 2.63–72 [*NE* 332–4]). His letter gives an account of the origins of the dispute, and describes a pointless and useless question by Alexander about a passage from the 'Law' (i.e. the Scripture), and a rash and improper answer. Neither was edifying to the people, or even within human rational capacity. Both question and answer should be withdrawn, and the public dissension laid aside. Whether or not that was psychologically practical advice, the formal synodical condemnation had already taken place, and it was not possible in ecclesiastical terms to restore the *status quo ante*; if Arius and his colleagues were to be restored, it would have to be as laymen. If it were now to take place, it must be on the authority of the Emperor their 'fellow-servant'. While the effort does Constantine much credit, as Eusebius of Caesarea points out in his biography of the Emperor, it failed to resolve the dispute.

The Council of Antioch, 325

In the spring of 325 a council met at Antioch, the second city of the East, probably to appoint a bishop. Since the local bishops were in dispute, Arianism was discussed. The majority found for Alexander, and the bishop they appointed, Eustathius, became a leading anti-Arian till he was deposed between 326 and 330. The Council is known only by a synodical letter (*NE* 334–7). This first states that the Council supports Alexander's condemnation, then sets out a statement of faith, and finally describes its condemnation of three dissenting bishops. The statement of faith is longer than that of Nicaea, and deals directly with the issues. It asserts that 'One God, Father almighty, incomprehensible, immutable and unchangeable' is Creator and Lawgiver. Jesus Christ his only-begotten Son is begotten in a way different from the creation of all other beings, a mysterious way known only to Father and Son. The key to his relation to the Father is 'Image' (Gk *eikon*): since he replicates the Father he also is immutable and unchangeable, and cannot be thought of as Son by volition or adoption, or as ever non-existent. The birth and passion of Christ in the flesh are also stated, and his resurrection and future judgement.

Specifically denounced are the views that Christ is a creature, or that there was when he was not, and that his immutability is 'by his own act of will'; 'For just as our Saviour is the image of the Father in all things, so in this respect particularly he has been proclaimed the Father's image.' In all this the Council seems to follow the concerns of Alexander, fixing on the co-eternity of the Son with the Father, his status as begotten not created, and his immutability, where the subtlety of distinguishing kinds of changelessness overcomes the contradictory statements of Arius and Alexander. Only in the predominating theme, linking all to the Image of God by scriptural texts, do we depart from Alexander's expressed ideas. This is a move associated with Antiochene traditions, as we shall see.

The final part of the letter records the dissent of Theodotus of Laodicea, Narcissus of Neronias, and Eusebius of Caesarea; they are provisionally excommunicated, but a final opportunity is allowed them at 'the great and priestly synod at Ancyra' to repent and recognize the truth. That opens a new topic.

Marcellus of Ancyra

We do not know who planned the episcopal ('priestly') synod at Ancyra; it may have been Constantine's scheme after the failure of his letter. Others, led by Marcellus the Bishop of Ancyra, may have proposed it with his approval. Marcellus helps explain why so many in the East favoured a position resembling Arianism. His view became clear in later years, but was certainly not like that adopted at Antioch (see the polemics of his letter to Julius of Rome in *CCC* 6–8). The Son shared the Father's characteristics because he was Word, Wisdom and Power of the Father, and thus existed in the Father's one Being (substance, hypostasis) from eternity. The notion that there were three distinct hypostases in or of God was quite unacceptable.

What Marcellus' Eastern colleagues found most offensive was his habit of interpreting passages from the Old Testament, which traditionally were used to prove that Christ was another divine being beside the Father, so as to refer to his incarnate life on earth. So 'The Lord created me the beginning of his way, the first of his works' (Prov. 8.22, as the Greek Bible read it) refers not to the generation of the Son before the world existed (as both Alexander and Arius would assert), but to the birth in the flesh, which was the beginning of the 'new creation'. In fact he thought of God as in eternity a single being (monad), with immanent Word and Spirit, which emerge at appropriate historical points to form the duality and trinity (dyad and triad), only to be reabsorbed when the creation is rolled up.

Marcellus was also criticized for his use of 1 Cor. 15.24–8 to mean that, after his second coming in judgement, Christ's reign would come to an end when he submits himself to the Father, 'so that God may be all in all'. In the end the Godhead reverts to its original monad. Marcellus insisted that all reference to the Son's action distinct from the Father belonged to a temporal sequence, from the conception in Mary to the final Kingdom on earth; apart from that he exists and reigns as the Logos and Mind of the Father. Marcellus' critics appealed to Luke 1.33, 'of his kingdom there shall be no end', and believed that it implied an eternal, distinct personal hypostasis. But the detail of that debate belongs to the years after Nicaea, when Marcellus wrote against the Arian philosopher Asterius and was lambasted by Eusebius of Caesarea. We must return to 325.

The Council and Creed of Nicaea

With Marcellus as bishop presiding, a meeting at Ancyra would favour Arius' bitterest enemies. Perhaps as a consequence Constantine moved the location to Nicaea, ostensibly because it was easier for Western delegations to reach it, because the air was good, and so that Constantine himself could attend (letter in *NE* 338). One must also suspect the advice of Eusebius of Nicomedia, since he was near the Emperor, and Nicaea had as bishop his own friend Theognis. Assisted by public transport, bishops travelled in from all over the world, though predominantly from the East. 230 were probably there when Constantine solemnly opened proceedings on 20 May 325 (though larger numbers are given in some sources). Unfortunately no minutes of the meetings survive, and we must understand what happened from fragmentary and biased recollections of participants and from a few formal letters of the time. Central to understanding the doctrinal decision is Eusebius of Caesarea, so recently condemned at Antioch. We may suppose that he went to meet Constantine armed with a version of his *Ecclesiastical History*, in which the old ending, celebrating the joint victory of Constantine and Licinius, had been hastily revised to record Licinius' crimes against the Church, and the reunification of the Empire under God's chosen, Constantine. His enemy Athanasius for his own purposes later recorded a letter which Eusebius sent to his church of Caesarea during or after the Council (*De decretis* 33 = Socrates, *HE* 1.8 [*NE* 344–7]).

Eusebius writes to explain two creeds, one presented by himself, and one drafted at the Council which he had after persuasion agreed to. His formal statement claims that he put forward the creed he had learned for his baptism and had always taught as presbyter and bishop; it is therefore commonly called the 'Caesarean Creed':

> We believe in one God, Father almighty, the Maker of all things visible and invisible.
>
> And in one Lord Jesus Christ, the Word of God, God from God, Light from Light, Life from Life, Only-begotten Son, firstborn of all creation, before all ages begotten from the Father, by whom also all things were made; who for our salvation was incarnate, and lived among men, and suffered, and rose again the third day, and ascended to the Father, and will come again in glory to judge living and dead.
>
> And we believe in one Holy Spirit.

It sounds inoffensive, and may well have grown up at Caesarea before the controversy raised by Arius. Eusebius added that he believed each of the three to be and to exist, 'The Father truly Father, and the Son truly Son, and the Holy Spirit truly Holy Spirit', citing Matt. 28.19 for the teaching of the Trinity. Like Arius when he insisted that the Son was begotten 'not in semblance but in truth', Eusebius saw his creed as opposed to the view that the Son existed only as the Wisdom or Word inherent in the Father.

Eusebius claims that this statement was incontrovertible (but not that no one contested it), and that the Emperor Constantine attested its orthodoxy, said he agreed with it, and advised that it should be generally adopted, with the addition of the one word 'consubstantial' (Gk *homoousios*, and usually so spelled in English, though some books prefer *homousios*). We may take this account as partisan but substantially true. Eusebius' bitter enemy, Eustathius of Antioch, told the story differently: Eusebius (he does not say whether of Caesarea or of Nicomedia) presented a creed which shocked those present into tearing it up, and they drafted a new one instead; we cannot be sure, but this may be another version of the same events. Constantine apparently commented on the meaning of *homoousios*, dealing with objections. Then Eusebius reports that 'they, on the pretext of [not 'because of' as in *NE* 345] the addition of Consubstantial, drew up the following formula':

> We believe in one God, the Father Almighty, Maker of all things visible and invisible.
>
> And in one Lord Jesus Christ, the Son of God, begotten of the Father, Only-begotten, that is, from the substance [*ousia*] of the Father; God from God, Light from Light, true God from true God, begotten not made, consubstantial with the Father, by whom all things were made; who for us men and for our salvation came down and was incarnate, was made man, suffered, and rose again the third day, ascended into heaven, and is coming to judge living and dead.
>
> And in the Holy Spirit.
>
> And those who say, 'There was when he was not', and 'Before his generation he was not', and 'he came to be from nothing', or those who pretend that the Son of God is of other reality [*hypostasis*] or being [*ousia*; some texts add 'or created', probably not original] or alterable or mutable, the Catholic and Apostolic Church anathematizes.

This is the original Nicene Creed, as agreed at Nicaea; the one which now usually bears that name belongs to the Council of Constantinople of 381.

Where did this creed come from? It used to be supposed that Eusebius had put his creed forward for adoption, and that the Nicene Creed (called 'N' for short) was based upon it. That was before the only record of the Council of Antioch of 325 was discovered and published in 1905, with the information that Eusebius was provisionally excommunicate, pending appeal to Ancyra. Now the 'priestly synod' had been moved to Nicaea, we may assume that Eusebius proposed his creed to clear himself; hence the Emperor's testimony that it was 'most orthodox' was a judgement admitting Eusebius to the assembly. The minor

differences of wording between the two creeds are so great, even in
non-controversial points, that one must assume that the drafting
committee started afresh. Eusebius implies that it differed
considerably, both by his introductory words and by his insistence
that he questioned its wording in detail. Some differences are
worth noting:

1. The anathema at the end attacks a series of statements
believed to be Arian. In fact Arius could evade most of them.
There is no evidence he actually wrote, 'There was when he was
not.' He would certainly deny 'alterable or mutable' as we have
seen. He appears to have written 'before he was begotten, he
was not', and, 'he is from nothing' (*Letter to Eusebius*, Theodoret,
HE 1.5.4 [*NE* 325]); but even there 'from nothing' may be what
he is accused of and not what he admits to asserting (note what
follows, 'this we do say, that he is neither part of God nor of any
lower essence'). 'Created' he did say, but it is not in the original
text of N. Eusebius of Nicomedia and Theognis later claimed,
'We subscribed to the creed; we did not subscribe to the
anathematizing; not as objecting to the creed, but as disbelieving
the party accused to be such as was represented' (Socrates, *HE*
1.14.3 [*NE* 354]). This probably means that they accepted the
whole creed, including the anathema at the end, but did not
accept that it applied to Arius.

2. Both creeds feature 'Only-begotten', but very differently. In
Eusebius it comes later in the description of the one Lord Jesus
Christ, after 'God from God, Light from Light', and is followed
immediately by reference to the creation and the ages. He is
unique (= only-begotten) in the sense that he is 'firstborn of all
creation'; these words from Col. 1.15 are taken by the Arians to
mean that Christ is head of all created things. Similarly he is
'before all ages begotten from the Father'; he is unique as
generated from the Father alone and before time. The drafters of
N would have found that unacceptable: bishops like Marcellus
and Eustathius could not accept 'only-begotten' in that sense,
since they took Col. 1.15 of Christ's manhood, the 'new creation'.
'Begotten from the Father, only-begotten' meant that Christ
originates 'from the being (*ousia*, 'substance' or 'essence') of the
Father'. In Marcellus' thought Christ is the means of creation
inasmuch as he is the immanent Logos, Wisdom and Power of

the Father himself; it is perhaps no accident that 'by whom all things were made' follows 'consubstantial with the Father' in N, whereas in Eusebius it follows 'begotten . . . before all ages'. N allows for a position in which God is a single being (*ousia*), who operates singly by his own unique Wisdom to make the world, and becomes two only in the incarnation.

3. One distinction is made clear, which Arians did not make and which Eusebius did not require: 'begotten, not made'.

4. Instead of, 'was incarnate and *lived among* men', we read, 'was incarnate, *was made* man'. Eustathius emphasized that Christ's humanity was complete with a rational spirit or mind; Arians thought in terms of the divine Son with a body, as did their Alexandrian opponents.

Eusebius found N difficult to accept. 'Consubstantial' could imply that Christ was generated out of the Father rather as a human son is sexually generated by his human parent, 'according to bodily affections'; or it could imply that some part of the Father was separated off by 'division' or 'severance', a view which had led Arius to repudiate the word *homoousios* as Manichaean (twice in his letter to Alexander, and in *Thalia* II.9 [*NE* 326, 327, 331]). Eusebius accepted reassurances on this point for the sake of peace (*Letter*, 5 [*NE* 345–6]), and positively interpreted the word as meaning 'that the Son of God bears no resemblance to the originated creatures, but that to his Father who begat him he is in every way assimilated, and that he is not of any other *hypostasis* or *ousia*, but from the Father' (*Letter*, 7). Thus he uses the idea used against him at Antioch: the Son is exactly like the Father, and has no other source. The Western tradition had spoken of one being or substance (*una substantia*) of Father, Son and Spirit; Eustathius and others took *homoousios* in that sense. It is plain that Eusebius (and many others like him) accepted the word, but in a very different meaning. This flexibility is perhaps the reason why *homoousios* was adopted in the first place. Eusebius ingeniously interpreted other clauses of the creed to suit his preferred meaning. One could anathematize 'before his generation he was not' by referring it to the human birth of Christ, before which he undoubtedly existed (*Letter*, 9): its proponents took it to refer to the Father's eternity which the Son did not share.

Homoousios means 'same in being', and is therefore ambiguous. 'Same' can mean 'identical', 'one and the same' (as two words are on the same page), or 'exactly like' (as when one word is the same as the other). 'Being' is also ambiguous. We speak of 'a being' as a concrete individual, as an angel is a spiritual being and a child a human being; but we might also say that the angel *has* spiritual being (essence, existence or nature), and the child has a human one. Eusebius' interpretation of N represents a position which many Eastern bishops shared, in which *homoousios* means 'exactly like in being', not 'one and the same being' as some would understand it. It is doubtful whether Arius' original critics would have found the positive parts of N congenial. The anathema certainly represents what Alexander opposed. But when Arius rejected *homoousios* in his letter to Alexander, he was claiming to agree with Alexander's habitual teaching. The bishop in his own letters (*NE* 322–4; 328–9) was concerned to state that the Son was coeternal, immutable, and not a creature, a position which the Council of Antioch had endorsed with none of the quasi-Marcellian features of N. The later Creed of Constantinople, as we shall see, was to retain *homoousios*, but avoided the other characteristic features of N.

The outcome and aftermath of Nicaea

The Council of Nicaea was almost unanimous. The Council reported its decisions to the churches concerned. To the Alexandrian church and to all the brethren in Egypt and Libya (see Socrates, *HE* 1.9.1–14 [*NE* 347–50]) it reported the condemnation of Arius for his views, and that the two Libyan bishops, Theonas of Marmarica and Secundus of Ptolemais, were also judged condemned; they had refused the creed. It then reported the other two issues settled. One concerned the Melitians, whose schism separated the Egyptian churches into two camps. Melitius was to be deprived of all powers and retain only a nominal dignity; those ordained by him might exercise their office but only as subordinate to bishops of Alexander's communion, and might succeed to episcopates, subject to the veto of the bishop of Alexandria himself. These humiliating terms of reconciliation did not in fact work. The other issue chiefly concerned the Antiochenes:

Easter was to be kept, not with the Jews, but according to the ancient practice of Rome and Alexandria. The Syrian churches appear to have kept the paschal fast ('Holy Week' in modern terminology) to coincide with the Jewish Passover, breaking their fast on the following Sunday, their Pascha (our Easter). The Alexandrians calculated for themselves the first full moon after the spring equinox, and reckoned Easter the Sunday after that. The Roman system was more complicated, and ensured that the fast finished no later than 21 April, when the City celebrated its foundation day. But usually it coincided with Alexandria. Constantine himself wrote to the Syrians, urging them to accept the Council's judgements. The Syrians soon abandoned their Easter rule.

Twenty canons were also produced at Nicaea (see *NE* 338–47). These touch on none of the three primary pieces of business, but appear to be genuine. They deal with several matters arising from the persecutions and the universal settlement, establishing uniform discipline for various classes of clerics and laity. Notably they recognize the provincial authority of Alexandria, Rome and Antioch over certain neighbouring churches (Canon 6), and ambiguously accord honour to Aelia (Jerusalem) without prejudice to its Metropolitan (Caesarea) (7). These decrees recognize the actual state reached in the churches. Novatianists were to be reconciled on very favourable terms, their whole clergy fully recognized provided only they will comply with Catholic penitential law (8). Those of the denomination of Paul of Samosata have to be baptized, but their clergy may then be ordained to office (19). This rule follows the general Eastern principle that the doctrine in which one is baptized determines validity: Paul's teaching, like that of the Montanists, is deemed corrupt and his baptisms consequently ineffectual.

The bishops dispersed in 325 after wining and dining with the Emperor to celebrate the twentieth year of his reign. But some constituted either a continuing committee or a more local ecclesiastical court. They may have been responsible for the twenty canons. They were certainly involved in grave affairs after the main Council. Before the end of the year Constantine had removed Eusebius of Nicomedia and Theognis of Nicaea, with or without support of a synod. These eminent bishops had apparently given communion to Arians condemned by the Council; Constantine accuses Eusebius of theological and political treason (Gelasius, *HE* 3 app. 1 [*NE* 351–3]). But Arius' supporters in Alexandria were not appeased, and Constantine received a statement of faith in which Arius affirmed his creed and swore that he believed 'as the whole Catholic Church and the Scriptures teach' (Socrates, *HE* 1.26.2–7 [*NE* 353–4]); the Creed of Nicaea was clearly not being used as a fixed doctrinal test, and his appeal was accepted by the Emperor and by the synod. Eusebius and Theognis appealed to the same court, pointing out that they had subscribed to N, and were restored too. The ecclesiastical court which permitted this may or may not be rightly called the 'second council' of Nicaea, and dated 327 or 328; scholarly opinion is divided. It is certain however that it marked the beginning of the dominance of Eusebius of Nicomedia and his party in Eastern church affairs, a dominance which persisted for over thirty years. Meanwhile the bishops of Alexandria, Alexander and his successor in 328 Athanasius, were not disposed to accept back Arius as a presbyter, when he had been formally deposed for heresy, and seeds of continuing dispute were thus sown.

It may be that behind the dispute about the time or eternity of the Son's origin there lay an issue as yet only obscurely seen. Arius felt that the only way to secure the deity of Christ was to set him on the step immediately below the Father, who remained beyond all comprehension. Arius is sometimes thought to be (like the Neoplatonist philosophers and perhaps Origen) ultimately a 'monist', who saw reality as a single graded continuum. The transcendence was made tolerable, since all reality was a series of steps from creatures to the Creator. Arius' enemies certainly attacked him as if he took this view, emphasizing that the divide between Creator and creature was ultimately significant, and that Christ is Creator, not creature. As the debate progressed, the topics which at first were less central than time and eternity, about whether the Son shared the divine 'substance' or was 'created', were to loom larger, and to make the issue clearer. Both parties understood the face of God as graciously revealed in Jesus Christ. Arius however was not really a monist; he did not perceive a smooth and almost natural transition from the transcendent One through the Son to the creation. In fact he saw himself as sharply opposed to such a view, as he shows by his strictures on those who see the Son as an 'emanation' or as an extension of the

Father's being, and posited a great difference between the Son and the beings he engendered. Instead he rested all upon the mere will of the Father, who is by definition incomprehensible and beyond description. At best the will which commanded the Son to be was mysterious; at worst merely arbitrary. For Alexander and Athanasius a miracle of condescension brought creating grace and saving pity down from an ultimate height of Godhead, where Father and Son dwelt in perfect communion. It was a richer gospel, even if they gave Arius less credit than he deserved.

14

COUNCILS AND CONTROVERSIES: 327–361

The Eusebian supremacy

For the remainder of Constantine's reign the party round Eusebius, many of whom had supported Arius against Alexander, grew in power. At an early but uncertain date (328?) Eustathius was forced out of the bishopric at Antioch, and the attempt to find a successor was accompanied by riotous disorder. Eustathius' crime was ostensibly an affront to the Augusta Helena, Constantine's mother, who was on a journey of imperial duties in Syria and Palestine. His real offence was perhaps theological: Eusebius of Caesarea, the greatest living scholar of the Church, an Origenist and a supporter of the dominant party, was bitterly opposed to his theology of 'one *hypostasis*' (Athanasius, *Hist. Ar.* 4 [*NE* 359–61]). The victors tried to make Eusebius himself bishop, but he declined to breach the Nicene canon against bishops changing their sees, and a series of less distinguished bishops occupied Antioch. The little body of loyal Eustathians, led by the presbyter Paulinus, were to cause much trouble later.

Athanasius was appointed Bishop of Alexandria in 328, possibly in controversial circumstances. He was soon quarrelling with the Melitians. On his own testimony they were formally reconciled as Nicaea had decreed shortly before Alexander's death, and a list of the reconciled clergy was in his office. But the Melitians accused Athanasius of rough and unfair treatment, and they soon called for support from Eusebius of Nicomedia and the wider Church (Athanasius, *Apol. sec.* 59, 71 [*NE* 357–8]). The ex-Melitians, led by one John Arcaph, alleged that Athanasius had campaigned against a bishop Callinicus and a presbyter Ischyras; his agents had committed sacrilege to an altar and a sacramental chalice, and he had put a deposed presbyter in charge of a church, and caused various imprisonments and beatings. He had obtained the episcopate by perjured testimony to his innocence of other alleged crimes, and the ex-Melitians could not conscientiously regard him as bishop. Some more spectacular crimes of cutting off a man's arm for magic purposes and suborning a woman for sexual purposes were easy to refute, and Athanasius cleared himself of these when it came to the point, as he himself is pleased to report (see Sozomen, *HE* 2.25.3–12 [*NE* 362–3]). The use of force, intimidation and imprisonment by bishops of Alexandria is quite common from this time onwards, and is confirmed in Athanasius' case by original papyrus letters recovered in modern times (an example in *NE* 359); while difficult to understand in detail, they undoubtedly attest the imprisonment and the terror which Athanasius induced in his opponents.

Constantine was involved in vain attempts to reconcile in Egypt. Eventually he decided that the peace of the churches must be restored in time for the dedication of his great new Church of the Resurrection (the *Anastasis*) in Jerusalem, the remains of which form part of the existing Church of the Holy Sepulchre. His mother Helena, visiting and restoring holy sites, had been present when the Hadrianic temple over the alleged site of the resurrection was excavated, and the actual tomb of Christ exposed. In the oldest account (Eusebius, *Vit. Const.* 3.25–40) nothing is said of the simultaneous discovery of the wood of the true cross of Christ, which figured very large in the cult of this church in Jerusalem from the middle of the century; it is uncertain whether Eusebius did not know this story in 338 when he wrote, or deliberately suppressed it. The dedication was to be a gathering of bishops from all parts at Jerusalem in his own thirtieth year, 335, as part of Constantine's Tricennalia festivities. But unity must first be restored, and the upshot was a trial of the charges against Athanasius at a council in Tyre.

Athanasius knew he would be convicted. Whatever the truth of the allegations of episcopal tyranny, many of the councillors who would judge him were those who had backed Arius against Alexander; he himself still resisted the restoration of Arius. He tried to avoid attending, but finally went. He refuted what accusations he could, but left when the judges (scrupulously, one might think), decided to send a commission to investigate the charges on the spot in Egypt. Athanasius played the imperial card, and presented himself before Constantine at Constantinople, and Constantine sent for the leading bishops to come and explain themselves (Constantine in Athanasius, *Apol. sec.* 36 [*NE* 363–4]).

Athanasius alleges that they then said he had threatened to stop the grain ships from Egypt to Constantinople, and for this he was exiled (Socrates, *HE* 1.35.1–4 [*NE* 364–5]). Eusebius and company hardly needed such an unlikely tale to persuade the Emperor that while Athanasius remained there could be no peace. He was banished to Trier in Gaul, and the Anastasis was consecrated with joyful magnificence.

From Trier Athanasius established links with Latin churchmen, sustained contact with his numerous supporters in Egypt, and probably wrote a two-volume book, *Against the pagans* and *On the incarnation*, a sort of theological manifesto. The idea that these were written about 318 before the Arian controversy is now generally discarded. If Arianism is not mentioned, it is because it was now a dead issue. Soon Athanasius would revive it, to claim that his condemnation by the Eastern churches was a conspiracy of Arian heretics and Melitian schismatics. But while Constantine lived, he was discreet. It was not his theology, but violence, that he was banished for.

About the same time another bishop fell, tried for heresy at Constantinople, and banished. Marcellus of Ancyra was stung by the hostile preaching in Syria of a layman called Asterius, and issued a comprehensive rebuttal. Asterius is regarded as 'Arian', and is notorious for making the point that the term 'power of God', applied to Christ in 1 Cor. 1.24, is also applied to caterpillars and locusts in Joel 2.25 ('my great power'). His point was that the mere title did not mean that Christ was, as Marcellus held, internal to the Father; but it supplied a ready handle to Asterius' critics. Marcellus' refutation itself shocked the moderates in the East. We have already described his teaching (pp. 127–8). Marcellus, not Arius, was for the Eusebian party the great Christ-denying heretic; to Athanasius he was a fellow-sufferer and campaigner for the truth.

The division of East and West

Constantine died at Pentecost 337, as he prepared for a Persian war. First, however, he was baptized by his leading bishop, Eusebius of Nicomedia, and, after courtly ritual, was laid to rest with Christian rites in a specially constructed Church of the Apostles. He left the Empire divided between his three sons and two nephews. A military *putsch* disposed of the nephews and their kindred, and left the three sons, Constantine II in the West, Constans in the centre, and Constantius II in the East. While Constantius was busy fighting the Persians in a war that was to drag on till 350, his brothers quarrelled, and Constantine II was killed. That left Constans with two thirds of the Empire, and Constantius comparatively weak. In ecclesiastical matters, Constans persistently pressed the claims of Rome and the Westerns, while Constantius kept to his Eusebian policy. When Paul, Bishop of Constantinople since 336, was deposed in 338, Eusebius was translated from Nicomedia, and was bishop of the capital till his death in 341, his dominance publicly confirmed.

Athanasius returned to Alexandria in 337 under a kind of amnesty (Socrates, *HE* 2.3 [*CCC* 1–2]). But there was local opposition, and soon the Eusebians elected a new bishop, Gregory, who was installed with military support; Athanasius fled to Rome. He and Marcellus appealed to the new bishop of Rome, Julius (337–52), who reviewed their cases and quashed their convictions at a council in 340 (see Julius' letter in Athanasius, *Apol. sec.* 35 [*CCC* 5–6], and Marcellus' cunning theological appeal, Epiphanius, *Haer.* 72.2–3 [*CCC* 6–8]). It was questionable, however, whether the Bishop of Rome could overrule the decisions of properly constituted synods in the East; the Easterns did not think so. Thirty-seven bishops assembled at Antioch in 341, to dedicate the new 'golden church', whence the name 'Dedication Council' is used. The credal statements of this Council (*CCC* 8–11) deserve special study, especially the second, which was regarded by many as the definitive credal foundation for the Eastern churches.

In circumstances we do not know much about, the bishops at Antioch in 341 published in letters two creeds. Antioch 1 (*CCC* 8–9) is a defensive document. Athanasius and Marcellus have put it about at Rome and elsewhere that they are Arian heretics, so they begin by disowning such an idea: 'How should we who are bishops follow a presbyter?' But the mud has stuck. In fact even today most modern literature labels the church of Constantius 'Arian'. That is to accept the label their enemies gave them. Hanson in *The search for the Christian doctrine of God* makes a determined effort to escape the scholarly tradition, and avoid labelling the whole dispute 'the Arian controversy'; but even he relapses into the conventional terminology. The bishops at Antioch were simply representative of the Eastern church. We should

accept their disclaimer on Arianism, particularly (as we shall see)
as their basic position was similar to that of the anti-Arian council
of Antioch in 325 (see pp. 126–7). The other point of interest in an
innocuous creed is their emphasis on 'one only-begotten Son of
God before all ages, subsisting and co-existing with the Father
who begat him'. This idea, suppressed by the Creed of Nicaea and
rejected by Marcellus, is one the Easterns constantly champion.

Antioch 2 (*CCC* 9–10) is more important, expressing more fully
their positive faith, and intended for that position as a foundation
for orthodoxy which the Nicene Creed eventually attained. It is
sometimes called the 'Lucianic Creed', because in some traditions
it is associated with the martyr Lucian. But the idea that it went
back to him is probably false; more probably this idea arose
because it was the basic creed of those for whom Lucian, buried at
Helenopolis near Nicomedia, was the patron saint. It is typical of
the Eastern position, which defines the deity of Christ in terms of
his exact likeness to the Father: 'begotten before the ages from the
Father, God from God, whole from whole, sole from sole, perfect
from perfect, King from King, Lord from Lord, . . . exact Image of
the Godhead, substance (*ousia*), will, power and glory of the
Father . . .'. It should be noted that the italics in *CCC*, 'exact *Image
of the Godhead*', are misleading, since not a single word is the
same as the biblical reference given, Heb. 1.3, though the thought
may be there. The words are nearly those of Col. 1.14, 'image of
the unseen God'; see also 2 Cor. 4.4. The term 'exact image'
(*aparallaktos eikon*) was actually used by Alexander of Alexandria,
and was regarded as orthodox by Athanasius. It was not exactly
Origenistic; Origen knew the Son as Image of the Father, but the
precise or exact similarity lay in the will. Here it is not only will,
but godhead and being which are the same in each, Father and
Son. Clearly Origenist, however, is the list of aspects of the Son's
being which intervenes between the parts of the quotation above:
'living Word, living wisdom, true light, way, truth, resurrection,
shepherd, door, both unalterable and unchangeable . . .'. It should
be noted that the term 'living' opposes the idea of a Word or
Wisdom merely immanent in the Father, and not a distinct being.
The last two words make him unchangeable in the same way the
Father is, thus distinguishing their position from that of Arius (see
p. 125). Furthermore, they are at pains to insist on the Holy Spirit
as a third, distinct *hypostasis*, and to insist on the real distinctions

in the Trinity: 'three in subsistence, and in agreement one', just as Origen had said. Finally they denounce a number of propositions associated with Arianism, which are basically two: that there was time before the Son existed, or that he is a creature like other creatures. This Creed clearly asserted the deity of Christ in terms of his exact likeness to the Father, and expressed well the beliefs later held by the party labelled 'homoiousian' (see p. 146).

Antioch 4 (*CCC* 10–11) was a negotiating position, not a creed of the whole council; it differs from others in condemning explicitly, 'that the Son is from nothing, or from another hypostasis and not from God, and that there was a time when he was not'. These anathemas bring them close to those of the Creed of Nicaea. Other parts of the document however seem to have more to do with the error of Marcellus: Christ is 'begotten from the Father before all ages', and 'will be sitting on the Father's right not only in this age but also in the coming one'. Even their expanded words on the Holy Spirit as Paraclete, sent after Christ's ascension, can be seen as opposed to Marcellus' tendency to identify the deity of Christ personally with the Holy Spirit.

In 343 or perhaps 342 a general reconciliation was attempted, at the instigation of Constans. The reluctant Easterns gathered at Sardica (modern Sofia), in Constans' territory, to meet more numerous Western colleagues. Ossius of Cordova presided, assisted by Protogenes of Sardica. They never sat down together, because the Easterns objected to the presence of the deposed bishops Athanasius and Marcellus, with whom were now Paul of Constantinople and Asclepas of Gaza. They withdrew across the frontier to Philippopolis in Thrace, and there decreed the deposition of all the supporters of Marcellus and Athanasius, including the leaders of the council. Meanwhile at Sardica the Westerns did the same, taking the trouble to examine the teachings of Marcellus before declaring him orthodox, reinstating all their allies in the East and deposing all their opponents (Socrates, *HE* 2.20.7–11 [*CCC* 11–12]). But with some copies of their circular letter is preserved a statement of faith, apparently drafted to deal with a document from Ursacius of Singidunum and Valens of Mursa, Latins who were the recognized rising stars of the Eastern party. Unfortunately the text of this document is corrupt, and the English version in *CCC* 13–14 misleading (new translation and exposition in S. G. Hall, 'The Creed of Sardica', *Studia patristica* 19 [1989]

173–84). Its drift is however clear. God is one *hypostasis* (= *substantia* in the original Latin), and Valens and Ursacius are heretics in maintaining that the Father, Son and Spirit are distinct *hypostases*; the *hypostasis* of the Son is exactly that of the Father. The English of *CCC* 13–14 fails to make clear that the Creed seems also to repudiate the idea of the begetting of the Son before the ages, and to identify the Holy Spirit with the Logos, though it is clear at the end that the Holy Spirit is identified with the divine person in Christ. Both parties slammed the door on each other doctrinally, but the Westerns especially damned the Origenist tradition. They also passed some canons, which were soon thought to derive from Nicaea; the most interesting is the third (*CCC* 15–16) which asserts the right of condemned clerics to appeal to Rome over the heads of the local hierarchy, reflecting the position of Athanasius, Marcellus and others like them, who had been condemned in the East.

Pressure for reconciliation continued, however, and the Easterns sent a further deputation to Rome, armed with lengthy defence of their position, the 'Creed of the long lines' of 345 (Athanasius, *Syn.* 26 [*CCC* 18–21]). While this did not achieve its purpose, it again made clear the Eastern fears of Marcellus' thought. Its first two propositions abjure the 'Arian' propositions that the Son is from nothing, and that there was when he was not. Much of the rest defends the concept of the Trinity of three real persons, and especially in propositions 4–8 they reject the idea that before the incarnation the Son somehow lacked personal being distinct from the Father, and was immanent within him. All this resists the Marcellian and Sardican pressure. Two biblical citations figure illuminatingly: Gen. 1.26 in section 18, which is taken to mean that God said to the Son, 'Let us make man in our own image', a position generally held since Justin but repudiated by Marcellus; and in section 22, Prov. 8.22, 'The Lord created me the beginning of his ways for his works', which Marcellus and Athanasius applied to the humanity only of Christ, is still applied to the generation of the Son from the Father, though not as making him like other creatures. Though peace was not made, Constantius and his bishops yielded to pressure: Athanasius returned to Alexandria in triumph in 346 on the death of Gregory.

The Eastern dominance

In 350 Constans was murdered by a group of officers, and the Western Empire was usurped by Magnentius. Constantius advanced to avenge his brother. The most important, though not the last, battle of the bloody campaign was fought in 351 at Mursa in Pannonia, the seat of one of the leading bishops of the Eastern party, Valens (see *CCC* 29–30). Magnentius finally perished in 353, and Constantius was sole Emperor. Until his death in 361 he strove, rather as his father had done, to cajole the bishops into accepting a common standard of faith. While prepared to use both bribery and exile to achieve his results, he was not wicked or violent towards the clergy, even when they wrote and spoke bitterly of him. It was because they believed his policies to be doctrinally destructive that bishops like Athanasius, Hilary of Poitiers and Lucifer of Calaris would call him Antichrist and Persecutor of the Church. Advised by such men as Valens, Ursacius of Singidunum and Macedonius, who was Bishop of Constantinople 351–60, Constantius generally tried to impose a broad framework of belief which almost anyone could subscribe to. Unfortunately for him, a large body of Western opinion would not abandon Athanasius, and shared his attachment to the principles of Sardica and the Creed of Nicaea. New questions were also to arise in the East, especially 'Neo-arianism', which alarmed many of the moderate churchmen there.

At a council at Arles in 353 Constantius secured the agreement of most of the bishops of Gaul to the deposition of Athanasius. Trying to widen the assent by a meeting at Milan in 355, the Emperor's bishops faced the resistance of Paulinus of Trier and a few others. Among them was Eusebius of Vercellae. He produced the Creed of Nicaea, and suggested that they should all sign it first and then condemn Athanasius. Valens prevented this being done, and the dissidents (Eusebius, Lucifer and others) were themselves condemned (see Hilary, *Ad Constantium* 1.3 [*CCC* 31–2]). The significance of this is that the Creed of Nicaea was thus clearly raised as a rallying-standard. While ratified by the Western Council of Sardica (see pp. 142–3), it had been until 355 merely an historic formula by which Arius had been condemned. It now became a point of principle for those who wanted to state that the Father and Son share the same divinity; and alternative formulae, however well-meant and innocuous in themselves, were rejected as refusing the principles of Nicaea and therefore 'Arian'. Constantius did obtain some success, however, and important figures who in 355 still resisted his policies (Liberius of Rome and Ossius of Cordoba) had by 357 yielded to persuasion (see *CCC* 33–7; 39–40. Ossius was officially responsible for the 'Blasphemy of Sirmium'.).

With the verdict of Milan against him, Athanasius went into hiding. From his hiding place he continued his literary campaign, tirelessly attacking Arianism as he understood it. Arius and the Eastern bishops who supported his views made the Son a creature just like other men, separated him from the Father, and deprived him of divine being and saving power. In Athanasius' doctrine, which increasingly came to reflect on and develop the words of the Nicene Creed, the Son was the Father's 'own' Son in a way no others are. He has his being 'from' the Father, and not from nothing or from any other source. He therefore shares every aspect of the Father's nature, and communicates true divinity to mankind by the incarnation. Once the political difficulties could be set aside, and he himself was prepared to make the necessary accommodations and qualifications to avoid misunderstandings, the power of his doctrine asserted itself. But other serious problems first emerged.

In 357 Eudoxius, Bishop of Germanicia, was promoted to be Bishop of Antioch. He was prepared to countenance quite extreme views, and promoted among his clergy two sharp young theologians, Aetius who was already a deacon, and Eunomius whom he ordained. These two were to elaborate a set of doctrines which caused great offence, and was nicknamed 'anomoian' (often spelled 'anomoean'; from the Greek *anomoios*, 'unlike'). They insisted in Aristotelian fashion that the words used of the divinity, and especially 'unbegotten' and '(only-)begotten', are precise descriptions of the essence or nature of the Father and the Son. They differed from Arius, who had a mystical conviction of the unknowability of God, in this belief that God could be clearly and accurately understood. But they drew from it conclusions like his, only sharper, and are consequently called 'Neo-arians'. If Father and Son are designated chiefly by the terms 'unbegotten' and 'begotten', then these essences are contrary at their most significant point. They are therefore unlike each other. Any likeness can only be in their outward works or activities, not in their own nature.

What is said of the Son is even truer of the Spirit. It will be seen that such a doctrine contradicts not only the Athanasian and Western idea that the Father and Son share the same being, but also the main Eastern doctrine that the Son is divine by being *like* the Father in being, will, power and glory (as in the Second Creed of Antioch, see pp. 141–2).

The Eastern majority reacted strongly. Led by Basil, Bishop of Ancyra (not to be confused with the younger and more famous Basil of Caesarea), they gathered at Ancyra in 358 and agreed to send a deputation to the Emperor, asking him to support the view that the Son was *like* the Father *in being* (Gk *homoios kat' ousian*) (see *CCC* 41–2); they were consequently named 'homoiousians' (or 'homoeousians') as supporters of the doctrine of *homoiousios* (Gk *homoiousios*, 'like in being'). It is important to note that this differs from the *homoousios* ('same in being') of the Creed of Nicaea only by one letter, iota. At first the deputation had some success with the Emperor, and was supported by the respected and longstanding Bishop of Constantinople, Macedonius. But Constantius' advisers rallied to resist, and eventually won.

The official position, argued by Valens and Ursacius (see p. 144), was represented by the Second Creed of Sirmium (*CCC* 39–40). It is often referred to as 'homoian' (or 'homoean'; from the Gk *homoios* 'like'), as holding that the Son is merely *like* the Father. This expression did not actually come into public use till after 358. It seems innocuous, but as a partisan term it went with the rejection of any terms about essence or substance: this Creed rejects both *homoousios* and *homoiousios*. The court party of Ursacius and Valens arranged for the whole to be settled by two large councils, a Western one at Ariminum (Rimini) and an Eastern at Seleucia. A creed was brought from the court to both councils, the Fourth Creed of Sirmium or 'Dated Creed' of 22 May 359 (*CCC* 45–6); this respectfully rejected the use of *ousia* or 'essence' to refer to God, and said that the Son was 'like the Father who begat him, according to the Scriptures'. In both respects it contradicted the position of Eunomius and the anomoians. But although it gathered some support in the East, it did not satisfy the majority. Those at Seleucia wanted it clear that the Son was like the Father 'in being' (*ousia*), or 'in all things' (Gk *kata panta*), which included 'being'; their opponents saw that this would exclude the Eunomians, and resisted it. After struggling for the older

Antiochene formula, the Easterners eventually yielded, and those who remained at the council subscribed to a version of the Dated Creed. The resistance of the Westerners at Ariminum, who wanted the Creed of Nicaea, crumbled even more quickly. So as AD 360 began the Dated Creed and the homoian doctrine it enshrined became the official faith of the Empire with the approval of the greatest gatherings of bishops and was to remain so for much of the following twenty years.

The official doctrine was not Arian. It was intended to be all-embracing. But it was taken as a surrender to 'Arianism' not only by the Western and Nicene supporters, who held that the Son was of the same essence or being as the Father, but also by the Eastern majority, who favoured 'like in essence' and the Second Creed of Antioch 341. 'The whole world groaned and was astonished to find itself Arian', wrote Jerome in a famous remark (see *CCC* 46). Many churchmen agreed with the Emperor, or yielded to the pressure. Some stood firm and were exiled, including Macedonius of Constantinople, into whose place Eudoxius moved from Antioch, his pre-eminence sealing his party's victory. But imperial events soon overtook the bishops.

15

TOWARDS SYNTHESIS: 361–380

The reign of Julian, 361–3

The last emperor of the house of Constantine was Julian, known as 'the Apostate'. He rose to power as a colleague of his cousin Constantius with responsibilities in Gaul from 355. In 360 his army drove him to rebellion, but Constantius died in 361 before it came to war. As sole emperor Julian revealed that he had turned in his youth against Christianity, and he tried to reinstate the old pagan religion by various means (details in CCC 52–68).

As part of his policy Julian allowed exiled bishops back to their sees, apparently believing that the resulting disputes would damage the faith he was attacking. In fact he precipitated some remarkable reconciliations; the threat of persecution made some doctrinal arguments seem suddenly less important. The most significant of the many church activities which followed was a council held at Alexandria in 362, presided over by Athanasius. Its synodical letter deserves close study: see CCC 80–3.

The object of the Council was to reconcile two parties at Antioch. One was the old dissident Nicene congregation, loyal to the memory of Eustathius (see p. 137) and led by Paulinus; to them Athanasius addressed the synodical letter. The other was the main congregation, described as 'those who assemble in the old town', who were led by Meletius, and also willing to subscribe to the Creed of Nicaea. Meletius (who has no connection with the earlier Melitian schism in Egypt) had been appointed in the last year of Constantius to replace Eudoxius, but shocked the authorities by commending the *homoousios* doctrine; he was exiled the same year, and replaced by Euzoius, a genuine Arian of the old school, who had shared Arius' exile. Meletius recovered the main church once Constantius was dead, but his congregation and leadership were not accepted by the Eustathian congregation, partly because Meletius had been appointed under the 'Arian' regime, and ordained by bishops out of communion with the true churches, and partly because of different theological formulae. The theological issues in debate were two: whether it is right to speak of God as one *hypostasis* or three, and whether Christ had a human soul. Representatives of various groups from Antioch were in attendance, and so were two Western bishops, exiled to the East for their Nicene loyalties, Eusebius of Vercellae and Lucifer of Calaris.

The first matter to be settled was the terms on which those tainted with heresy were to be accepted by the party of Athanasius and Paulinus. In this the synod's decision was generous by the standards of the day. On older canonical principles, lay persons could be received back into orthodox communion as penitents, or, if their baptism was thought doctrinally unsound, as candidates for baptism. Clergy might be accepted as clergy only where there was no doctrinal error, as Nicaea did with the Novatianists and the Melitian schismatics of Egypt. Where the mortal sin of heresy was involved, they were treated as laymen. Whole communities of the Eastern church were, however, regarded as 'Arian', and could not be accepted simply by subscribing to orthodox doctrine now. That was one reason why the Paulinians refused to recognize the Meletian party at Antioch. But now the Council of Alexandria laid down only three conditions for acceptance of laity, clergy and whole communities:

to anathematize the Arian heresy

and to confess the faith confessed by the holy fathers at Nicaea

and to anathematize also those who say that the Holy Spirit is a creature and separate from the essence of Christ (Athanasius, *Tom. ad Ant.* 3 [*CCC* 80]).

The first two conditions are obvious enough. The third reflects a new issue which had recently come to the fore, on which the parties were not apparently divided: the heresy of the Pneumatomachi or 'Spirit-fighters'; see below pp. 153–4. At Alexandria it was agreed that to make the Spirit a creature was a form of Arianism. The Meletians were invited to restored communion on these terms alone (*Tom. ad Ant.* 4), a generosity some thought scandalous. Lucifer of Calaris was so incensed that he went to Antioch and consecrated Paulinus as bishop, to make sure that his congregation could not simply be incorporated into that of Meletius. His ploy was wholly successful, and the schism among the Nicene supporters at Antioch lasted till 388 (*CCC* 268).

The first doctrinal issue was that of God's *hypostasis* or substance. The Eustathian tradition held that God was one substance or being, in agreement with the Western terminology since Tertullian, which spoke of 'one substance'. The Creed of Nicaea ('N') seems to take this position, denying that the Son is 'of another *hypostasis* or *ousia*' than the Father, and it was certainly interpreted so in the Creed of Sardica (pp. 142–3 and *CCC* 13–14). Here Athanasius denies that such a creed was approved at Sardica (*Tom. ad Ant.* 5), and claims that the Creed was an informal attempt turned down by that council. Athanasius may be lying. He is certainly now in the position of wanting to insist on the Nicene Creed *and no other*, and of wanting to be allowed 'three hypostases', which Sardica had rejected. Those who spoke of 'three hypostases' were questioned as to whether they meant quite separate beings, like the Arians, or three separate gods or beginnings. The Meletians made it plain that they used this traditional Eastern terminology 'because they believed in a Holy Trinity, not a trinity in name only, but existing and subsisting in truth', so that each of the three exists and subsists distinct from the others: that the Son is co-essential (*homoousios*) with the Father, and that the Spirit is proper to and inseparable from the *ousia* of the Father and Son, they also acknowledged. This terminology suggests a deliberate, and rather new, distinction between the essence (*ousia*) common to Father, Son and Spirit, and their individual or personal existence (*hypostasis*).

The same distinction emerges in the questioning of those who assert 'one *hypostasis*', that is the Paulinians. Their position was not to be understood as that attributed to Sabellius, implying that God is a single person, but in the sense of the single divine essence (*ousia*), Godhead or nature (*physis*) present alike in Father, Son and Holy Spirit. On this basis the two parties anathematized various well-known heretics, and agreed with each other. For theological purposes this agreement overcame the division of the main body of Easterns, who were allowed to speak of three beings or subsistences (*hypostases*) in an Origenistic way, and the Eustathian/Nicene party who had always insisted on a single divine being or essence (*ousia*). The problem of translation into Latin would still trouble some, especially Westerns: three *hypostases* still seems to contradict 'one substance'. But from now on this distinction of *hypostasis* from *ousia* would form the basis of the Eastern theological vocabulary.

The second theological issue concerned the soul of Christ. Like that over the Holy Spirit, this question was emerging as a new source of contention. Scholars disagree about the cause of the issue at Alexandria: was it the beginning of the heresy of Apollinaris of Laodicea (see pp. 154–6)? Was it Arianism, which some held to be implied by the other's position? It is also not clear that the matter was resolved: rather it was fudged, as we shall see.

The idea that in Christ there is a created and rational human soul was not new. It was held by Tertullian and by Origen. The alternative was to hold, in one way or another, that in Christ the functions of the soul are performed by the divine Word. The latter position was held by the Arians, though not directly attested for Arius himself, and became the chief point of the heresy of Apollinaris. But it appears also to have been held by Athanasius and all the other opponents of Arianism, except one: Eustathius of Antioch alone pitted the idea of a created human soul in Jesus Christ against the Arian argument. Whereas the Arians proceeded on the assumption that Christ was the Word with his flesh (*Logos–sarx* Christology), Eustathius developed the thought that Christ was the Word with his man (or, more accurately, with his human person; the *Logos–anthropos* Christology). So the sufferings, ignorance, and sorrow of Christ, and his advancement to glory, are not to be attributed to the Word, who shares the impassible divine essence, but to the man he dwelt in. The followers of Eustathius would see the denial of Christ's created human soul as a surrender to Arianism.

The party round Meletius, however, had an eminent biblical theologian in Diodore of Tarsus, who took a rather different view. Like Eustathius, he came to distinguish sharply between the divine and the human in Jesus: the Word of God cannot be called 'Son of David', as Christ is. He used the distinction of two essences (*ousiai*) in Christ to resist, among others, the emperor Julian himself, who poured scorn on the Christian idea that Jesus could be the divine Logos. Nevertheless, 'Diodore, at least for a long period, built up his "divisive" theology within the "Logos–sarx" framework' (Grillmeier, 358). He does not argue for a created soul, but writes of the Word dwelling in his flesh. Diodore's position, and the publicity of his controversy with the emperor, make it reasonable to assume that this topic was a bone of contention between the Meletians and Paulinians whom Athanasius tried to reconcile in 362. It is not necessary to assume that the argument involves (very early) Apollinarianism, or is merely directed against Arians.

The synodical letter from Alexandria achieved a compromise (Athanasius, *Tom. ad Ant.* 7 [CCC 82-3]). It was so successful a piece of theological ambiguity that modern scholars differ widely in their assessment of its 'real' meaning. That may be because it was a fudge, deliberately designed to mean different things to different people. The 'Economy of the Saviour in the flesh' (i.e. what modern writers refer to loosely as 'the incarnation') is not like the case of a prophet, a mere man indwelt by the Word of God. The Word himself 'from Mary after the flesh became man for us'. That might satisfy the Meletians, who would suspect the Paulinians of teaching an inspired prophet. The second point would be on the other side: 'they confessed also that the Saviour had not a body without a soul, nor without sense or intelligence (Gk *ou soma apsychon oud' anaistheton oud' anoeton*)'. That appears to say that Christ has a human soul and mind, and has been used by some to prove that Athanasius denied the main tenet of the Apollinarians (see p. 155). But it is not really so, since the text continues: 'For it was not possible, when the Lord himself had become man for us, that his body should be without intelligence: nor was the salvation effected in the Word himself a salvation of body only, but of soul also.' This gloss says first, 'Christ was not without intelligence, because he was God become man'; it can be accepted by those who think that the Word *replaces* the created intelligence in Jesus, which is exactly what Apollinaris would later hold. It says secondly, that the presence of the divine Lord in the man Jesus ensures that the human soul is saved. That is wholly ambiguous, not just about what sort of soul, since animals and even vegetables have 'soul' (*psyche*) in some sense, or they would not be alive; it is also ambiguous about whether the Lord *constitutes* the soul or life-principle in Jesus, or *possesses* such a soul. Christology had progressed, but was still relatively unsophisticated. It seems likely that both the principal parties, and perhaps some of their quarrelling members, found that they could subscribe to the formula. It is also not surprising that the controversy over the soul of Jesus was not laid to rest.

The Spirit-fighters

After Constantius died in 361, some members of the party of Basil of Ancyra (see p. 146) began to be active in promoting a new solution to the vexed trinitarian question. They were prepared to accept the deity of the Son and the Creed of Nicaea, but denied that the Holy Spirit belonged to the divine Being. The Creed merely said, 'We believe . . . also in the Holy Spirit'; it made no more specific statement. By 364 or 365 a deputation reached Rome, led by Eustathius of Sebaste, and persuaded the bishop Liberius that they represented a hope of reconciling the Easterns to the Nicene doctrine. They were well received, and for a time had some success in the East. Later writers were to associate them with the name of Macedonius, the Bishop of Constantinople who was exiled in 360, and they are hence called 'Macedonians'. Their own contemporary critics called them *Pneumatomachi*, or 'Spirit-fighters', since they opposed the Holy Spirit.

It was not difficult to find biblical texts which supported the idea that the Holy Spirit was a creature, like the created angelic spirits, only superior. If all things were made through the Son, it could be argued, so was the Spirit. But the Pneumatomachi were attacked on two fronts. By 365 the new Eastern emperor Valens was sustaining the official position reached under Constantius, the so-called Homoian doctrine of Eudoxius and those like him (see pp. 146–7). Eudoxius would never tolerate the Nicene Creed. On the other side the main body of moderates had always been committed to the idea of a divine trinity or triad, which the Pneumatomachi seemed not to recognize, and the Nicene Athanasius was deeply offended. By 360 he had written to his friend Serapion at some length on the subject, treating the whole movement as implicitly Arian: the godhead is indivisible (*Ep. ad Serap.* 1.1 [*CCC* 79–80]). The doctrines and arguments faced by Athanasius in the party he nicknames *tropici* ('allegorizers') are no different from those of Eustathius' group (in spite of the note on *CCC* 79). We have already seen the Antiochenes and Athanasius unanimous against those who denied the Spirit's divinity at the Council of Alexandria in 362.

The Pneumatomachi survived, and were to cause much division in the decade before 381, when they seem to have struck a compromise with the government and dominated large areas of Asia Minor about 375. The doctrine that the Spirit is truly God would soon be developed by the Cappadocian Fathers. But first we must consider the other issue, Christology.

Apollinarianism

To understand the issues involved in the heresy of Apollinaris (or, Apollinarius) of Laodicea, it is helpful to read the credal argument of a typical Homoian (or 'Arian'). Probably while he was still at Antioch (before 360) Eudoxius stated his Arian faith to take account of christological issues in the narrow sense, that is, the question of the relation of godhead and humanity in Jesus Christ:

> We believe in one the only true God, the only Nature unbegotten and fatherless, . . . and in one Lord the Son, religious because he worships the Father, . . . made flesh, not made human (Gk *sarkothenta ouk enanthropesanta*); for he has not taken a human soul, but has become flesh, so that through the flesh, as through a veil, he might deal with us human beings as God; not two natures, since he was not a complete man, but instead of the soul God in the flesh; altogether one composite nature; able to suffer by condescension (Gk *di'oikonomian*), for he could not save the world by a soul or a body which suffered.

Eudoxius goes on immediately to draw a trenchantly 'Arian' conclusion: 'Let them tell us, then, how the suffering and dying one can be consubstantial with the God who is superior to these things, transcending suffering and death' (text in Hahn, 261–2; see also Grillmeier 264–5). All the debates of current Christology are exposed: Is the divine Son made flesh or made human (the Creed of Nicaea said, 'made flesh and made man')? Has he a human soul, or does the divine Son replace the soul? Should we speak of two natures or of one? – the word 'nature' (Gk *physis*) can in Greek mean 'being', just like *ousia*. Eudoxius goes for 'one composite nature', because only so can the death of Jesus have saving value.

Both the chief Nicene groups in Antioch, those of Paulinus and Meletius (see above pp. 148–52), took a different position. The Paulinians asserted the soul of Jesus; the Meletian theologian Diodore strongly asserted the two natures – he wrote of two 'beings' (*ousiai*), and discerned in Jesus both the Son of God and the Son of David. Both groups acknowledged 'made flesh, made human' with the Creed of Nicaea. By attributing all the weaknesses, suffering and death of Christ to his humanity and not to his divine nature, these Nicenes evaded the force of the Arian and Eudoxian argument, which was also used in his campaign against Christianity by the Emperor Julian himself. But in so doing they caused distress to one of the ablest of the old Nicene theologians.

Apollinaris was Bishop of the Syrian seaport of Laodicea. From early in the post-Nicaea disputes he had given strong support to Athanasius, enduring hardship and excommunication on his account. Athanasius even consulted him on Christology, and although some works against Apollinaris are attributed to Athanasius, it is generally held that Athanasius shared his views, though not in their precise elaboration. By his concise and lucid presentation of the consubstantial Trinity Apollinaris seems to have converted Basil of Caesarea, the chief of the Cappadocian Fathers, to Nicene orthodoxy. Yet in 375 this pillar of rectitude was to confuse and shock the Nicene camp by ordaining one of his own associates, Vitalis, as bishop in Antioch, as though Meletius and Paulinus did not exist, let alone their official Homoian rival Euzoius. His reason was a simple doctrinal one. The Arians were wrong about the deity of Christ, and both the other two parties were wrong about the humanity.

Apollinaris could not allow that there was any mind in Jesus Christ except the divine mind of the Son of God: he is 'God enfleshed' (Gk *theos ensarkos*). Apollinaris constantly writes of the 'incarnation' or 'enfleshment'. Any created human soul was inevitably changeable, 'enslaved to filthy thoughts', whereas the divine Mind is immune to passion, and untouched by death. So through all the human activity of Jesus, the divine Word was absolutely and wholly in control, adjusting the body to the conditions appropriate to a human being, but not an actual human being. He was complete (or 'perfect') as man, but with a divine, not a human, completeness. He cannot possibly be described as 'two persons' or 'two natures (beings)'. In short, he is 'one incarnate nature of God the word' (for these propositions, see *CCC* 87–8).

It is fair to say that Apollinaris held what many Christians down the centuries have in practice believed: that Jesus was not a man, but God the Son with a human body. 'Veiled in flesh the Godhead see, Hail the incarnate Deity!' sums it up perfectly. Yet although ideas of Apollinaris were to be promoted by his disciples after his condemnation, and his writings circulated under false but respectable names, and although Cyril of Alexandria in the next century would constantly use these Apollinarian writings as if they were orthodox, the Church condemned him. First, some Easterns, reacting to the outrageous uncanonical appointment of Vitalis, then a Roman council in 377 (*CCC* 94–5), and comprehensively the Council of Constantinople in 381 and the imperial government of Theodosius I (*CCC* 119). The grounds for this condemnation were to be elaborated by the Cappadocian Fathers.

The Cappadocian Fathers

Cappadocia constantly produced church leaders in the fourth century, involved in different theological parties. Those known as 'the Cappadocian Fathers' are chiefly three, Basil of Caesarea (*c.* 329–79), his younger brother Gregory of Nyssa (died about 395), and his older friend Gregory of Nazianzus (died 390). Their theological background was that of the Eastern majority, who emphasized in Origenist fashion the distinctions between the three persons of the Trinity, and based their concept of Christ's deity on the idea of 'image' – he is like his Father in all things, including being and eternity. Their position is often called 'Neo-Nicene' (or 'new Nicene'), being an adaptation of the doctrine of the Creed of Nicaea to these Eastern emphases.

Basil was from a Christian family, educated in the classics in Constantinople and Athens, converted in his youth to Christian asceticism, and a life-long promoter of monasticism (see pp. 179–80). Ordained Bishop of Cappadocian Caesarea, he was the Metropolitan, in other words had ecclesiastical jurisdiction over the whole province. He spent much time and effort resisting Eunomian doctrine, rallying support for the Nicene cause on a basis that the Creed expressed the traditional Eastern doctrine, and trying to win over those attracted by the Spirit-fighters. He organized his province strenuously in defence of his cause, and in a famous episode was believed to have faced down the emperor Valens himself (Theodoret, *HE* 4.19(16).1–6 [*CCC* 100–1]). He backed Meletius of Antioch strongly; and the position of Paulinus, with Western and Athanasian support, was a major stumbling-block which he could not overcome (Basil, *Ep.* 214.2; 239.2 [*CCC* 102–3]). He did, however, begin a movement, developed by the two Gregories, which led to the victory of Neo-Nicene theology at Constantinople in 381.

Gregory of Nazianzus, the oldest of the three, was the son of a bishop. He studied in Palestine, Alexandria amd Athens, where he met Basil. After co-operating with Basil in monastic experiments in Pontus, and compiling with Bail a florilegium of Origen's writings of great value to us, he was made Bishop of a village called Sasima in 372 to strengthen Basil's clergy against the Homoian government and other disputes. After his uncomfortable mission at Constantinople (see pp. 165–7) he retired to Cappadocia and spent his last years in monastic quiet, producing a vast literary output on theological subjects in prose and verse.

Gregory of Nyssa seems to have learned rhetoric from his brother Basil in Caesarea. A married man and a professional teacher, he too was promoted to a bishopric in 372 as part of Basil's campaign for orthodoxy. His writing is fluent and stylish, and besides carrying on Basil's campaigns against Eunomius and Pneumatomachi he wrote a splendid *Catechetical Oration* as a handbook of doctrine for teachers.

The Cappadocian Fathers on the Trinity

In resisting Eunomian doctrine, the Cappadocians first attacked the view that the essence of God can be perfectly known. Eunomius held that in theology words mean what they say: God is unbegotten because by definition he has no originator; since that is not true of the Son, he is essentially distinct and different. For Basil, 'We know the greatness of God, his power, his goodness, his providence over us, and the justice of his judgement; but not his very essence . . . we know our God from his operations, but do not undertake to approach near to his essence' (*Ep.* 234 [*CCC* 106]). This mystical approach (curiously resembling the attitude to the divine mystery of Arius) is sometimes called *apophatic*, denying that God's being can be known and defined; that of the Eunomians is called *cataphatic*, asserting that God can be described or defined exactly. Basil's approach is developed in a favourite idea of Gregory of Nyssa: God's being is infinite, and so the more that the finite mind knows of him the more it becomes aware of its ignorance. Those who seek him therefore strive ever more eagerly to know him more, and to know and enjoy him is to want him more.

Within the transcendent divine being (*ousia*) there are three persons (*prosopa*) each existing as a concrete individual with its own *hypostasis*. This is an adjustment of the Nicene emphasis on one *ousia* to the Origenist principle of three individuals. To identify *hypostasis* with *ousia* is a mistake (see Basil, *Ep.* 210.5; 236.6 [*CCC* 104–5]). In nature and being the three are absolutely the same, coeternal and infinite, and utterly distinct from created being, which is finite and exists in time. But they are distinguished from each other by the characteristics of each: the Father is distinguished as the Cause, the Son by being only-begotten, the Spirit by proceeding from the Father. They can use the model (originally put to Basil by Apollinaris) of Adam, Eve and Seth: they are distinct persons of one (human) nature consubstantial with each other, in which Eve and Seth are derived from Adam (cf. Gregory of Nazianzus, *Orat.* 5.9–11 [*CCC* 84–5]). So although the works and nature of the three persons are indistinguishable, they have distinct functions in relation to each other, and the Father has a certain priority.

This classic idea of the consubstantial Trinity obviously entails the deity of the Holy Spirit, of the same substance as Father and Son. This was apparently an advance on what had been defined before, even at Nicaea, and was recognized as in a sense a development of doctrine (Gregory of Nazianzus, *Orat.* 31.27 [*CCC* 85–6]). But it was necessary to persuade many who felt it went too far. Eustathius of Sebaste, an early friend of Basil and associate in his monastic enterprise, was Metropolitan of the neighbouring province; but he was a leader, perhaps the leader, of the Pneumatomachi, and Basil tried hard to contain him and his like within the orthodox camp. It is therefore notable that, while adopting formulae and language which plainly imply the consubstantial Trinity, Basil does not write of the Holy Spirit as 'God' or as 'consubstantial with the Father'. So in a letter asserting the one essence, he concludes, 'God the Father' and 'God the Son' (Gk *theon huion*), but 'the divine Holy Spirit' (Gk *to theion pneuma to hagion*). He does not want to expose his case to the retort that it adds unbiblical titles to the Spirit, though there can be no doubt about what he believes.

This classic understanding of God as Trinity, embodying the essential insights both of Athanasius and of the Eastern Origenist tradition, won the day at Constantinople in 381, and has never been seriously questioned in the East. Rapidly taken up in Milan by Ambrose, it prevailed in the West also. Augustine was to put a particular gloss upon it which has caused complication and dispute since. Its great claim on Christian faith and imagination is that it relates the works of God in time – creation, revelation and salvation – to the divine being itself. God does not appear in Jesus Christ and in the working of the Spirit as something other than he is in himself. The 'economic Trinity' (God as we perceive him in his works) is no other than the 'essential Trinity' (God as he is in himself); the infinity which puts knowledge of his essence beyond our grasp is an infinity of generous, creative and redeeming love.

The Cappadocian Fathers on Christ and salvation

In the midst of their other battles the Cappadocians had to cope with the perplexity of Apollinarianism, forced to the fore in 375 when their fortunes were lowest. Basil had to find grounds against his old mentor, because he had to defend Meletius against the new threat; but his awareness of the christological issue was slight. It was Gregory of Nazianzus who elaborated most strongly and clearly the arguments for the complete humanity of Jesus, for example in his *Letter* 101 to Cledonius (*CCC* 88–92). His famous sentence sums it up: 'That which he has not assumed, he has not healed; but that which is united to his Godhead, is also saved' (181C [*CCC* 90]). His actual wording of the first phrase is more concise. 'The untaken is unhealed' (Gk *to aproslepton atherapeuton*). He works it out especially in connection with the idea that the created mind or spirit of human beings is corrupt. Far from making it impossible for Christ to have a human mind, it is precisely in the mind that sin lodges, corrupting the will; it is what most needs redeeming, not just the body or the lower, animal soul. The biblical verse, 'The Word became flesh', does not imply that Christ was the Word with only a fleshly body, because 'flesh' in Scripture can be used to mean 'human being' (189A [*CCC* 92]).

The two natures of Christ are not two persons; but just as the Trinity has three distinct persons in one essence, so Christ is two elements in one person (180AB [*CCC* 89]).

This 'soteriological argument' – an argument based on the saving effect of Christ's work – is generally regarded as decisive, and it is certainly potent. But soteriological arguments were used on the other side both by Eudoxius and by Apollinaris, as we have seen. What must be noted with critical care is the distance theology has travelled since St Paul. It has in fact shifted into a Platonic vein, where salvation for humanity as a whole is achieved by the union in the body of Jesus Christ of divine being with human being. Humanity, which we tend to view as abstract, was to the Gregories a reality more concrete than any individual human being. With that, godhead unites itself in Jesus Christ, and so the whole of humanity is infused with the characteristics of divine life, including immortality. This is heady medicine:

> It seems that the perishable nature is recreated by commixture into the divine, since the divine prevails over it; and thus it partakes in the power of the Godhead; as if one should say that a drop of vinegar mixed in the ocean is turned into sea by that mixture, since the natural qualities of the liquid do not remain in the infinity of the prevailing element. (Gregory of Nyssa, *c.Eun.* 5.5 [III.68.Jaeger] [*CCC* 93])

The death of Christ crucified is not rejected, nor entirely neglected; but somehow a different perspective prevails, and incarnation (in this sense) is the decisive act of salvation, rather than the death and rising of the Messiah.

16

THEODOSIUS I AND THE
COUNCIL OF CONSTANTINOPLE

Theodosius and the Western theology

On 9 August 378 invading Goths overthrew a powerful Roman
force at Adrianople (in what is now Bulgaria), and the Eastern
Emperor Valens died in battle. Gratian, who with his infant son
held power in the West, sent a promising soldier from Spain to
rescue the East. He came to be known as Theodosius the Great,
and was a military success. But his reign also marked changes in
the relation of the Empire both to Christianity and to other
religions. He identified Christianity with the Empire in an
unprecedented way, presided over much destruction of temples,
and tried to settle and enforce orthodoxy by anti-heretical laws
and action.

The classic example of Theodosius' policy is the edict *Cunctos
populos* of 380 (*CCC* 150), in which he expresses his determination, 'that all the peoples who are ruled by the administration
of our Clemency shall practise that religion which the divine Peter
the Apostle transmitted to the Romans'. Peter's martyrdom in
Rome has been transformed into a formal communication of
divine truth by the prince of the apostles to the Empire as a whole;
his fellow-martyr Paul is of no consequence. Theodosius goes on
to define that religion as he knew it: 'It is evident that this is the
religion that is followed by the Pontiff Damasus and by Peter,
Bishop of Alexandria, a man of apostolic sanctity.' At this point
Theodosius adopts a typically Western view of the divisions of the
Church. The orthodox communion is that of Damasus, the
powerful political Bishop of Rome, who had succeeded Liberius
amid scenes of strife and carnage in 366 (Ammianus Marcellinus,
Res gestae 27.3.12–15 [*CCC* 71]). His position was ostentatiously
Nicene and trinitarian, against rivals in Rome and those Latin
bishops, especially in the Balkans, who stood by the decrees of
Rimini-Seleuceia and the 'Arian' policies of Constantius II and
Valens. Peter of Alexandria had succeeded to Athanasius' policies

and see in 373, but had immediately been exiled in favour of Lucius, a government supporter; Peter returned to his throne on Valens' death. Damasus and Peter thus represented a Nicene alliance. Theodosius goes on to express the content of this faith: 'That is, according to the apostolic discipline and the evangelic doctrine, we shall believe in the single Deity of the Father, the Son and the Holy Spirit, under the concept of equal majesty and holy Trinity' (*CCC* 150). Damasus had presided over a Council at Rome in 377, which had condemned Apollinaris' Christology, and expressed loyalty to the faith of Nicaea with the affirmation: 'We do not separate the Holy Spirit, but together with the Father and the Son we offer him a joint worship as complete in everything, in power, honour, majesty, and Godhead' (*Ep.* 2 frg. 2 = *CCC* 94–5). Peter also, as heir to the later position of Athanasius, expressed at Alexandria in 362, confessed the consubstantiality of the Spirit.

Nicenes divided in the East

Theodosius soon found that his understanding of churchmanship needed some development in the East. In the West the Nicene party had, since Constantius died in 361, a comparatively easy time. Bishoprics might be in the hands of government sympathizers, but Valentinian I was indifferent to their replacement by Nicenes, as happened at Milan when Auxentius died and Ambrose succeeded him in 373 (Ammianus Marcellinus, *Res gestae* 30.9.5; Paulinus, *Life of Ambrose* 6; see *CCC* 70, 120). In the East the opponents of the government orthodoxy suffered badly under Valens, when the decrees of Seleucia 359 were urgently enforced. Among the heroes of the opposition were Basil of Caesarea (see Theodoret, *HE* 4.19 = *CCC* 100–1), recently dead, and the twice-exiled Meletius (Melitius) of Antioch (see *CCC* 49–50). Round Meletius now gathered the Eastern majority, expecting the new regime to change the official ecclesiastical policy. Meletius' supporters included the great exegete Diodore of Tarsus and the Cappadocians Gregory of Nyssa and Gregory of Nazianzus. The last in 379 accepted an invitation to begin ministering in a suburban church at Constantinople, with a view to being enthroned as bishop (Socrates, *HE* 5.7.1–2 = *CCC* 111).

The Cappadocian version of trinitarian theology prevailed in this Eastern majority, asserting the one substance of Father, Son and Holy Spirit, but speaking of three personally distinct *hypostases*. There was opposition to this in Antioch itself. The old Nicene group, led by Eustathius' faithful lieutenant Paulinus, asserted 'one hypostasis' in a way which chimed in with the Western tradition of 'one substance', but was hard to reconcile with the doctrine that Christ was an eternal person distinct from the Father in any of its forms; they regarded the Meletian/Cappadocian Neo-Nicenes as Arian. In 362 Athanasius in the Synod of Alexandria had tried in vain to reconcile the Antiochene parties. The *Tomus ad Antiochenos* 3–6 (see pp. 149–51) declared that both parties agreed that 'one hypostasis' could refer to the single deity of the three persons, and that 'three hypostases' did not entail separating the persons into three Gods or making the Son and Spirit mere creatures. On that understanding all those who condemned Arianism, confessed the Nicene faith, and rejected the doctrine that the Holy Spirit was a creature, could be united. Since 363 Paulinus, ordained bishop by Lucifer of Calaris in order to prevent this reconciliation with those he regarded as Antichrist, had been steadily supported by Rome, and Athanasius had been unable to recognize Meletius (see Basil's frustrated protest in *Ep.* 214.2 = CCC 102). The division of the 'Nicene' parties made reconciliation with other groups more difficult, whether they were the Pneumatomachi, who professed the Nicene Creed but held the Holy Spirit to be a creature of the Son and outside the divine being, or the 'Arians' like Demophilus of Constantinople, or the Anomoeans like Eunomius.

But there was another group to contend with. The Apollinarians were seen as orthodox on the Trinity, but bitterly opposed by the other parties at Antioch. Diodore in fact had used the formula 'two beings' (Gk *ousiai*) in distinguishing the deity of Christ from his humanity, and this was one of the expressions which provoked the protest of Apollinaris. The Paulinians also opposed Apollinaris; their hero Eustathius had been the first to use the idea of the human soul of Jesus in his anti-Arian arguments. In 362 these Christologies were already a cause of division, and Athanasius had attempted an ambiguous compromise in the *Tomus ad Antiochenos* 7. The issues had been pressed to schism in 375, when Apollinaris concluded that none of the existing bishops (Paulinus, Meletius and Euzoius the Arian) was sound, and ordained his colleague Vitalis as bishop of Antioch. After that, the others were all out for his blood, and found various ways to vilify his doctrines.

To Damasus' credit, the Council at Rome in 377 reached judicious statements both on Christology and on the Trinity (*PL* 13.352-3 = *CCC* 94-5). Complaints from the East about Apollinaris' schism led to a studied condemnation of those who say that Christ 'took from the Virgin Mary human nature incomplete'. On the Trinity, the Council affirmed Nicaea, and denied that it separates the Holy Spirit; Rome had in the past given some support to the Macedonian Pneumatomachi, who affirmed the Nicene faith while denying the deity of the Spirit. But further, the Council sided with those who attribute distinct personal being to the Son before his action in the world:

> We believe that God the Word in his fulness, not put forth but born, and not immanent in the Father so as to have no real existence, but subsisting from eternity to eternity, took and saved human nature complete.

The Marcellian and Eustathian insistence on 'one hypostasis' is thus significantly modified in a direction compatible with the Meletian and Cappadocian view: the Son is not immanent in the Father, but subsists from eternity to eternity. This position was apparently communicated to the Antiochenes along with Theodosius' edict, designating Damasus a criterion of orthodoxy. We have a story, highly partisan and not to be taken as literal history, to the effect that Paulinians, Apollinarians and Meletius' friend the presbyter Flavian all claimed to be in compliance with the edict, which was required if they were to be allowed to keep their church buildings (Theodoret, *HE* 5.3.9-15 [*CCC* 103-4]). Flavian rebuts Paulinus on the ground that Damasus 'openly preaches three *hypostases*', and Apollinaris on the ground that 'Damasus maintains our nature to have been taken in perfection by the Word of God'. Each of the non-Meletian parties was thus disqualified. The story goes on with an understanding between Meletius and Paulinus that their congregations would unite on the death of either one of them.

Deep hostility in fact remained. The Meletians generally resented the way in which the Eastern majority had for a long time been treated as Arian, and Rome had stubbornly supported the Paulinus faction. Matters were made worse in the ensuing months.

Theodosius, now a baptized Christian since a critical illness at Thessalonica, had moved to reorder affairs. Demophilus of Constantinople, a loyal and popular defender of Valens' church policies, refused to conform to Theodosius' decree and was removed from his see. But replacing him was complicated by an intervention from Alexandria. Gregory of Nazianzus in the suburban church of Anastasia had been preparing the ground for restoring Nicene orthodoxy. There he welcomed the support of a converted Alexandrian philosopher, known as Maximus the Cynic, who arrived and joined his congregation. To Gregory's consternation, this man was suddenly ordained Bishop of Constantinople by a group of bishops with the connivance of Peter of Alexandria, with a view to acquiring control of the capital for the Alexandrian party; Maximus was to retain the support of Alexandria, Rome and Milan for some time. Theodosius now led the churches towards a comprehensive settlement by calling a general ecclesiastical council in Constantinople. This met in 381, and after 451 this came to be recognized as the 'Second Ecumenical Council'.

The Council of Constantinople: Canons

Unfortunately there is no accurate record of the proceedings. 150 bishops were present, all from the East. There was undoubtedly a concerted attempt to be comprehensive, and to win the assent of as large a body as possible. In effect it barely succeeded in uniting the two chief parties, the Meletians and the Alexandrian Nicenes; though it laid the basis for a settlement once some loose ends were tied up. The most important documents we have are a set of Canons (Hefele-Leclerq, *Histoire des Conciles* II.1 pp. 18–35 [*CCC* 115–18]) and a Creed of great ecumenical consequence but uncertain history (*CCC* 114–15). The preamble and the first Canon ratify 'the faith of the 318 Fathers who assembled at Nicaea', and put under anathema all heresies, and specifically, 'that of the Eunomians or Anomoeans, and that of the Arians or Eudoxians, and that of the Semiarians or Pneumatomachi, and that of the Sabellians and Marcellians, and that of the Photinians, and that of the Apollinarians'. Despite reference to 'some short definitions' in the preamble, there is nothing which suggests a new version of the creed other than that of Nicaea 325. The second Canon authorized more precisely than Nicaea had done the jurisdiction of the great sees of the East, pointedly confining the Bishop of Alexandria to 'the affairs of Egypt only'; his intervention in the case of Maximus had perhaps reflected an Alexandrian claim to primacy in the whole East. The third Canon stated: 'The bishop of Constantinople shall have the primacy of honour after the bishop of Rome, because Constantinople is new Rome.' This gave ecclesiastical precedence to the capital on grounds of state. It could be seen as offending the traditional precedence of Alexandria, and even more seriously as implying that Rome too derived its primacy from its civil rank as capital, and not from its divinely ordered foundation by the chief apostle. Not surprisingly it was a part of the proceedings which neither of the offended sees accepted. The fourth Canon declares that Maximus the Cynic 'neither was nor is the Bishop' of Constantinople, and any ordinations of his are deemed invalid. The fifth Canon acknowledges 'the tome of the Western bishops', which appears to report or be based on Damasus' Roman council; the bishops accept 'those in Antioch who confess the one Divinity of the Father, Son and Holy Spirit', probably referring to the Paulinian party. The sixth regulates accusations brought against bishops, which have been numerous in the disordered times recently past.

It is clear that these Canons reflect overwhelmingly the interest of the Meletian group. That is not surprising, even if things did not go entirely their way. Meletius himself presided. When he died in the course of the Council, the presidency was taken over by Gregory of Nazianzus, who had by then been imposed upon the see of Constantinople by the Emperor. Controversies ensued over both bishoprics, Antioch and Constantinople. The bishops from Egypt and Macedonia, close to the Western view on controversial matters, impugned Gregory's standing. He was already Bishop of Sasima in Cappadocia, and the Nicene Canons ruled that bishops could not move from one see to another. Gregory eventually gave in and resigned (see Socrates, *HE* 5.7.1–2; Sozomen, *HE* 7.7.6–9; Gregory, *Or.* 42.24–7 [*CCC* 111–13]). He was a literary theologian, with little stomach for politics, and scarcely fitted for the task of presiding over the greatest see of the East. He was also disgusted at his own party's unforgiving attitude to the problem at Antioch. There Flavian was made bishop by the Meletian majority, who would not implement the understanding that the congregations should unite under Paulinus if Meletius died. The schism in fact trailed on for seven years. The immediate effect of Gregory's withdrawal was, however, that Constantinople was without a bishop. A venerable senator called Nectarius, unbaptized and committed to no party, was duly nominated, baptized and installed as bishop. He doubtless performed his task thereafter to the satisfaction of city and Emperor.

The Council of Constantinople: the Creed

We are left with the problem of the Creed. In 451 at the Council of Chalcedon the government party produced 'the Creed of the 150 assembled at Constantinople', and used it to justify their own new formulary (see *CCC* 350–2). The fathers of Constantinople, they said, had published the new Creed, 'not as though they were supplying some omission of their predecessors, but distinctly declaring by written testimony their own understanding concerning the Holy Spirit, against those who were endeavouring to set aside his Sovereignty'. This explanation is plausible. Whereas the Creed of Nicaea (designated N) goes on from 'and in the Holy Spirit' to curse various supposedly Arian doctrines, the creed attributed to Constantinople (commonly designated C; *CCC* 114–15) has none of the anti-Arian anathemas, but enlarges instead upon the Holy Spirit: 'And in the Holy Spirit, the Lord, the giver of life, who proceeds from the Father, who with the Father and the Son is together worshipped and together glorified, who spoke through the prophets.' Having thus affirmed the Person of the Spirit, C then adds clauses of a kind which was common in baptismal creeds, but which could also be regarded as affirming the effects of the Spirit's working: 'In one holy catholic and apostolic Church; we acknowledge one baptism for the remission of sins; we look forward to the resurrection of the dead and the life of the world to come. Amen.' This substitution of detail about the Holy Spirit for the out-of-date anathemas is not however enough to justify the theory asserted in the Chalcedonian Definition. Difficulties abound.

If the Chalcedonian theory were true, one would expect the remainder of C to be more or less identical with N. The bishops at Chalcedon, and some of the scribes who copied the proceedings later, were quite conscious of this. To make N and C look more alike, N was presented with a number of additional words, here italicized (these words are bracketed in the Chalcedonian version of N at *CCC* 350-1): came down *from heaven; from the Holy Spirit and the virgin Mary; and was crucified for us under Pontius Pilate;* suffered *and was buried;* rose again the third day *according to the scriptures; whose kingdom shall have no end;* the Holy Spirit *the Lord, the giver of life.* The Chalcedonian version of N also lacks 'the things in heaven and things on earth', which stood in the original after 'by whom all things were made'. These changes alone make the Chalcedonian theory suspect. But they do not exhaust the list of differences. In addition to those adjusted in the Chalcedonian text, C has other additions: it adds to the clause on the Father, 'Maker *of heaven and earth and* of all things visible and invisible'; it omits 'God from God'. It also arranges differently the clauses about the Lord Jesus Christ, omitting 'that is, from the substance of the Father' and substituting, 'from the Father before all ages'.

For some of these differences one can perceive a plausible theological purpose. If that were true of them all, one might suppose that the Chalcedonian theory was basically correct, but that a few other alterations were made to update the theology in the light of Marcellian and Apollinarian doctrine: 'of his kingdom there will be no end' (from Luke 1.33) was certainly used against Marcellus, and 'from the Holy Spirit and the virgin Mary' has been thought to be anti-Apollinarian. An account can also be given of the new statement of the Person of Christ, as we shall see. But for too many of the variations of C from N, including minor points of wording not listed here, there is no perceptible theological significance. It is therefore to be assumed that C is a different creed from the original N, though it includes a number of expressions and ideas derived from N (notably of course *homoousios*, 'of one substance').

There is a further problem. If, as Chalcedon asserted, C was authorized in 381 at Constantinople, how does it come about that no reference is made to this creed until 451? There are one or two references to the doctrinal statement or position of the Council which imply that they went further than the mere ratification of N. But since in their Canons they condemned the Pneumatomachi, Marcellians and Apollinarians, all of whom accepted N, it is plain that they affirmed N with important interpretative qualifications. The text of C does occur in the manuscript tradition of a work of Epiphanius of Salamis, written before the Council, the *Ancoratus.*

But it is now demonstrable that originally Epiphanius' text had N and not C. One must therefore face the possibility that C had nothing to do with the Council of 381, but was a different baptismal creed falsely represented at Chalcedon as from the Council of 381. C was so important at Chalcedon however, that scholars have found it difficult to believe that the bishops there would have accepted an absolute fiction. They have therefore sought to explain how the Council of 381 could assert the authority of N, but also be responsible for C. It was suggested, for instance, that it was the baptismal creed used for the baptism of Nectarius, the new bishop. But that is purely speculative.

J. N. D. Kelly suggested that an expression like 'the faith of the fathers of Nicaea' could be used with reference to any creed with basically Nicene content, and could have been so used of C in the preamble and first Canon of Constantinople in 381. Later Kelly adopted the theory propounded by A. M. Ritter, that C was authorized by the Council, but as part of its negotiations with the Pneumatomachi, and not as its own formal conclusion. That is certainly credible. A body of those supporting the position of the Pneumatomachi was originally present, but they were unable to agree with the dominant party and withdrew to hold a council of their own. C could have been an 'olive branch', a proposed basis of union between those who affirmed that the Holy Spirit was inseparable from the divine essence of the Father and the Son, and those who held him to be created.

The terminology used of the Spirit has the same ambiguity found in the trinitarian writings of Basil of Caesarea, who always had an eye to winning over former friends, like Eustathius of Sebaste, who denied the deity of the Spirit. He never called the Spirit 'God', nor said he was *homoousios* with the Father or the Son. C avoids any but biblical terminology: the Spirit is Lord (2 Cor. 3.17) and Lifegiver (2 Cor. 3.6); he proceeds from the Father (John 15.26). The statement that he is jointly worshipped and glorified with the Father and Son, while perhaps reflecting the decree of Damasus' Council of Rome 377 (*CCC* 94–5), can be justified on the basis of the traditional doxologies of the Church and the New Testament verses where Father, Son and Holy Spirit are mentioned co-ordinately (Matt. 28.19; 2 Cor. 13.14). That the Holy Spirit speaks through the prophets is a commonplace of Scripture (e.g. Acts 28.25), yet implies that his action in revelation is divine. Each clause can be taken as affirming the Spirit's consubstantial deity in one way or another, while, being purely scriptural, it can be subscribed to by those who resist such terminology and doctrine. This is perhaps the best historical explanation of C's status at the Council of 381. It does not, however, explain everything. Unlike N it is suitable for liturgical use in baptism, and it later became a baptismal and a eucharistic creed. It may have originated in Constantinople for just such use; whether or not connected directly with the proceedings of the Council of 381, it could have come into use about that time, and its capacity to make things easy for persons of Pneumatomachian background could be useful. More significantly, it modifies the ideas enshrined in N.

The churches which accept the authority of the Council of Chalcedon – and that includes the majority of Christians in East and West – are committed both to N and to C, which is sometimes called 'the Niceno-Constantinopolitan Creed'. The theological differences of C from N thus represent an important modification or explanation of N's doctrine, even if the history is not quite as Chalcedon stated it. We should observe what the modifications are:

1. The person and work of the Holy Spirit are set out, as we have noticed, in terms of their biblical foundation. The trinitarian faith is thus expressed without controversial words. From the point of view of church unity, it is sad that the Western churches from the sixth century began using an altered version of the Creed by introducing the Augustinian (and strictly unscriptural) development, 'who proceeds from the Father *and the Son*'. Whatever theological merits this idea has, the change in an ecumenical Creed divided the churches over a document which is still the most promising foundation for doctrinal unity.

2. The position of the Son is stated differently, in ways which avoid the Marcellian tone of N, which had been made explicit by the Creed of Sardica in 342/3. Christ is now described as 'the Only-begotten Son of God, begotten from the Father before all ages'. Thus 'Only-begotten' is interpreted in the old Eastern way, as Eusebius did in his creed at Nicaea, to refer to the birth of the Son from the Father before time and the world began: he exists as a distinct person beside the Father and derived from

him. N had spoken differently: 'the Son of God, begotten of the Father, Only-begotten, that is, from the substance of the Father'; in conformity with the prevailing Marcellian influence in N, 'Only-begotten' is referred to the common divine being of Father and Son, 'before all ages' is suppressed, and the idea that the begetting is the same as the incarnation is implicitly allowed. C gives the necessary corrective, implying the Cappadocian principle of the distinct eternal hypostases of whom the Father is the cause. This was the principle which Rome had already adopted in 377, when the Council there spoke of 'God the Word in his fulness, not put forth but born, and not immanent in the Father so as to have no real existence, but subsisting from eternity to eternity'. Other adjustments also correct the Marcellian aspects of N. The anathema which could be taken to deny that the Son was a distinct hypostasis beside the Father has also disappeared.

3. We have already noticed that 'Of his kingdom there shall be no end' quotes a biblical text thought to refute Marcellus, who held the Kingdom of Christ to be earthly and temporary until he yields it up to the Father, 'that God may be all in all' (cf. 1 Cor. 15.23–8). Apollinaris of Laodicea also believed in the earthly Kingdom of Christ before the end of time, and may also have been in mind. If the addition, 'incarnate *from Holy Spirit and the virgin Mary*', is theologically significant at all (which is doubtful), it could subtly lay a foundation to oppose Apollinaris: Christ is of two natures, one divine (called Holy Spirit in Scripture [cf. Luke 1.34–5], but regularly understood by the Fathers to refer to the godhead of the Son or Word) and one human. Apollinaris held firmly to '*one* incarnate nature of God the Word' (see *Ad Jov.* 1 [*CCC* 88]).

The West

Neither the Council nor the Creed affected the West much. At this time Ambrose of Milan established Cappadocian-type orthodoxy by his own teaching, and, in a series of ecclesiastical negotiations in the Western provinces near enough to Milan for his will to prevail, he got rid of the enemies of Nicene orthodoxy (for the Council of Aquileia 381, see *CCC* 124–5). Ambrose resisted attempts by the Roman aristocracy to reverse the christianization of the West, and had great success in open confrontations with the emperors (*CCC* 126–32, 135–40). These important affairs did not seriously affect the development of doctrine, for Ambrose was an excellent communicator and administrator, but not an original thinker.

Theodosius ultimately prevailed not only over the East, but against the enemies of the established power in the West, and especially the forces of the pagan revival. His reign saw great progress in the suppression of paganism (law of 391; *CCC* 151), and the imposition of unprecedented constraints on heretics, once they had been clearly defined by the Council of 381 and given the opportunity to conform. The policy went back to the original decree, *Cunctos populos*:

> We command that those persons who follow this rule [of trinitarian faith] shall embrace the name of Catholic Christians. The rest, however, whom we adjudge demented and insane, shall sustain the infamy of heretical dogmas, their meeting places shall not receive the name of churches, and they shall be smitten first by divine vengeance and secondly by the retribution of our own initiative, which we shall assume in accordance with the divine judgement. (*CCC* 150)

It was Theodosius' laws against heresy which Augustine and his colleagues were to call upon to suppress Donatism, with some success.

17
NEW SPIRITUALITY:
THE MONASTIC MOVEMENT

Monastic beginnings

The fourth century was marked by an enormous growth of the monastic movement. This had its anticipations and counterparts in pre-Christian times. There were Cynic philosophers among the Greeks, who lived in studied poverty and preached indifference to material goods. The learned ascetics of the Qumran community in the desert by the Dead Sea and their counterparts (called *Therapeutae*) in Egypt, attempted a rigorous observance of the Law of Moses, which they held to be incorrectly followed by the Jerusalem authorities. Some Christian circles, especially in the Syriac-speaking East, required the baptized all to be sexually celibate; the majority of the Christian adherents lived as unbaptized catechumens, an arrangement which prevailed among the more serious gnostic sects, as well as Marcionites and Manichees. Even where doctrine was otherwise orthodox, this form of sexual discipline was dubbed 'Encratite' heresy by others in the Church; *enkrateia* means 'continence' or 'holding in'. But the monastic movement as generally understood began just as the age of persecution was about to reach its final climax. Men and women tried to live out the gospel message by separating themselves from the society around them and from the increasingly worldly churches, and turned to do battle alone with the devil in tombs, cells and deserts.

The famous *Life of Antony*, written about 357 shortly after his death, and attributed to Athanasius, illustrates the kind of life which some monastics envisaged and more or less successfully lived. About 270 Antony heard the call of Christ, 'If thou wilt be perfect, go, sell all that you have, and give it to the poor, and come follow me, and you shall have treasure in heaven.' He sold his estates, except enough for his sister; later he heard the word, 'Be not anxious for the morrow', and gave that away too, sending his sister to a nunnery.

We must come to terms with the fact that very little information
survives about early women's monasticism. Some reports indicate
that in some places it was on a larger scale than that of males. But
our literature is almost all written by males, for males and about
males. Women could not be pioneers because of their social
dependence upon men: Antony's sister became a nun because
Antony felt obliged to put her in a safe place so as to be free for his
own spiritual adventure. One or two women of wealth, like Melania
and Paula of Rome, disciples of a Rufinus or Jerome, became
ascetics and used their wealth to build and endow monasteries in
Jerusalem and Bethelehem, and to set up houses for women.
Gregory of Nyssa praises his sister Macrina for her spiritual
leadership, and knows the spiritual sisters who lived with her in
the family house. Later rules are made for women as well as men,
as by Augustine and by Caesarius of Arles. But for monks generally
women represent a threat to their own chastity, or at their best
manage heroically to live down the misfortune of their weak and
dependent nature.

Antony began like others, we are told, learning ascetic ways
from an older man in a nearby village. He was a pioneer in going
further afield, and especially into the desert. Here there is a
difference between the account of Antony which emerges from the
Apophthegmata patrum or *Sayings of the Fathers* (extracts in
CCC 170–2), and the Athanasian *Life*. In the former, which is
probably more reliable, the purpose of the retreat is to find solitude.
That was why his sister was an embarrassment to him, as would
be all the other worldly encumbrances which go with marriage,
possessions and family. In the *Life* the same escape is needed, but
it is to do battle with the powers of evil. He is depicted from the
standpoint of the observer in the town or village, who knows the
desert only as the abode of evil demons. So we read of Antony
being attacked by demons, who tried various devices to distract
him from the holy life. He therefore went and lived in a tomb (or
cell) for many years, where he was fed occasionally by a friend;
there, after still fiercer demonic attack, a divine light came to him.
Later he crossed the Nile, and went into the mountain, the devils'
own domain, where he lived for twenty years, to return fit and
healthy in body, and glowing with a kind of divinity within him,
'like an initiate emerging from a shrine'. He now had gifts of
healing and prophecy. For twenty more years he travelled,

promoting asceticism and helping people. To escape pressure, he withdrew again to the inner mountain. Even there he was pursued by disciples, who settled near him, each in his own cell, pursuing his own battle with the devil and his fleshly implements. Antony came out of the desert to make himself available for martyrdom in 311, and again in 338 to support Athanasius against his 'Arian' enemies in terms which read suspiciously like Athanasius' personal propaganda. The story is full of visions, miracles and demonic assaults; his holiness attracts the admiration of pagans, and leads emperors to consult him. The *Life of Antony* may be more a programme for monastic life in co-operation with the bishops than a strictly historical account. But it was none the less effective for that, and rapidly circulated in both East and West; it played a significant part in the conversion of Augustine in 386.

Antony may be regarded as typical of the great leaders of Egyptian and Alexandrian monasticism. The *Sayings of the Fathers* (see *CCC* 170-1) name him as one of several great leaders of the early *anachoresis* ('withdrawal' or 'retreat', from which comes the word 'anchorite'). Soon thousands of monks populated the deserts near the Nile delta, and though their ideal remained essentially individual, this was promoted by elements of necessary industrial and commercial organization: if basic needs were met, spiritual single-mindedness was promoted. The movement spread rapidly in Palestine and Syria. A little later tighter organizations originated with Pachomius in upper Egypt, and were developed in Asia Minor by such enthusiasts as Basil of Caesarea.

In the early days the monks, shutting themselves in isolated places or enclosed cells, possessed nothing and could have nothing to read. Their prayers were repetitive, and Scripture was heard rather than read, and in some cases recited by heart as a religious duty, rather than studied for its meaning. An attempt was made to live by what the Bible prescribed, but to some extent ignorance was regarded as a virtue in the face of biblical mysteries (cf. *Apophth. patr.* 15.1-4 [*CCC* 171]). For guidance in their spiritual journey the young monks learned to treasure the wisdom of experts in the monastic way. Visitors to famous monks sought a word, which was often reluctantly given by an old man who had made silence a virtue. Sayings of the wise were remembered, taught, and finally written in collections (such as those quoted in *CCC* 170-2), which survive in various forms, as they constantly accrued new material and were repeatedly edited. Round famous teachers, like Amun, Pambo, Macarius of Egypt, Macarius of Alexandria, and Antony himself, circles of disciples would gather, each pursuing holiness in his own cell. Of Antony we read, 'When the persecution ceased, . . . he went back to his solitary cell; and there he was a daily martyr of his conscience, ever fighting the battles of the faith' (*Life* 47). The ideal of this life is described too:

> He fasted continually, his clothing was hair on the inside, while the outside was skin, and this he kept to his dying day. He never bathed his body in water to remove filth, nor did he as much as wash his feet or even allow himself to put them in water without necessity. No one ever saw him undressed, nor did anyone look upon his bare body till he died and was buried. (*Life* 47)

Another one of the early heroes of this war with the flesh, Macarius of Alexandria, was noted for his feats of asceticism, living on a diet made deliberately sparse, and attempting to conquer sleep until his brain became fuddled (Palladius, *Hist. laus.* 18.1–3 [*CCC* 169–70]). This attitude to the flesh also affected the attitude of monks to prayer. Whereas in the great Church generally the apostolic command to 'pray without ceasing' (1 Thess. 5.17) was taken to mean that prayer was offered at set hours three or four times a day, the monk saw stopping for food or sleep as a concession to the flesh; his object was a life like the angels, where such things were not needed.

The monks of northern Egypt (Wadi Natroun [Nitria], Kellia, Sketis) lived nominally as solitaries, but by the time Palladius visited them in 390 (*Hist. laus* 7 [*CCC* 168–9]) there were about 2000 near Alexandria and 5000 in Nitria alone, besides 600 further out in the desert, but fed from their bakeries. They had buildings and a good church. There were meetings for worship on Saturdays and Sundays, and there was co-operative baking and industry. The sick might be visited by a nearby brother. Some discipline was imposed: visitors were shown three palm-trees outside the church, where transgressors were flogged, one for monks, one for robbers, and one for visitors. Virtue and vocation however lay with the individual in his cell. Even the word 'monk' (Gk *monachos*) means 'solitary', and only by development has come to refer to a member of an ordered community.

Pachomius and life together

Further south at the bend in the Nile lived the first monks to follow a Rule. Their founder was Pachomius, a soldier converted to Christianity, who at first lived with an older ascetic, and then gathered a group of brothers. His movement caught on and spread: the mother house at Tabennisi is reported to have had 1300 monks in Pachomius' lifetime, and about 7000 spread through other monasteries throughout Egypt (Sozomen, *HE* 3.14.16–17 [*CCC* 164]). Pachomius' Rule plainly spread among those who had already committed themselves to the solitary life in general. Each settlement had an Abbot ('Father') in charge. Monks lived three to a cell, but with cells grouped in houses, with a high wall enclosing them all. Each house had a trade, mat-making, weaving, laundering and so forth, and the houses would take it in turns to fulfil the duties of cooking, care for the sick and dealing with visitors, novices and traders (see Jerome's *Preface* to his version of the *Rule* [*CCC* 165–6]). The house was the focus of worship twice daily, with psalms, prayers and scripture readings, and meals (where conversation was discouraged). Sunday washing was allowed, and Sundays (perhaps Saturdays too) saw a general meeting for instruction under the Abbot, and a eucharistic celebration. Life was hard, but not cruel. They slept on hard couches, not the floor, and beating was used only for serious offences. Aspirants were kept in the visitors' lodging to learn basic prayers and psalms, and admitted only after careful screening. Some of these Pachomian practices became general in monasticism; they were learned in Egypt by John Cassian, and promoted by him in the West (see Cassian, *Inst.* 4.3 [*CCC* 164–5]). Jerome's Latin version of the *Rule* is the earliest extant version; Pachomian Coptic monasteries still survive today, but their versions of the *Rule* have developed and changed over the centuries.

Syrian movements

While Egypt saw progression towards orderly monasticism, both through episcopal interest and Pachomian organization, Syria was noted for extreme individualism. Jerome is a defective witness to the misdeeds of those he disliked; his praises of the coenobites (those who lived a corporate life on the Pachomian style) and his fulminations against the Remoboth, always quarrelling, boasting and visiting virgins, are equally exaggerated (*Ep.* 22.34–5 [*CCC* 166–7]). He rebukes those who engage in sweeping doctrinal condemnations:

> I blush to say it, but from the caves which serve us for cells we monks of the desert condemn the world. Rolling in sack-cloth and ashes, we pass sentence on bishops. What use is the robe of a penitent if it covers the pride of a king? Chains, squalor, and long hair are by right tokens of sorrow, and not ensigns of royalty. (*Ep.* 17.2 [*CCC* 174])

Needless to say, these were monks he disagreed with. So were those who lived with women in what purported to be a purely spiritual and continent marriage (*Ep.* 22.14 [*CCC* 184–5]); Jerome, highly sexed himself, found their continence impossible to believe.

To John Chrysostom in Antioch shortly after, the Syrian monks coming in from the desert were heavenly visitants at church festivals. When we get to the *Religious history* of Theodoret of Cyrus about 440, we find him praising the exploits of saints so heavily loaded with chains they cannot stand up, or living shut in a cylinder of laths and suspended from a gallows, or standing for days or weeks on end on bare mountain-tops. Symeon the Stylite ('pillar-man') left his monastery in 412 for a mountain cell, spent three successive Lents walled in, chained himself for a period to a mountain-top, and finally began living on rocks and pillars; he stayed on his last pillar, 18m. high and about 4m. square on top, for 30 years. He continuously abased himself in prayer, and became very famous for his holiness. There he was consulted by emperors and bishops, and visited by savages seeking conversion. Theodoret's history is full of miracles worked by the saints, often modelled on biblical events. We should not pour scorn either on the rigorous exploits of the monks, or on the credulity of those who wrote of their spiritual gifts. Theodoret was a thoroughly well-educated and worldly-wise scholar, as were the author of Antony's *Life* and Sulpicius Severus, who wrote similarly of Martin of Tours. To them it was not incredible that God worked miracles again for those who put their whole selves in his hands, as he had in biblical times, and it was certainly regarded as virtuous to believe it.

Syria also produced the 'singing monks', founded about 400 by one Alexander. He tried to find them a place at Palmyra, then at Antioch and Constantinople, but they were treated with hostility or suspicion. They finally settled on the Bosporus, and as the *Acoemetae* (unsleeping ones) they survived many centuries, becoming quite influential in Byzantine religion. 490 times a day they sang, 'Glory to God in the highest, and peace on earth to men of good pleasure.' They took it in turns to rest from this perpetual prayer.

Another movement was officially condemned, but remained influential. The Messalians or Euchites ('Praying ones') tried to pray continuously, believed in absolute dependence on God, studiously took no thought for the morrow, and lived rough in streets and byways on what people gave them. Some of the practices condemned by the Synod of Gangra (Canons in *CCC* 2–3) have been associated with Messalianism, as has the name of Eustathius, Bishop of Sebaste (Sebasteia) in Armeina, a leader of the Pneumatomachi; but in fact the movement arose in Syria and at a rather later date. At Ephesus in 431 they were directly condemned on doctrinal grounds. But the material used at that Council shows that Messalian works written by a little-known Symeon are in fact the same as various writings which have come down to us attributed to Macarius the Egyptian. These homilies and other writings are spiritually interesting. The Messalians were condemned for asserting that the devil continues to reside in the baptized, and that by prayer perfection is possible. But the writings of Macarius/Symeon give a different picture: sin continues deep rooted even in the baptized, and against it only God's Spirit can prevail; any claim to perfection reflects an unjustifiable pride. It is for the believer to pray continuously for the divine deliverance. This pessimistic but ardent spirituality is an Eastern equivalent of Augustine's conception of continual confession in the face of persistent sin. Not surprisingly, graced with the pseudonym of one of the great founders of Egyptian monasticism, Macarius, Symeon's work has continued to be widely read in Greek monastic circles.

Basil's contribution

The strongest influence, however, in Greek monasticism is Basil of Caesarea. Friend and fellow-enthusiast of Eustathius of Sebaste, Basil parted from him, not only on the question of the deity of the

Holy Spirit, but on monastic life. While Eustathius was criticized for promoting extreme ascetic views, and was posthumously associated with the recklessness of the Messalians, Basil insisted on control, organization, service and social life. Basil's conversion to 'philosophy', that is, to the life of an ascetic, is attributed by Gregory of Nyssa to his elder sister Macrina (*CCC* 96). After a pilgrimage to the holy places in Egypt with Eustathius, Basil tried to set up monastic life with friends in Pontus. Then as bishop he wrote rules for his monks, who were associated closely with the bishop and his congregation. They were not to meet or worship except in the bishop's church and under his authority. This meant that the church's life would be adapted to monastic ideals. From this time onwards we find more extended and frequent hours of worship developing in cathedral (episcopal) churches, with monastic choirs. At the same time the monks are brought under firm episcopal control, and their goals shaped by less individualistic ideals. Among the church buildings a hospital was set up where Basil and his associates could serve the community (Basil, *Ep.* 94; Gregory of Nazianzus, *Orat.* 43.61 [*CCC* 96–8]). But the most important feature of his spirituality was the doctrine that corporate life was not merely a help towards individual perfection, but essential if Christ was to be obeyed (see *Reg. fus.* 7 [*CCC* 98–100]). Life must include work in order to have the means to be charitable. And if the Lord set the example of love and humility by washing the feet of the disciples, 'Whose feet will you wash? Whom will you care for? In comparison with whom will you be last, if you live by yourself?' Hermits and anchorites did not cease to exist; but now a plain call to evangelical maturity bound monks again to the Church Catholic.

Evagrius of Pontus

Among the circle of Basil's Cappadocian associates was Evagrius of Pontus (345–99). He was made deacon by Basil's close colleague Gregory of Nazianzus at Constantinople in 379, but soon left public church life to pursue monasticism. He stayed briefly in Jerusalem, at the monastery of Rufinus and Melania on the Mount of Olives. The rest of his life was spent in Egypt, first in Nitria and then in the Kellia of the Nitrian desert, a close disciple of Macarius of Egypt; he figures in the *Sayings of the Fathers* 1.4–5[3–4] (*CCC*

170). Whereas Basil was a great administrator and organizer, Evagrius' contribution was in scholarship, expressing the primitive monastic spirituality in a systematic and learned manner. He was not alone in this, since the exegete Didymus, known as 'the Blind', worked near Alexandria and shared Evagrius' commitment to Origenism. Together with Didymus and their spiritual forefather Origen, Evagrius was condemned at the time of the second Council of Constantinople in 553. His works were consequently destroyed. But they had already been widely translated into Latin and Syriac, and some survive in Greek under the names of other authors. In line with the tradition of the desert fathers he wrote *Antirrhetikos*. This is a survey of the eight evil thoughts or demons (he uses both terms) which attack monks: gluttony, sexual indulgence, love of money, grief, wrath, sloth (or *accidie*), vainglory, arrogance. In dealing with these he offers a series of sayings from Sctipture, to be used (as Jesus used scriptural sentences when tempted) to defeat the demon. Through the work of Evagrius' friend and admirer John Cassian, these were to become basic to the Latin spirituality of the West (see his *Inst.* 10 [*CCC* 172–4] on sloth) and engendered the traditional 'seven deadly sins' in the work of Gregory the Great. The demons figure also in *Praktikos*, which deals with the same spiritual stage. But Evagrius had more to offer than simple biblical and moral ascesis, and that is where the trouble began. He saw such practical obedience (Gk *praktike*) as only the beginning, leading to control of the passions of the soul. For this the Stoic term 'passionlessness' (Gk *apatheia*, 'apathy') is used; it goes with a loving and true awareness of the nature of the world. Once the passions are conquered, true prayer becomes possible, the 'continual intercourse of the spirit with God', as he says in his most popular book *On prayer*. It corresponds to the Sabbath of the Kingdom of Heaven, the new creation, the second stage of the spirit seized by love and true understanding of the world (Gk *theoria*). Beyond it lies the realm of the knowledge of God (Gk *theologia*), not to be achieved in this creation, but the goal of the true intellectual (Gk *gnostikos*, Gnostic). Like Origen, he saw the spirit of man as eternal, fallen by deviation from God, and being trained for ultimate restoration to absolute contemplation of God who is pure Spirit.

Western developments

Evagrius was a captivating writer. He captivated John Cassian, a visitor to Nitria from the West, who wrote the influential *Conferences* and *Institutes* for the guidance of Gallic monks. The *Conferences* are ostensibly discussions with desert fathers, and contain much Evagrian teaching on sin and salvation: he notably substitutes for Evagrius' Stoic term *passionlessness* the biblical virtue of *purity of heart*. His *Institutes* are more concerned with the organization of a monastery, and reflect Pachomian influence. Looser forms of monasticism had already reached Gaul, notably in the career of Martin of Tours. The date of Martin's birth is widely disputed, but by 360 he was founding a monastery at Ligugé, and about 370 became Bishop in Tours. He became the subject of hagiographic writing by Sulpicius Severus, and both in his lifetime and afterwards was the inspiration both for the spread of Christianity and for the planting of monasteries (extracts from *Life of Martin, Chronicle,* and *Dialogues* in *CCC* 158–63). In his time he offended the worldly bishops of Gaul and Spain by continuing to live the impoverished life of a monk even as a bishop, and by supporting the passionate asceticism of the Priscillianists, whose leaders were executed on trumped-up charges in 385. Meanwhile orderly monasticism developed from the south. The settlement at Lérins, founded in 410, provided a series of monk-bishops, of whom Caesarius of Arles (502–42) was perhaps the most notable for the theory and practice of the ascetic life in conjunction with the episcopal church.

Before we assess the contribution of the early monastic movement to the life of the Church, we must consider some remarkable events in Egypt, Palestine and Constantinople in which Jerome and John Chrysostom were involved.

ORIGENISM, JEROME AND JOHN CHRYSOSTOM

Origenism and Jerome

In the East an unpleasant controversy caused much destruction among the monks of Egypt. The learning of Evagrius and those like him did not appeal to those who made ignorance and simplicity a virtue. The majority of the monks rose up to destroy 'Origenism'. Those opposed to Origenism are usually dubbed 'Anthropomorphite'. This reflects their view of God as having a human form. It is based not only on Gen. 1.26-7, but on the incarnation: God incarnate is man-shaped. Origen, and Christian thinkers like Augustine who followed the same Platonic way, placed the likeness in man's rationality (Gk *logos, nous*). So of course did Evagrius and his friends. The wily Bishop Theophilus of Alexandria at first sided with the Origenists, but found it tactically wiser to switch to the majority. In 399 the Origenists were forcefully driven out by their enemies, their monasteries pillaged, their books destroyed. One precious dossier of books by Origen and Didymus was hidden in an old tomb at Toura, to be rediscovered when the British army used the same tomb to store ammunition in 1941. The refugees fled abroad, and with them Origenism and controversy. By then the dispute had already split the Latin-led monks of Jerusalem and Bethlehem. Jerome (*c.*347–*c.*420) and Rufinus (d. 410) were long-standing friends. Both were well-educated Latins; both came from the Adriatic area, and were fellow-students in Rome.

Jerome is known to us chiefly through his own tendentious letters (see *CCC* 178-90). After travels in the West to Trier and Aquileia, he studied and was baptized in Rome before visiting the East in 372. He narrates a dream in which Christ accused him of being a Ciceronian rather than a Christian (*Ep.* 22.30 [*CCC* 180-1]), whereat he parted with his secular library. If this is a true account, he did not keep his vow absolutely, and continued to acknowledge the benefits of discreetly used secular learning; but the episode is probably coloured in retrospect. It belongs to his early time in Antioch (373?), or as a monk in the Syrian Chalcis (374-8). He was ordained priest in Antioch by the dissident old Nicene Paulinus, who had the support of Damasus of Rome (see, but do not trust, *Ep.* 15.1-4 [*CCC* 181-2] for his difficulties with the trinitarian disputes there). He composed the *Life of Paul*, a fictitious romance about a monk even earlier than Antony, written (like so much else by Jerome) more with an eye to elegance and edification than to historic truth. But he also began more serious theological polemic, and the engagement with exegesis in translating Origen. By 382 he was in Rome, where in addition to advancing the study of the text, Latin translation and interpretation of Scripture, he promoted asceticism, conspicuously among ladies of wealth, the widows Marcella and Paula, and Paula's daughter Eustochium (for Jerome's letter to Eustochium, and letters about Marcella and Fabiola, see *CCC* 185-6, 195-200). He also made enemies among the clergy, of whose foppish behaviour he was critical. In defending the perpetual virginity of Mary against Helvidius he went too far by asserting the superiority of virginity to marriage, as he was to do later in his attack on Jovinian (*CCC* 195). The nature of his relations with Damasus the Bishop of Rome is not certain, since we know it only from his own letters, which were possibly improved, or even written, for publication after Damasus' death in 384. Being highly gifted as a speaker and writer, he may well have expected to be elected Bishop of Rome. But perhaps because of his sharp arguments about the superiority of the ascetic life, he had made enemies. Siricius was preferred, and Jerome found himself obliged to leave Italy, bitter about the imputations against his character, the unfairness of which can be readily parallelled in the savage things he often wrote about others (see his complaints in *Ep.* 45 [*CCC* 187-8]).

Jerome went to the East again with his brother Paulinian and some other aspiring monks, and teamed up with Paula and Eustochium in Palestine. After a visit to the monks in Egypt, they settled at Bethlehem, where monastery and convent for nuns flourished together, sustained by Paula's vast wealth. Jerome was able to devote the rest of his long life until 419 to writing, and his output was enormous. Not only did he find time to write many letters of spiritual advice and consolation, but he translated most of the Bible afresh into Latin, revising or replacing the old versions. He based his Old Testament work directly on the Hebrew, instead of the Greek Bible which had been the basis of the existing 'Old Latin' version, and his work became the basis of what is called the 'Vulgate', the official Bible of the Roman Catholic Church to this day. His principle, that truth lies in the Hebrew ('*Hebraica veritas*'), was to become the basis of the later Protestant Bibles, which bypassed the official Vulgate to translate afresh from the 'original tongues'. This principle of discarding the Septuagint was to cause offence and anxiety to many, however, including Augustine, who disapproved of removing in this radical way the landmarks planted by the Fathers. Jerome also produced detailed commentaries on many biblical books, and these were widely read and appreciated for their learning. But here we come to a point of controversy. Jerome confessed his admiration for Origen as man and scholar (*Ep.* 32.4 [*CCC* 190–1]), and translated commentaries of his into Latin, thus enabling them to survive. Throughout his career Jerome continued to use Origen's work as the basis for his own, often unacknowledged, especially after he became a bitter anti-Origenist. One modern scholar (P. Nautin) holds that Jerome's claims to have learned Hebrew are fictitious, and that he owed all his information about the Hebrew Bible and its meaning to lost works of Origen; but this view of him is not widely held.

Origenism in Palestine; Rufinus

The dispute about Origen was already brewing up in 393, and had reached Palestine. A venerable patron of monks called Epiphanius, Bishop of Salamis in Cyprus, visited Palestine in 394. He had been an ardent supporter of Paulinus, the old Nicene Bishop of Antioch, as Jerome had also been. In 374–7 Epiphanius had written two books, *Ancoratus* and *Panarion*, in which he had elaborated a system of heresies, eighty in all plus subdivisions, with morbid enthusiasm for detail. Among them, not surprisingly in view of his hostility to the Eastern (Cappadocian) doctrine of the Trinity, he had included Origen. Origen was charged with a number of vicious errors: he had denied that the Son could see the Father, postulated that souls exist as rational spirits before being imprisoned in the body, predicted the repentance of the devil and demons, held 'the coats of skins' put on by Adam and Eve after their fall to mean their physical bodies, denied the resurrection of the flesh, and allegorized Paradise so as to deny its historicity (see Jerome, *Adv. Joan. Hier.* 7 [*CCC* 192]). These charges had some foundation in Origen's views or speculations; though most of us might share Socrates' opinion that the general attack was outrageous (*HE* 6.13 [*CCC* 193–4]). The rumblings of dispute about Origen were already present especially among the monks. In Palestine, Epiphanius did two more improper things. First, he used a sermon in the cathedral church at Jerusalem to preach against Origen, knowing that the Bishop John was an Origenist: Jerome sided with Epiphanius (*Adv. Joan. Hier.* 2 [*CCC* 191–2]). Secondly Epiphanius ordained Jerome's brother Paulinian as presbyter, to cater for the needs of the monastery at Bethlehem, an uncanonical act (Jerome, *Ep.* 51.1–2 [*CCC* 188–9]). Thereafter Jerome became a fervent anti-Origenist, and this led to his quarrel with his friend of student days, Rufinus.

After a career in monasticism and scholarship Rufinus of Aquileia had settled in a monastery at Jerusalem, where like Jerome he had a wealthy patroness, one Melania. Rufinus was a great translator, responsible among other things for a Latin edition of Eusebius' famous *Ecclesiastical history*. But his great work in this field was a version of Origen's *On first principles*, the only complete copy to survive. Jerome and Rufinus let off furious polemical works against each other. Jerome gleefully pointed out the many ways in which Rufinus improved the theology of Origen by smoothing over his more provocative speculations, and himself produced a more accurate – and more 'heretical' – version. Rufinus' friends campaigned on behalf of Origen in the West. But Jerome and Theophilus of Alexandria ultimately prevailed at Rome, and a condemnation was issued there of 'everything written in former days by Origen that is contrary to our faith', a delicate compromising formula which does not appear to condemn Origen outright (Anastasius of Rome in Jerome, *Ep.* 95 [*CCC* 193]). Jerome was perhaps reconciled to Bishop John, but not to Rufinus. One ancient lover of monasticism took a more favourable view of Rufinus than of Jerome (see Palladius' remarks in his *Lausiac History* 36.6–7; 46.5 [*CCC* 205]). Later in life Jerome found other victims to lash with his ferocious pen, such as Pelagius. But he also left a huge legacy of careful biblical scholarship, in which the influence of the great Origen pervades, not only in erudite learning, but in allegorical interpretation. Jerome himself thus became one of the principal purveyors of the spiritual exegesis of Origen to the West, where his influence as a biblical interpreter came to prevail. Western saints like Gregory the Great and Bernard, who read the Song of Songs as a love affair between the soul and its Saviour, had learnt their spirituality through the commentary of Origen that Jerome made available.

John Chrysostom

One other monastic career was seared by the controversy over Origen. John, posthumously surnamed *Chrysostomos* ('golden-mouth'), was born about 350 and died in 407. After baptism in 372 he pursued biblical and ascetic studies. After starting an ecclesiastical career John withdrew to a monastery, where his self-imposed regime was so harsh that it damaged his health. Reverting to a public career he was made deacon in Antioch by Meletius in 381, and presbyter by Flavian in 386. By then he had already composed his famous book *On priesthood*, in which the merits of monasticism and ministerial priesthood are set out together. The privileges of the priest, whose ministry lifts him into heaven, are clear; and perfection is achieved not in solitary strife, but in loving service to the neighbour. John's gifts as a preacher were soon apparent, and he began a ministry which fills many volumes of modern collections with his sermons and biblical commentaries. He cannot be considered an original theologian; his principles must be gleaned from works written with other, often practical, goals. He accepts the authority of the councils, the coequal Trinity, and the divine Christ whole in his manhood. God's condescension is a constant theme. This is revealed in the Scriptures, which express the divine will, exhorting and chiding in terms appropriate to the condition of the ignorant and erring, rather than to God's own perfection and glory. The text is read for the most part practically and literally, though allegory and typology certainly appear. Jesus Christ was (as might be expected for a disciple of Diodore of Tarsus) clearly twofold: John does not hesitate to depict him as sometimes speaking with the voice of a man, expressing want, distress or ignorance, and sometimes with the voice of God, in commanding miracles and affirming his authority. There is strong emphasis on human freedom to respond to the laws of God: conscience is the inner tribunal which judges us. From the Scriptures emerges a pattern of Christian perfection which every Christian must aspire to. His characteristic theme is the duty of those with wealth to give to the poor: true wealth is not possessing, but giving. But he spoke on a multitude of subjects, reassuring and rebuking in time of public anxiety (as in his sermons after the Antioch riots of 387, CCC 264–8), attacking heresy, Judaism, and horseracing, promoting Christian education on a biblical basis, and many more. His fame grew, and in 398 he was taken off to be ordained Bishop of Constantinople.

From the start it was a more perilous ascent than he perceived. Theophilus of Alexandria had hoped to promote his own presbyter Isidore to Constantinople. But a court official had incriminating papers to blackmail him with, and the tough Alexandrian had to consecrate John as bishop himself. John's rigour and sanctity won admiration from some; his sermons offered divine pity to the poor, while chiding the rich, and the people loved him. But the monastic fare set before visiting ecclesiastics, the absence of episcopal banquets, his deposing of two deacons for serious offences, and the nagging of the rich of the imperial city about luxury, soon made enemies. He offended the empress Eudoxia with the implication that she had conspired in a palace murder and with a reference to Jezebel. He responded in the 'Home Synod' at Constantinople to appeals from Asia, where Antoninus of Ephesus was accused of shocking corruption. John went to Ephesus, and finding Antoninus had died, held a council of bishops from the neighbouring regions. This not only elected a replacement for Antoninus, but deposed six bishops for simony (Palladius, *Life of St John Chrysostom* 14–15 [CCC 269–70]). Not very culpable; but Constantinople had no formal authority over Thrace and Asia Minor until it was established by the Canons of Chalcedon in 451, and the tale of John's enemies grew accordingly.

Finally, John received in his city the Tall Brothers, a group of monks who had fled from Theophilus and the Anthropomorphites as they overthrew the Origenist monasteries near Alexandria. He gave them hospitality but not communion, and consulted

Theophilus (Palladius, *Life of St John Chrysostom* 7-8 [*CCC* 271-2]). John was no Origenist himself. His biblical training was in the Antiochene school, quite opposed to Origen's spiritual exegesis; his spirituality was essentially practical, and he did not aspire to realms above *praxis* as Evagrius did. He responded to the Tall Brothers, as some of the imperial court responded, because they seemed honest, learned and devout. Theophilus was summoned to answer charges. But John's tactlessness and Theophilus' bribes took their toll, and it was finally John himself who stood trial at the Synod of the Oak in 403, and was condemned and exiled (see John's own account in *CCC* 273-6). But the people rose in protest, and John returned triumphant.

Once again, however, his principles got the better of him. A silver statue of the Empress was erected amid scenes of jubilation outside the church of St Sophia. She was likened by the Bishop to Herodias (Socrates, *HE* 6.18.1-5 [*CCC* 276-7]); in June 404 he was exiled. At first he continued to teach and preach at Cucusos, and exercised a ministry by letter in the capital; to this period belongs his correspondence with Olympias, a lady who had followed his teaching, liberated her slaves and given away her wealth. He died in 407 on the way to a remoter exile.

Monasticism had begun with men escaping to serve God perfectly in solitude. Some achieved heroic feats of self-imposed spiritual martyrdom in their cells and on their mountain-tops. Even there they were sought out as inspired guides, as counsellors who would know the mind of God, as examples to others of God's sanctifying power in the world. But most learned from Pachomius that to achieve perfection they needed the help of others. Basil taught them that to achieve perfection one needed someone else to help, a neighbour to love. In their strife with sin they learned like the Messalians the persistent need for divine grace sought in prayer. From Origen descended the exploration of the inner realm of spirit through the Bible, aspiring to realms above this world. In their different ways Didymus, Evagrius and the Cappadocian Fathers helped this process. Directly through Rufinus and Jerome, indirectly through John Cassian, Ambrose of Milan and Augustine, Origenism became pervasive also in the West. It broke the friendship of Jerome and Rufinus, and unjustly toppled John Chrysostom from his throne. Alongside the movement went the determined efforts of bishops to harness monks to the cause of the larger Church, as Athanasius deployed the *Life of Antony*, and Theophilus connived with the Anthropomorphites, and Basil built his hospital and rallied his team. But some might suppose that under the clumsy arrogance of John Chrysostom, so out of place in the imperial city, lay a purer testimony to the Kingdom of God and its judgements than all the rest.

19

AUGUSTINE OF HIPPO

Career and Confessions

The greatest single contributor to the thought of the Church in the early period was Augustine of Hippo (so called to distinguish him from Augustine of Canterbury, who was named after him). Born in 354 at Tagaste in Numidia of a devout Christian mother, Monnica, and an unconverted father, he was sent to Carthage in 370 for higher education, through the munificence of a rich patron. Brilliant at Latin, he became a teacher of grammar, first at Tagaste, then at Carthage, and in 383 at the age of twenty-nine he tried his fortune in Rome. Problems with students (and perhaps with himself) led him to seek a move, and he was recommended by admirers for a public appointment as professor of rhetoric at Milan, then virtually the capital of the West. At Milan in 386 he underwent a conversion, and for a few months lived and wrote in philosophic retreat. Baptized the next Easter, he returned to Africa, where he tried again to live in monastic seclusion. He was reluctantly dragged into the ministry of the Church when Valerius, Bishop of the sea-port Hippo, needed a teacher and preacher in his old age. As presbyter (391) Augustine began this work, which he continued first as coadjutor and then bishop in 395. As bishop he helped the African church through various crises and controversies. He died in 430 while his city was besieged by the Vandal armies which had invaded Africa from Spain.

We know a great deal about Augustine's earlier life from his *Confessions*, an original book of meditations on his early life and present spiritual state, which he began in 397 and completed over two or three years. It takes the form of an address to God, but is aimed to communicate with the growing company of intellectuals attempting the spiritual and monastic life, those he calls 'the spirituals' (*spiritales*). There are thirteen 'books'. Eight trace and muse upon the years before his baptism, and the ninth recounts his baptism and the last days with his mother on the way back to

Africa. The tenth book recounts his present state of mind. The last three books begin an exposition of Genesis, dwelling strongly on the nature of time and God's relation to it. He speeds up towards the end, but only covers the first chapter of the Bible.

Confessions is thus not autobiography, though it contains autobiographical material. It is a theological meditation chiefly about himself and God's dealings with him. This means that it reflects strongly Augustine's concerns and attitudes when he wrote it. Critical opinion at one time disparaged the historical value of the accounts it contains. In particular, it has been held that in 386 he was not seriously Christian in his beliefs and attitudes, but held a more optimist Neoplatonic philosophy revealed in the 'Cassiciacum dialogues', a set of philosophical works written in his retreat in Italy during 386 and 387. When he wrote *Confessions* he was anxious to make himself appear more Christian than he was, and much of the work, including the famous scene of conversion (8.12.28–30 [*CCC* 213–14]) is a fiction. Scholarly opinion is now more positive. While the work reflects the pastoral and controversial concerns of the bishop of 397 and his commitment to the monastic movement, and while he has come to a more pessimistic view of human nature as the result of his experiences, there is a central desire to be honest before God. His representations of early attempts to understand God, as a philosopher and as a Manichee, and his improper opinions about the Scriptures (as in 3.5.9 [*CCC* 207]) are an unparalleled confession of his own disgrace. They do not fit the theory of deliberate fabrication. Nor do features like the frank preference for the speaking style of Faustus the Manichee over that of Ambrose, the distinguished Bishop of Milan who helped convert Augustine and baptized him (5.13.23 [*CCC* 208]).

Confession in the biblical texts (especially Psalms) is praise, confessing to God his greatness and merits, or of sin, confessing what has been done wrong, whether in hope of reconciliation or not. Augustine's *Confessions* certainly include these. But in Christian terms confession is also confession of faith, like the profession of those being baptized, confessing God as Father and creator, as Son and Lord in his saving work, and as Holy Spirit; this kind of confession may be found in the later, more directly theological, books. Augustine's model may be the confession which the convert was expected to make. In a small book, *On catechizing beginners* (*Cat. rud.* 5.9), Augustine recommends a junior clergyman to begin by asking the convert what led to the desire for baptism; if he or she answers in terms of divine miracles or judgements, the convert is to be taught not to rely on such signs, but on the invisible miracle of the Scriptures, which are then to be taught beginning with Genesis. So his books recount the wonderful works of God which drove him to baptism, and then turn to Genesis to begin the systematic account of the whole Scripture. If this was his plan, we should be relieved that he stopped after Genesis 1 and got on with other things.

Youth in Africa; Manicheism

Within *Confessions* we may trace both an intellectual and a moral development of the young Augustine, which set the scene for much of his later theology. He begins with a background of African Catholicism. He was registered as catechumen in infancy, but not baptized (1.11.17). He wonders whether his mother did right in deferring baptism (1.11.18). Baptism was held in strong religious awe, as the behaviour of one of his wild friends showed; he changed his attitude to life when he heard he had been baptized while unconscious and thought to be dying (4.4.7–8). Church people enjoyed picnic parties at martyr–shrines, as Monnica started doing at Milan, but Bishop Ambrose forbade them (6.2.2). They also held boozy anniversary parties for the saints in the churches themselves; Augustine was to find it difficult to abolish these at Hippo (*CCC* 214–16). Astrology was widespread, and Augustine was attracted by it, until argued out of it (4.3.4–5; 7.6.8–10). With Old Testament passages taken literally, God was regarded as of human shape and corporeal. As a Christian bishop Augustine regards such interpretations of God's body and voice as childish (12.27.37). But as a young man he had no answer to the Manichean heretics, when they objected to the Old Testament statement that humanity is created 'after the image of God': 'Is God bounded by a bodily shape, and has he hair and nails?' (3.7.12 [*CCC* 207–8]). Thus the Scriptures literally interpreted by the Manichees killed him spiritually (5.14.24 [*CCC* 208–9]); he found none to undeceive him until he was in Milan (6.3.4). With this simple-minded reading of the Old Testament went a view of God as personally the source of evil as well as good, something incompatible with the rational philosophies of the day, and of great personal concern to Augustine, who repeatedly reverts to the problem of where evil comes from (so 5.10.19–20; 7.3.4–5).

Early in his time as a student he began to think seriously about the philosophic life of virtue. He read *Hortensius*, a lost work of the Roman rhetorician and philosopher Cicero, which led him to aspire to truth; but he found it unsatisfying, because it lacked the name of Jesus, which he had learned to love 'with my mother's milk'. Cicero's polish, however, made the ungainly Latin of the current Old Testament quite distasteful, and he did not know the New Testament at all (3.3.6–5.9 [*CCC* 206–7]).

The Manichees were a different matter. Not only did they deal comprehensively with the difficulties of the Old Testament by rejecting its authority; they offered an explanation for evil, as originating in a separate power alongside the Kingdom of Light where God reigned, and impinging upon it. They also encouraged rational discussion, whereas the churches demanded intellectual submission (at least as it appeared in Africa), and had beautiful works of art, books, music, poetry and oratory; and though as a Catholic bishop Augustine would find grounds to criticize the conduct of the Manichees, we may suppose that many of their 'elect' lived chastely as monks just like many Christians. Their mythology was complicated, like that of other dualistic gnostic sects (see Chapter 4), but it went with some fundamentally attractive ideas.

Mani was born in AD 216 in Babylonia, and brought up in the religion of Elkesai, a Jewish–Christian sect. After two conversion experiences he parted from them and composed a universal religion based on the traditional dualism of Persian Zoroastrianism. He travelled widely, preaching his faith and building up schools of followers and missionaries. Like Muhammad later, he had enormous success in his own lifetime. During a period of military success by the Persians against their Roman rivals in the Middle East, however, there was a resurgence of state Zoroastrianism, which led to a persecution, in which Mani was himself arrested, and died in prison a martyr for his cause (277; the date 272 given in *NE* 265 is a mistake). Mani consciously named the Buddha, Zoroaster and Jesus among earlier revelations of the Light (*NE* 265), but claimed that the one accorded to him was not local, but for all the world, as was the church he founded (*NE* 266). In fact

Manichees assimilated to the religions around them, resembling Buddhists in the East and looking like a Christian sect in the West.

Mani taught that beside the good God, who is Light, there was a realm of darkness, which had managed to invade the realm of light and seize particles of it. This world is the result of that malevolent event, and of subsequent actions by the realm of light to preserve and recover the lost portions, and by the agents of darkness to counter those efforts. Two practices in particular kept the Light imprisoned: flesh-eating and sexual reproduction. The Paraclete promised by Jesus, the heavenly Twin (of Jesus rather than Mani), had communicated to him the detail of pre-mundane history, and of the heavenly machinery (like the phases of the moon) by which light-particles were recovered from the damaging mixture. The heart of the message was knowledge (*gnosis*) that the spirit in humanity is superior to the matter in which it is imprisoned. Those chosen to know this truth ('elect') were released from the evil passions which suppress the spirit in others: they sang jubilantly of their release in words taught by Mani (*NE* 266–7), and lived celibate and vegetarian, eating especially luminous fruits like melons and cucumbers, in order to accumulate light in themselves before their spirits returned to the realm of Light. Most adherents were not elect, and lived more normal lives; in fact the Manichean communities, especially in the East, resembled oriental societies centred on Buddhist monasteries.

Augustine was attracted by this creed partly because he was a man of taste: the poetry was pathetically moving, the language, music and books were beautiful, the lives of the elect pure. Theologically it offered a God he could understand, of Light in physical particles like Tertullian's God, but one who (unlike the God of Scripture) was free from imputations of human shape or evil. The Manichean God was infinite except on the one side which faced Darkness. Sin and suffering had another source, from which the God of Light delivered those to whom his knowledge came. There was no moral judgement, only salvation. Jesus was constantly spoken of, since he too had revealed the Light. His suffering was that of the Light everywhere imprisoned by the power of darkness: he is crucified on every tree. Later Augustine reproached himself for docetic Christology as a Manichee (for all this, see especially *Conf.* 5.10.20).

Augustine remained a Manichee, and intended to become an

elect, until disillusion set in. He had problems with Mani's astronomy. Christians could be wrong about astronomy: for Manichees, the mistakes were in the holy books of revelation, and disastrous. He waited for the promised expert, the Manichee Bishop Faustus, to visit Carthage, expecting him to clear up the difficulties. Faustus, though Augustine loved and respected him, failed, and so the rational appeal of the religion lessened (5.3.3–5.6.11). Augustine remained with the Manichees for his period in Rome, and was indeed sponsored by some of them for the chair in Milan. But by then he had turned philosophically sceptical, doubting Mani but not believing anything else. He was ready for something new. He found it at Milan.

Ambrose and Neoplatonism

Attending the sermons of Ambrose the Bishop, Augustine met the allegorical exposition of Scripture. Ambrose knew the Origen tradition well, both directly and, more particularly, through the Origenistic theology he borrowed from the Cappadocian Fathers. In addition to laying to rest particular problems, moral and historical, of the Old Testament taken literally, this untied one particular knot: man was made in the image of God, not in a literal sense as Augustine had supposed was meant by Genesis 1.26–7, but spiritually (see 3.7.12 and 5.14.24 [CCC 207–9]). We know from Ambrose's surviving sermons that he interpreted this image as referring to 'power of mind' (Ambrose, *Hexaemeron* 1.8.31). In the same sermon he attacked the Manichees on another theme near Augustine's heart: freedom of the will. The Manichees believed that the elect were mysteriously predestined, and that sin was the effect of forces outside human control. Ambrose argued that we are in command of ourselves, not subject to such external constraint in moral choices. Augustine has such teaching in mind when he writes, 'I directed my attention to understand what I now was told, that free will is the cause of our doing evil and that thy just judgement is the cause of our having to suffer from its consequences' (7.3.5). Both these ideas of Ambrose were expressed in terms partly derived from Neoplatonic philosophy, a system which Augustine was to meet from another source.

The Christian intellectuals of Milan, like many of their pagan contemporaries, read philosophy in the light of the mystical

Platonism of Plotinus (about 204–70), especially as popularized by Porphyry (about 232–304) and Iamblichus (died about 326). One of these intellectuals introduced Augustine to what he calls 'Platonic books', probably the writings of Plotinus himself. Augustine found these very illuminating. The 'Academic' or sceptical Platonists argued that there could be no real knowledge, only probable opinions; in his doubts about Manicheism this was the position Augustine had adopted. The Plotinian school however claimed that it was possible for the mind to rise above the crowded pressure of matter and its transient images to a purely mental or spiritual reality beyond. Above and beyond the World-soul was Mind (*nous*), in which inhered the Forms or Ideas familiar in Platonism (see p. 5), and beyond Mind in utter transcendence the One or Good. The Forms impose themselves upon matter, in itself a characterless abstraction not truly conceivable without form. This relation is elaborated by Augustine in *Conf.* 12.7–13. Such notions had already infiltrated Christian thought, as in Origen's system, and among the Cappadocians. It was peculiarly relevant to Augustine's predicament at Milan, because Plotinus is strong against the Stoics for saying that fundamental spiritual reality is material; against the sceptics who asserted that it is unknowable; and against gnostic dualists who point to no one original source. Neoplatonism also resolved Augustine's problems over evil: all that exists is as a totality perfect, but as a series of graded beings. It is for individuals to determine their place in this totality by their own free choice.

Augustine thus suffered a conversion, and in a spiritual ecstasy was caught up to a vision of God as Truth:

Being admonished by these [Platonic] books to return into myself, I entered into my inward soul, guided by thee . . . And I entered, and with the eye of my soul – such as it was – saw above the same eye of my soul and above my mind the Immutable Light . . . He who knows Truth knows that Light, and he who knows it knows Eternity . . . And thou didst beat back the weakness of my sight, shining forth upon me thy dazzling beams of light, and I trembled with love and fear . . . I realized that I was far away from thee in a land of unlikeness, as if I heard thy voice from on high, '. . . grow and you shall feed on me; . . . you shall be changed into my likeness'. (*Conf.* 7.10.16)

This conviction that there is an ultimate Reality, and that it is man's proper destiny to become like it, is deeply Neoplatonic, but is also at the heart of the spirituality Augustine now read in Scripture, where humanity is created in God's image and likeness, designed to see and enjoy him.

Monastic call and conversion

Augustine now accepted much of Christian doctrine. He did not sustain the spiritual ecstasy, because of the sins of the flesh, and especially sexual desire. Back in Carthage he had taken a wife or concubine (he never tells her name), who gave him a son. In Milan he sent away the woman, because his mother was scheming for him to make a marriage in a family which would improve his career. But the new bride was too young to marry, and he was unable to live without sexual activity, and took a mistress. Both the worldly marriage and the mistress seemed to offer insuperable obstacles to the one who sought to know only God: 'I was transported to thee by thy beauty, and then presently torn away from thee by my own weight, sinking with grief into carnal habit' (7.17.23). He still thought of Jesus as a man of pre-eminent wisdom, and therein lay the key that would unlock the door for him (7.17.24–18.25). He started taking counsel from a wise presbyter called Simplicianus, who had himself taught Ambrose and was to succeed Ambrose as Bishop of Milan.

Simplicianus congratulated him on reading the Platonists, and probably urged him to make the comparison between those works and the apostolic writings, which are graphically presented in 7.9.13–15. He found the teaching identical in substance, but always the apostles offered that bit more which referred to the grace of Jesus Christ. All of the Prologue of John 1 he found in the Platonists, but not that the Word 'came unto his own, . . . and as many as received him, to them he gave power to become the sons of God', nor that 'the Word became flesh and dwelt among us'. But Simplicianus did more, and deliberately told him the story of Victorinus, the philosopher who had embraced Christianity, and had insisted on professing his conversion by public ceremonies after his baptism (8.2.4–5 [*CCC* 210–11]). This tore at Augustine's conscience, since he was already a believer. Soon other pressures came upon him. It was, he recognized, a matter of *will*: he knew what was right, but could not do it (8.5.10–12). To his house, where he was resting because of a chest complaint (perhaps a psychosomatic asthma), an old friend told Augustine and Alypius about the monastic movement, and how two young men at Trier had forsaken political advancement and marriage to become monks, after reading the *Life of Antony* (8.6.14–15 [*CCC* 211–12]). He vividly describes the conflict this precipitated. He went out into the garden of the house, torn between the appeal of his old fleshly loves and the voice of continence, 'not barren, but a fruitful mother of children', who spoke of the men and maidens who had followed the monastic way (8.11.25–7). In a storm of passion he fled from Alypius and flung himself down in floods of tears under what he calls a 'tree of fig', an unusual phrase reflecting the biblical account of the fig-leaves which his the sexual shame of Adam and Eve after their sin in Genesis 3.7. This passionate grief he describes as a prayer like that of the Psalmist: 'How long, O Lord, wilt thou be angry for ever? Remember not our former iniquities' – in fact a prayer of confession. The divine response is immediate: 'I heard from a neighbouring house a voice, as of a boy or girl, I do not know, often repeating in a sing-song, "Take up and read; take up and read."' Obeying this mysterious voice (not human, but *as of* a child), he took up the New Testament to read where it should open, and saw about forsaking fleshly sin, and putting on Jesus Christ (Romans 13.13–14); with those words, his burden was lifted, and serenity replaced hesitation. Together with Alypius, he consecrated himself to the celibate life, and prepared for baptism the next Easter (8.12.28–30 [*CCC* 213–14]).

Unquestionably Augustine saw himself as lifted by the grace of Christ from passions he could not control: he had understood Paul. Equally he saw the process not as perfected: this release was into a life of continual mortification and confession. But perhaps above all it was to a life of monastic or 'spiritual' celibacy, in which marriage and those cares of this world that went with property and family were firmly excluded. By identifying the grace of Christ with release from sexuality Augustine set out on a road which was to prove unhealthy for theology and the Church. All else apart, conversion comes to be identified with entering the monastic life, and not with baptism, for the medieval Church, with consequences most Christians have never escaped from. We shall see it in Augustine's conclusions about original sin.

Augustine on the Trinity

Augustine's mind and heart were fixed upon God. He thought of God as absolute spiritual being, beyond description. If we know God it is because he stoops to us in the grace of Jesus Christ, and makes himself known. Consequently Augustine's book *On the Trinity*, which appeared in 414, is not an attempt to demonstrate the truth about God. He takes for granted the one being and three persons of God, and tries to elucidate the meaning. He does so in a way which embodies features of the Western theological tradition, as it had come down since Tertullian and especially in the work of Hilary of Poitiers, 'the Athanasius of the West', who had written important treatises mediating between the old Nicene position and the thought of the Eastern majority. Augustine probably ignored, if he knew it, the rather personal trinitarian philosophy of Marius Victorinus, the writer who had translated Plotinus into Latin and whose conversion story had once so affected him.

For Augustine, God is the Trinity. As with Origen and the Cappadocian theology he met through Ambrose, he combines biblical with Platonic thought. God belongs to the intelligible realm, and is immutable. And God *is* the Trinity: Father, Son and Spirit are the single source of all being (5.15). Whatever can be said of the divine being, that is of God as God, belongs to all three: each is God, each is Lord, each is almighty, but there is only one God, one Lord, one Almighty. He uses the kind of formulae which later were put into the credal hymn which is called 'The Athanasian Creed' or *Quicunque vult*: so he writes, 'The Father is almighty (*omnipotens*), the Son almighty, the Holy Spirit almighty; yet not three almighties, but one Almighty' (5.8.9). One of the effects of this equalization is to distort biblical texts. The same passage continues, 'from whom are all things, through whom are all things, in whom are all things; to him be glory'. One might contrast this with 1 Cor. 8.6, where all things are 'through' the Son, and 'from' the Father, or Eph. 4.6, where the subject is the Father. He similarly turns the point of Luke 18.19, where Jesus declares that only God is good, by insisting that 'good' applies to all three persons of the Trinity alike, as belonging to the nature of God. One of the more remarkable features of his book is that Augustine turns round many of the 'theophany' passages which theologians had used to demonstrate that the Son or Word existed and operated in the Old Testament, and claims them as manifestations of God the Trinity (see 2.12–31).

As to trinitarian terminology, Augustine understands and accepts much of the Cappadocian resolution of the conflicts precipitated by Arianism. He quotes '*mian ousian treis hypostaseis*' ('one *ousia*, three *hypostases*'), and its Latin equivalent ('one essence, three substances'); but he notes that the Latin tradition is to speak of 'one substance, three persons' (5.8.9). All of this he regards as a word-play in an area where human speech is defective: 'When it is asked, "Three what?", human speech labours under great difficulty. Nevertheless "Three persons" has been said, not in order to say just that, but to avoid saying nothing' (5.9.9). So he sees the Latin tradition, *una substantia, tres personae*, which goes back to Tertullian (see p. 72) as not contradicting the Greeks.

Augustine made a technical logical advance by writing of what are called 'real or subsistent relations'. This is a modification of the theory of distinguishing characteristics of the persons, which the Cappadocians had used. They taught that the Father is distinguished by fatherhood or unbegottenness, the Son by sonship or begottenness, the Spirit by sanctification or proceeding. Current logic, exploited by the Neo-Arians, reasoned that any attribute (like 'being a son') applied either to the essence of a thing, or was an 'accident', not essential to it. In the case of God, who is eternal, nothing can be 'accidental' (or as we might say, 'incidental'). Hence the Eunomian argument: a son has a source ('begotten'); if that is 'accidental' he cannot be God, since there are no 'accidents' in God; if it is 'essential' it contradicts the essence of God, who has no source or origin ('unbegotten'); therefore to be Son is not to be God. Augustine defines the differences of the persons as neither essential nor accidental, but relational: all are equally God and equally eternal, but they are related to each other in a certain way. So the Son is Son because that is his relation to the Father, and the Father is Father solely by his relationship to the Son (see 5.2.3–5.7.8). Hence the expression, 'real or subsistent relations' in some books.

A similar argument applies also to the Spirit, the Spirit being 'given' by the Father and the Son and so related as 'gift'; but he is given by them coequally, not by the Father alone (5.14.15). The Spirit is also sometimes identified with the love that binds Father and Son together, and is the essence of God himself: God is Spirit, and God is Love, and the Spirit is the Spirit of both Father and Son. Such meditation leads Augustine to teach that the Spirit proceeds from both the Father and the Son, as from a single source. Only rarely does he refer to the Father as holding any priority in the relationships, in contrast to the Cappadocians for whom the Father is the 'cause' of the Trinity. The consequence is the doctrine of 'double procession', that the Holy Spirit 'proceeds from the Father *and the Son*'. This doctrine was later clearly asserted in the 'Athanasian Creed', and in 589 was added to the Nicene–Constantinopolitan Creed by the Council of Toledo in Spain. The Eastern churches came to repudiate it, and whether the Spirit proceeds from the Father only, or from Father and Son, divides the Churches to this day. Augustine was clearly responsible for the Western doctrine.

The most remarkable contribution of Augustine to trinitarian thinking was yet another point. He devotes much space to psychological analogies: God's being as Trinity is modelled by the human mind. Undoubtedly he was driven to this by his Neoplatonic assumption that God is pure intellect and that the human mind is a replica of God. If therefore the Church's revelation stipulates a coequal Trinity in God, it must be replicated in the human mind. In working this out, Augustine produces brilliant philosophical analysis of how the mind works, which we cannot consider in detail. Augustine has prolonged analyses based on:

Mind, self-awareness and self-love (9.2.2–9.5.8);

Memory, understanding and will (or love) (10.11.17–10.12.19).

This last is the more fruitful: for the mind to remember, understand and love God is wisdom; to remember, understand and love itself is foolishness (see especially 14.12.15–16). This fits with his notion that a person's place in God's design is determined by whether he looks up to God or down to self.

Brilliant and influential though it is, Augustine's work on the Trinity is flawed. The distinctions which Scripture makes between the persons of the Trinity are lost in the conviction that the Trinity always operates together. In the New Testament, for instance, 'God' normally refers to the Father, not to the Trinity. Furthermore, the psychological analogies point to a God who is one Mind and one Person, as Augustine himself recognizes. It is true that such models are intrinsically imperfect, but this seems to be too fundamental to be allowed. The general process of equalization, or homogenizing the persons, is one of the reasons for the doctrine of double procession of the Spirit, which has been so divisive.

Donatism and the Church

Donatism (see pp. 114–17) still prevailed in North Africa. Despite some internal splits, even over the bishopric of Carthage (*CCC* 217–18), it was in many places the chief church, and had able leaders. As a bishop Augustine campaigned against it, using all kinds of methods, especially public disputations (Possidius, *S. Aug. vita* 9 [*CCC* 216–17]).

Augustine proceeds on the basis that God has established the Catholic Church throughout all the world, that is, the Roman Empire, and the Donatists belonged solely to Africa (though they appear to have had an expatriate congregation in Rome with a bishop; Optatus, *De schism. Don.* 2.3–4 [*CCC* 225–6]), and could not be the universal or Catholic Church. 'The verdict of the whole world is certain', writes Augustine ('*securus iudicat orbis terrarum*', *c. Ep. Parm.* 3.4.24, sometimes mistranslated).

Augustine would take the arguments of the Donatists and use documents and rhetoric to refute them. The arguments he so identified are well illustrated by the letters of Petilian, Donatist bishop of Constantine, which Augustine refuted point by point in a book (Petilian's arguments in *CCC* 222–5). Notably it begins with baptism, which was at the heart of the original dispute. Following Cyprian's logic (see pp. 92–4) they baptized other Christians who came to them, reckoning their former baptism demonic and invalid. They were a persecuted minority church with martyrs; their enemies relied on secular, not spiritual power, which was the source of persecution. Augustine took the contrary view of the sacraments, and reckoned the baptisms and ordinations of the Donatists valid, like their ascetic commitment and faith in the Trinity; but he reckoned them to be of no effect without charity (love), quoting 1 Corinthians 13.3 (*Ep.* 61.2 [*CCC* 218–19]). It was in this connection that Augustine could claim to be truer to Cyprian than his opponents, since Cyprian used precisely the argument from charity in attacking schismatics. Donatists, said Augustine, excommunicated far-distant churches; they tried to anticipate the divine judgement, when wheat and weeds would be separated at the last day.

From Augustine's arguments both about baptism and about ordination the main lines of Western sacramental theory were to develop. The Donatists argued that it was the spiritual state of the officiant at a baptism which determined its validity (so Petilian, *CCC* 222). For Augustine it was the command and word of Christ. Similarly a sinful priest remained a priest, and however scandalous and improper his behaviour, those baptized or ordained by him were validly appointed.

Augustine invoked the civil power to support his campaign. An unsuccessful rebellion by an African magnate called Gildo in 397–8 attracted some Donatist support, and they could be portrayed as rebels. In 404 a council of bishops asked for imperial protection for Catholics against Donatist violence, and for Theodosius' anti-heretical law of 392 to be implemented against them (*CCC* 219–20). The government responded positively, but the measures were patchy and only partly successful; at the same time the *Cirumcelliones*, some kind of terrorist organization sympathetic to Donatism, became very active. In May 411 Augustine's work bore fruit in a conference of bishops at which the imperial tribune Marcellinus presided over equal representatives of Donatists and Catholics. Judgement was given for the Catholics, and the next year Donatism was banned and severe repressive measures were used. Though he counselled moderation in punishing those found guilty (*Ep.* 133.2 [*CCC* 226-7]), Augustine favoured state compulsion. He argued from Scripture texts ('Compel them to come in', Luke 14.23, among others), from the violence and terror used by the Donatists themselves, and from the successes with genuine conversion which compulsion achieved; he also claims that he had originally not believed in force, but had been driven to it by experience (*Ep.* 93.5,17–18 [*CCC* 220-1]). Scholars disagree about how honest he is: some suggest that he always believed in repression, and made a virtue of not using it only so long as the state would not intervene. Others point to his increasing pessimism over human nature, as he met frustrations as pastor and preacher in trying to persuade people to love God. This pessimism contributed to the particular self-analysis of the *Confessions*, and was to come to a head in the Pelagian dispute. Whatever accounted for it in Augustine's lifetime, it had the unfortunate effect of giving theological authority for all kinds of vicious repression in the Middle Ages and the sixteenth century, and to some extent since.

Pelagianism

Pelagius, probably British, was a revivalist who preached for many years in Rome. He left, like many others, when it fell to the Goths under Alaric in 410. But before that he had succeeded in persuading many people, not only in Rome, that it was possible to fulfil Christ's command, 'Be perfect, as your heavenly father is perfect' (Matt. 5.48); God would not have commanded it if it were not possible. The power of his words in encouraging people to take the Bible seriously can be seen from his letter to Demetrias, a wealthy heiress who in 414 gave up wealth and impending marriage to devote her life to God (extract in *CCC* 233–4). Demetrias' spectacular renunciation called forth letters also from Jerome and Augustine, aimed perhaps more at the public than at the lady herself.

Augustine attributes the dispute to Pelagius, who criticized words used repeatedly by Augustine in *Confessions*: 'Give what you command, and command what you will' (*Conf.* 10.29.40 and *Don. pers.* 53 [*CCC* 230]). Pelagius' difficulty is understandable, since he held that God never commands what people cannot perform. The possibility is always there, because God makes it possible: the will and the action have to come from human beings (see quotation in Augustine, *Grat. Christi.* 5 [*CCC* 232–3]). It was not true (as is commonly said) that Pelagius denied the grace of God – Jerome even accuses Pelagians of resting too much upon it. On the contrary, Pelagius believed that mankind is created with the ultimate grace of freedom, and to it is added the grace of the divine commands in Scripture teaching us what we should do and sacramental release from past guilt in baptism. He sustained his argument by close exegesis of Paul's letters, on which he wrote commentaries, and by quotations from revered theologians like Hilary, Ambrose, Jerome and John Chrysostom, and even the early Augustine, whose book *On free will* had been written against the Manichees, whose fatalism was one of Pelagius' chief targets. That was the point at which Augustine's involvement became serious, since it called in question his own more recent position.

A disciple of Pelagius called Celestius, fleeing from Rome in 410, applied for ordination in Carthage. Faced with doctrinal questions he stirred up a hornet's nest by bald assertions based on his master's principles: Adam was created mortal; Eve's sin affected only Eve, and all babies are born sinless; law and gospel equally prepare men for eternal life, and some of the Old Testament characters were sinless; the rich must give their wealth to the poor to be saved. Celestius was condemned. Augustine responded with a book, *On the letter and the spirit*, in which he works out the Pauline contrast between law and gospel. The law prescribed what must be done, but only the Spirit working in the heart to generate love can enable one to do it.

In the next few years Augustine issued many books and sermons on topics related to Pelagianism: infant baptism, nature and grace, the interpretation of Romans 7 and 8, and Pelagius' activities. Pelagius himself travelled in the East, where he was welcomed by John of Jerusalem and accused by Jerome of Origenism (see pp. 183–5), which was plausible because free will held a decisive place in Origen's system (see p. 107), and of Stoicism, which was not true. A Spanish priest called Orosius brought charges against Pelagius, and after various proceedings he was examined by twenty-four bishops at Diospolis in December 415. Pelagius denied all the doctrines for which Celestius had been specifically condemned, and explained his own position in favourable terms. Afterwards he claimed that 'the doctrine that man can voluntarily and easily live in justice had received approbation of twenty-four bishops'. The Africans were appalled, and Councils at Milevis and Carthage in 316 appealed to the Pope Innocent (402–17). His positive reply led Augustine to affirm that 'the case is closed', and to encourage active heretic-hunting (Innocent, *Ep.* 29 and Augustine, *Serm.* 131.10 [*CCC* 234–5]). But Celestius appealed to Innocent's successor Zosimus (417–18), and was at first successful. Pressure from a further council at Carthage, however, and Augustine's campaign of letters not only to eminent bishops but to members of the imperial government, led to a reversal. Pelagianism was condemned in the West by imperial edict in 418, and by the Council of Ephesus in 431 (see p. 219). The case was, however, not truly ended; features of Augustine's teaching were themselves only partly accepted, and 'Semi-pelagianism' continued for some time.

The issues are summed up by Augustine in *De haeresibus* 88 (*CCC* 239–41), which is accurate despite Augustine's heavy commitment. The propositions condemned as unacceptable by the Council of Carthage in 317 are those attributed to Pelagians, and are also a useful summary (*CCC* 237). Pelagians saw grace as aiding the good choices made by free will; the grace without which human beings can do nothing good is the gift of free will itself. To Augustine that was not enough. His own experience was of knowing the good and being unable to do it, until the divine grace released him from the flesh. Similarly, he argued that Pelagianism made nonsense of praying for the conversion of unbelievers and heretics; remembering the part played by Monnica's prayers in the *Confessions* one understands his point. Augustine took seriously Phil. 2.13, 'It is God who works in you both to will and to work for what pleases him.' The will itself is corrupt, and must first be cured before good works could please God. If most people did not repent and believe, and if they were consequently destined to burn in hell (a view which he shared with his contemporaries), that must be because God had so decided in his mysterious wisdom. They deserved it; the divine pity had determined to save a few 'vessels of mercy' (*Nat. et grat.* 3.3–5 [*CCC* 238–9]). These were perhaps enough to replace the fallen angels, but not so many that it might suggest that God's bliss was disturbed by the loss of all the rest. That God wishes all people to be saved and come to the knowledge of his truth (1 Tim. 2.4) cannot be strictly true; it must refer to all the elect. This doctrine of predestination was to be stated again by the Reformer John Calvin. Before Calvin it was accepted in the medieval Church with one important modification: the divine choice depended on merits which God could foresee in his eternal wisdom, and so was not absolutely arbitrary.

Apart from free will and predestination, Augustine developed the idea of original sin, which means the sin people are born with. It arose especially in connection with baptism. Africa had long practised infant baptism, and regarded it as essential if a little child was to be saved. Augustine rightly interprets this as implying that the child belongs to a lump of humanity which is all under God's condemnation: the child is born stained, and must be washed clean. Each is therefore born guilty. What they are guilty of is Adam's sin. That was particularly heinous, since it was committed freely and by one capable of doing otherwise. All those since Adam have lost that freedom not to sin, which is restored in the grace of Jesus Christ. Adam's sin is sexually tinged: Adam and Eve perceived that they were naked immediately after (Gen. 3.6–7). Adam's guilt is transmitted to all his progeny, who were 'in his loins' when he sinned (as Levi was in Abraham's when he paid tithes, Heb. 7.9–10); and that transmission occurs through sexual reproduction. Augustine uses various arguments:

> Scripture teaches it: two special texts are Ps. 51.5, 'In sin did my mother conceive me', and Romans 5.12, 'one man [Adam] . . . in whom all sinned'. The latter text was misrepresented in the Latin Bible Augustine used (see *CCC* 230–1).

> Earlier Fathers had taught it, and the traditional ceremonies of exorcism and renunciation used at infant baptisms imply it.

> In sexual intercourse even lawfully married Christians act with fleshly desire (concupiscence) overcoming rational control (specifically, the male has no muscular control over the erection of the penis).

Thus Adam's monstrous sin makes all children born by sexual reproduction guilty and deserving punishment. Adults who have added actual sin make hell a bit worse for themselves.

Augustine had one special problem, on which he sought Jerome's advice: the argument only works, and the baby only deserves punishment, if the soul, like the body, is passed on from generation to generation – the 'traducian' doctrine held in the past by Tertullian. If souls are created new for each person, there has to be a clean start. He seems finally to have adopted the view that the taint occurs when the new-created soul joins the body in the foetus.

Augustine continued till his death in an increasingly rancorous debate with the Pelagians, particularly the well-educated exile, Julian of Eclanum. Julian saw much of Augustine's position as Manichean: the denial of free will, the unmerited election, the corrupting entail of sexuality. Not all Julian's criticisms were valid. Even if the biblical and metaphysical detail of Augustine's scheme is too much to bear, he understood mankind's desperate condition and the graciousness of God in salvation better than his opponents. He knew the mind's deviousness and self-deception, and the impotence of mere intellect in the face of powerful passions. But the idea of infants being guilty at birth and deserving damnation is repulsive, and leads to an improperly superstitious view of the necessity to baptize infants. And the close bonding of sexuality with guilt has more to do with Augustine's past, and the complex of problems accompanying his conversion, than with the positive sexuality of the Bible.

The City of God

The fall of Rome in 410 was a crisis for Christians. Emperors had accepted the assurance of the Church that if God were honoured, their Empire would be secure. The Church had sanctified the notion of 'eternal Rome' by associating it with the chief apostles, Paul and Peter. Even if its military importance had diminished, the city of Rome could not fall and be plundered without minds being disturbed (see Jerome, *Ep.* 127.11–12 [*CCC* 201]). Augustine took up his pen to rebut the charge that Rome had fallen because of Christianity, and his massive *The City of God* appeared in instalments from 412 to 426. The first ten books are a destructive critique of Roman society and religion. The remaining eleven books analyse the present condition of the world. This is seen as one more stage in an agelong conflict between the divine city and the earthly city (samples in *CCC* 228–9).

The two cities are not to be identified as the physical and the spiritual realms, though the terminology might suggest it. Nor are they Church and State simply. Rather they are principles of human society: Augustine finally writes of them as that wherein reigns the love of God to contempt of self, and that wherein reigns the love of self to the contempt of God. In a sense they are Platonic ideas, with imperfect visible manifestations. The earthly city is represented by all the evil societies of the past: Scripture is full of them, Egypt, Babylon, Nineveh, Tyre, Jerusalem in some of its guises, and Rome – each of these is the earthly city, but none complete. The heavenly Jerusalem of Psalm 87.2–3, Gal. 4.26, Heb. 12.22 and Rev. 21 has also its earthly manifestations, and one of them is the Catholic Church. But even the outward Church is infected with sin, and this leads Augustine to his idea of an invisible true Church not identical with the visible Church, consisting only of the elect; this idea has been taken up in Protestantism.

In these terms the collapse of the Roman Empire is not the end of the world, even though Augustine respected the Empire and used its powers for ecclesiastical ends. Apart from the justice exercised within it, the Empire was no better than organized brigandage. But there was an end ahead, when the kingdom of this world would become the Kingdom of God. Augustine's work may appear too vast and rambling, or to resemble journalism rather than systematic theology. He certainly manages to work into his thesis not only apologetic, but fundamental philosophy both of humanity and of history, and as usual provides immense material for others to use, imitate and criticize. But he does achieve a vision which carried the Church through the next great crisis of its history. Having won the Roman Empire, it had to find a way of surviving its collapse. He directed people to a city which could not be shaken, when Rome fell.

20

CYRIL, NESTORIUS, AND THE
COUNCIL OF EPHESUS

Cyril and the rise of Nestorius

Cyril became Bishop of Alexandria in 412, succeeding his uncle Theophilus. He had probably been trained in Theophilus' household, and certainly attended him at the Synod of the Oak in 403, which found John Chrysostom guilty. He brought to his episcopal throne an experience of higher imperial and ecclesiastical politics which made him a formidable enemy. He showed this at the start of his episcopate, when he held on in the face of opposition from a rival episcopal candidate and the imperial government, and riots in the streets. A number of other disorders followed, as Cyril had schismatic churches suppressed and Jews expelled. He was blamed when people claiming to support him were involved in various riots, and in 415 lynched the philosopher Hypatia. But Cyril established himself, and for much of his long reign (till his death in 444) knew how to secure his base of domestic authority. His concerns were not, however, purely practical. He produced a steady stream of writing, including biblical commentaries, *Dialogues on the Trinity*, and an annual festal letter announcing the date of the next Easter and setting out his views on important contemporary issues. Before 428 he had at least begun a great work of apologetic, *Against Julian*, in which the arguments of the apostate Emperor are systematically refuted. He had inherited a longstanding, intellectually rich Christian tradition, in which Athanasius played a significant part; his confidence in attacking all its rivals, Jews, Pagans and heretics, was unbounded.

In 428 a new bishop was appointed to Constantinople, Nestorius, a monk of Antioch. Like John Chrysostom, now reinstated in official recognition even by Cyril, Nestorius was an ardent monk and a brilliant speaker. Honoured for his monastic life, and urgent in preaching serious religion (see the sermon on Heb. 3.1, quoted *CCC* 290-1), he came to see with even less experience of public affairs than John had, and with rather sharper theological convictions. He was apt to find heresy or deceit in others, and thus to offend honest souls, embarrass his friends, and give ammunition to his enemies. In his contest with Cyril he started with the considerable advantages of the episcopate in the capital and the Emperor's clear favour; Cyril defeated him by experience, diplomacy, and an unscrupulous determination.

From the start Nestorius attacked heresy. 'Give me the earth purged of heresy', he said in his first sermon to the Emperor, 'and I will give you heaven as recompense. Assist me in destroying heretics, and I will assist you in vanquishing the Persians', and he was nicknamed 'Firebrand' after an Arian church building which he was seizing caught fire (Socrates, *HE* 7.29 [*CCC* 287–8]). That he attacked Arians is interesting. While condemned for making Christ a mere man, Nestorius always saw himself as the defender of the deity of Christ against its Arian detractors and Apollinarian corrupters. He supported one of his clergy in criticizing the use of the title *Theotokos* to honour the Blessed Virgin Mary, and himself publicly rebuked its use by a distinguished preacher in Constantinople, one Proclus, who had been his rival in the election and later became bishop there. This began his downfall.

Theotokos

The Greek word *theotokos* literally means 'Godbearing'; not quite the same as 'Mother of God', but very nearly. Nestorius had been trained by the greatest of the Antiochene biblical theologians, Theodore of Mopsuestia, and it was from him that he had learned the objections to this title. It might suit the growing cult of Mary to be able to address her so, but it was not technically correct. The one born of Mary, said Theodore, was Christ, who was both God and Man. Mary was thus accurately called 'Christbearer' (Gk *christotokos*). If the title 'Godbearer' was used, it must be balanced with 'Manbearer' (Gk *anthropotokos*); or else she might be honoured as 'Godreceiver' (Gk *theodochos*), since the Word enfleshed dwelt in her. Theodore had in mind chiefly the peril of the Arian argument: the sort of God who suffers birth and death cannot be of the same order of being (substance) as the transcendent Father, but is a distinct kind of generated being; so if you simply call Mary 'Godbearer', you imply that his godhead is variable, inferior to the Father, not strictly speaking God at all.

One must attribute every aspect of the human weakness of the Word to the man Christ Jesus, who could be properly referred to as a man, 'the man assumed' by 'the Word assuming'; in other words, the divine Word takes to himself a complete human being, and the sufferings of Christ do not strictly speaking affect the Word himself.

The same concern led Nestorius to condemn the term *Theotokos*, but at first without the saving qualifications or positive features of Theodore's discussion. The result was that Nestorius was seen as making Christ a mere man, as Paul of Samosata and the older adoptionists were held to have done. Better informed persons noted that *Theotokos* had been used in the past by respectable writers of various opinions (Socrates, *HE* 7.32 [*CCC* 288–90]). If Socrates mentioned only Origen and Eusebius of Caesarea, he might have added Gregory of Nazianzus, who had used it against Apollinaris (*Letter* 101 to Cledonius [*CCC* 89]). Gregory seems to have thought that it entailed that Christ was 'at once divinely and humanly formed in her (divinely, because without intervention of a man, humanly, because in accordance with the laws of gestation)'. That interpretation was not far from the Christology which both Theodore and Nestorius attempted to defend. But the circumstances and sharpness of Nestorius' campaign made him easy to misrepresent; some eminent scholars to this day hold that the popular sense was right, and the Nestorian Christ no more than an inspired man, so far personally distinct from the divine Word that he cannot be called God at all.

Nestorius had need of friends, and had them in the Emperor and the Antiochene bishops. But he offended others. Like John before him, he offended princesses by preaching against luxury. He conducted his campaign against heresy in areas well within the political sphere of influence of Constantinople, but transgressing traditional lines of independent church jurisdiction. Thrace and Asia knew no rights of the civil foundation of Constantinople like those which made Italy depend on Rome or Egypt on Alexandria. More seriously, he took up the cases of persons condemned by Cyril of Alexandria for various crimes, acting as if he had appellate jurisdiction superior to Alexandria, and inflaming the old wound of rivalry between the traditional ecclesiastical primacy of Alexandria and the claims of the new Christian capital. And this coincided with the appeal to Cyril of the defenders of *Theotokos* in

Constantinople. Cyril could not avoid seeing his own position as under threat, since the word was known and loved already in his own provinces, and it fitted the traditional Alexandrian Christology. He might find himself subverted by the Emperor's bishop both for tyranny and for heresy, rather as Athanasius had been. Cyril became very active. He wrote to his local monks to justify *Theotokos* from Scripture, and he wrote letters to the Emperor and various influential persons at the court, including the royal princesses. He wrote also to Nestorius, first briefly, then at greater length to expound the truth of God in Christ. This second letter of Cyril to Nestorius (*Ep.* 4 [*CCC* 295–8]), sent early in 430, is one of the most important christological documents of the early Church.

Cyril's Second Letter to Nestorius

Cyril's *Second Letter to Nestorius* represents his moderate, well-thought-out position. It well illustrates not only the basis of the current conflict, but Cyril's fundamental way of thinking. He asks Nestorius to avoid offending the flock with error, and to base his teaching on the Creed of Nicaea 325. That speaks of the Only-begotten Son, true God from true God, who 'came down, was incarnate, and was made man, suffered, rose again the third day, and ascended into heaven'. This means, not that the Word changed, or was transformed into a human being, but that 'the Word, having in an ineffable and inconceivable manner personally united to himself flesh animated with a living soul, became man and is called Son of Man'. So the union is indescribable, but personal (or hypostatic; Gk *kath' hypostasin*); he means that the humanity of Jesus Christ belongs to the person of the Word, and is not another person distinct from or alongside him. Apollinarianism is ostensibly excluded, since the humanity is complete, flesh with soul. All the features of a man are there, an entire manhood; but there is not an individual human person, since the Person is divine. Above all, the Creed itself is seen as presenting a heavenly Person who remains identically the same in his incarnation. The conditions of the union are then spelled out. 'Not of mere will or favour', reacting to a strong feature of Antiochene Christology: Theodore had held that the union of God and Man in Christ was 'voluntary', represented by the divine 'favour' or 'good pleasure'

(Gk *eudokia*), like that bestowed on the saints, but specially applying to the Son, as announced at the baptism and trans-figuration of Christ. So God becomes man freely, and not by essence or activity, and Man serves God freely, sustained and directed by the divine indwelling, but not puppet-like preserved from fallibility by the divine core of his personality (see Theodore, *On the incarnation* 7 [*CCC* 291–5]). Cyril rejects such a voluntary union as intolerable. All that Christ is and does has God the Word as its subject: the conception is his, the birth is his, the passion, death and resurrection are his, though in his fleshly capacity; they do not impair his divine nature. He does not have a 'voluntary' association with his body, any more than any man does; it is his own. Again, Nestorius made much of the 'outward appearance' or 'role' of the God–Man, expressed by the Greek *prosopon*, and this is repudiated, 'nor again as if by the assumption of a mere role' (*CCC* 296 mistranslates 'by the simple assumption to himself of a human person'). There is a 'true unity', and only one 'Christ and Son'. Since the natures are diverse, it is miraculous and inexplicable, 'unutterable and unspeakable'. But the selfsame Jesus Christ exists first as begotten before all worlds from the Father, and as man is born of the Virgin: on this account the Fathers had called Mary *Theotokos*. The letter also discusses the passion, death and resurrection of Christ, which are attributed to the Word in his incarnate state, because it is his body, his flesh, which are injured and raised; as Word he remains invulnerable and immortal.

This *Second Letter to Nestorius* was to become one of the documents annexed to the Chalcedonian Formula, and thus a credal document of the principal churches to this day. A copy was immediately despatched to Caelestine, the Bishop of Rome, together with a Latin version; Caelestine had also received some specimens of Nestorius' preaching (possibly not entirely authentic). He was already irritated with Nestorius. Not only had Nestorius given hospitality to Pelagian refugee bishops expelled from their dioceses in the West; he had sent Caelestine a high-handed letter demanding to know why they were excommunicate. After a careful scrutiny of Cyril's letter in a synod, Caelestine sent back just the sort of reply which Cyril wanted. Cyril was to initiate action to get Nestorius to recant or be faced with excommunication: he was to have only ten days from the receipt of Cyril's letter, an unrealistic deadline which Cyril was too sensible to try to implement. Meanwhile Nestorius replied to Cyril's second letter in terms which were to prove fateful for them both (*CCC* 298–300).

Nestorius greets Cyril politely but superciliously, and proceeds to rebuke him for misinterpreting the Creed of Nicaea. With characteristic rashness, Nestorius seems to have worked with a copy which diverged slightly from N (the original) in the direction of C (the version of Constantinople 381; see Chapter 16). But it is the interpretation which is strikingly different from Cyril's, and characteristic of the Antiochene Christology. The Fathers, he says, begin their account of Christ by using the titles common to the divine and human natures: Lord, Jesus, Christ, Son, Only-begotten. It is on this basis that they proceeded to give an account of his incarnation and becoming man, his passion and other human experiences. So they prevent any misunderstanding that the visible, human events might be attributed to his deity, and his godhead be thought to suffer or die. Scripture texts from Phil. 2 and John 2 enforce the point: in the form of God he is superior to human things, in the form of a servant he goes to the cross; as divine Word he says, 'Destroy this body and in three days I will raise it up', not, 'Destroy my godhead and in three days it will rise.' These arguments are typical of the Antiochene method: first the One Christ, then the divine nature and the human nature which both operate in him. Things which Christ does and says on earth sometimes reveal one nature, sometimes the other, sometimes both; both operate in him fully and freely. We shall meet this Antiochene method again in the *Formula of Reunion* agreed in 433, and in the Chalcedonian Formula itself. Now it was pressed against Cyril with a clear note of warning: As in 2 Sam. 3.1 the house of David grew stronger and stronger, and the house of Saul grew weaker and weaker, so matters were prospering in the court and Church.

Cyril's Third Letter to Nestorius

The Emperor Theodosius II now took a hand, and in November 430 summoned Cyril to a council in Ephesus at Pentecost 431. Viewed from Constantinople, it was Cyril who was to be on trial. But he was not cowed. He redoubled his efforts, and composed the letter that was to turn defence into attack, his third to Nestorius

(*Ep.* 18 [*CCC* 301–9]). This was to carry out Caelestine's commission by forcing him to either retract or be deposed. It condemned the characteristic features of Antiochene Christology in uncompromising terms, and was intended to humiliate, not reconcile. He states his duty not to ignore damage done to the Church by false teaching, the support of the Roman synod, and the scandal that Nestorius has deposed upholders of the truth. Then comes a momentous step: it is not enough for Nestorius to assent to the Creed of Nicaea; he must abjure his false interpretation of it. That means that Cyril is asking for another doctrinal test besides the Creed of Nicaea, something which the Church generally was very reluctant to allow. It had happened before. The Eastern churches had repeatedly tried to enshrine a supplement or alternative. Even Athanasius, while repudiating the extreme document from Sardica, had required an affirmation about the Holy Spirit at Alexandria in 362; and the Council of Constantinople had by its anathemas and apparently by its Creed achieved a similar goal, though its decisions were not all recognized by the Alexandrians. But the theoretical position remained, and would be reasserted in Canon 7 of Ephesus in 431, that the Creed of Nicaea alone should be used to define orthodoxy. Cyril proceeds, after his theological statements, to sum up his points in twelve anathemas, renunciations of doctrines to which Nestorius must subscribe (*CCC* 306–8).

All the *Twelve Anathemas* express sharply the Alexandrian position, and appear to leave no room for the characteristic Antiochene approach, even though it should be said that Cyril makes them at once offensive and defensible. The first is against those who deny Emmanuel to be true God: even in his humanity the Lord is personally divine, and thus the Virgin is *Theotokos*. The second insists, 'that the Word which is of God has been personally united (Gk *kath' hypostasin henomenon*) to flesh, and is one Christ with his own flesh', setting out the usual Alexandrian starting-point, the heavenly Word as the subject of the human flesh. The third denies division after the union, and might be taken to deny any distinction, since it states a 'union of natures' (Gk *henosis physike*). Cyril elsewhere acknowledges a continuing distinction, but here he exposes himself to the later interpretation of Eutyches, 'after the union, one nature'; he could also be read as meaning that the union was 'natural' in the sense that it was not voluntary, but was part of the 'nature' of the divine Word.

The fourth anathema caused particular offence, since it seemed to forbid a familiar and nearly universal method of dealing with Scripture: the lowly things done and said by Christ (birth, growth, fatigue, sorrow, ignorance, death) are attributed to his human nature, while the glorious things (pre-existence, feeding multitudes, union with the Father, omniscience, raising himself) belong to his godhead. From Tertullian to Ambrose in the West, from Origen to Gregory of Nazianzus in the East, this method had precedents. It was very familiar among Antiochenes, notably John Chrysostom, and was a hall-mark of Nestorius' recent letter to Cyril. It enabled the lowly words to be taken seriously. From a modern perspective the idea of a Christ who switches from one capacity to another, speaking at one moment as God and another as Man, seems an unhelpful way of understanding the mystery of his person. Even so, it might be thought one degree better than Cyril's treatment of the same passages. Cyril implies and sometimes states that, if Christ says that he does not know the time of the end, it is a pretence, devised by the Word to show the apostles how humans should behave. For Cyril, as for Apollinaris, the Word restrains his powers voluntarily to the measures of humanity; even in his suffering he remains impassible. As he says in this letter (8), 'To one person must be attributed all the expressions used in the Gospels, the one incarnate *hypostasis* of the Word.' So the anathema runs, 'If anyone distributes to two persons (*prosopa*) or subsistences (*hypostases*) the expressions used in the Gospels and Epistles, or used of Christ by the saints, or by him of himself, attributing some to a man conceived of separately, apart from the Word which is of God, and attributing others, as befitting God, exclusively to the Word which is of God the Father, let him be anathema.' This seems to condemn the whole tradition, putting Cyril as far wrong as Nestorius in rejecting the traditional piety of *Theotokos*; even if he could defend it as directed only at those who attribute the words to the natures 'separately' or 'exclusively', and claim that the texts of humiliation belong to the Word *as incarnate*, the immediate damage was done.

Other anathemas reject 'conjunction' and other Antiochene theological ideas and arguments, and conclude with a statement about the passion: 'If anyone does not confess that the Word of God suffered in the flesh, and was crucified in the flesh, and tasted death in the flesh, and became the firstborn from the dead,

even as he is both Life and Lifegiving as God, let him be anathema.'
That summarizes the whole Cyrilline understanding of salvation
through Christ's death. In his letter, he insists that the Word
remained unchanged 'impassibly appropriating and making his
own the sufferings of his own flesh'. The theme is characteristic
Alexandrian thought, from Athanasius onward. The sharpness of
the anathema is injudicious.

Nestorius condemned

Nestorius saw to it that these shocking anathemas were read by
all his friends, chiefly John of Antioch and his dependent bishops.
They were duly shocked. But they failed to reach Ephesus on time,
as did the Roman delegates. The Emperor's deputy tried to defer
proceedings, but Cyril had the support of numerous monks
imported from Egypt, who terrorized opponents, and of Bishop
Memnon of Ephesus, and he opened the council. A deputation
was sent to fetch Nestorius with a dossier of charges, including
the third letter and its anathemas. The door was not opened.
Nestorius was judged to be in contempt, and declared deposed.
The second more moderate letter of Cyril was formally read and
approved, and thus became a document of the ecumenical faith. A
fortnight later the Antiochene party arrived, and held a smaller
council, which in turn condemned and deposed Cyril and Memnon
for their irregular proceedings (*CCC* 309). The Romans arrived and
backed Cyril, whose council reassembled and condemned Nestorius'
supporters; in addition various canons were passed, which among
other things condemned Pelagianism, and forbade the use of any
creed but the Nicene for doctrinal purposes (*CCC* 310-12). The
government, frustrated and puzzled by the deadlock, after six
weeks produced an imperial letter rebuking the bishops, and
upholding the depositions of Nestorius, Cyril and Memnon. There
then began a period of negotiations, leading to a settlement in 433.

Nestorius himself seems to have cracked under the strain, or
simply lacked the nerve and resources to stand his ground or
negotiate a compromise. He withdrew to Antioch, and ultimately
to the Egyptian desert, where among other things he wrote a self-
defence, known by its later disguise-title, *The book of Heracleides*
(brief polemical extract in *CCC* 312-13). The discovery of this
book in modern times has led to a renewed interest in and

appreciation of Nestorius' thought. With few exceptions, scholars this century, Roman Catholic, Protestant and in some cases Orthodox, acknowledge that he was orthodox in his thinking by the standards of Chalcedon, and not a 'Nestorian' in the conventional sense: he clearly did not hold that the man Jesus and the divine Word were two distinct persons, 'adding a fourth to the blessed Trinity', or that Christ was a 'mere man'. His fundamental christological concept is the *prosopon* of unity, in which the two natures, essences, concrete realities of God and man were joined. He invents or adapts a philosophical vocabulary, in which each nature (*physis*) or essence (*ousia*) exists in its own individual reality (*hypostasis*), but whereas other beings each have their own outward manifestation (*prosopon*), in Christ the two natures have only one; rather as body and soul in a human being have only one outward manifestation. Within the logic of this 'prosopic union' the divine Word generates and indwells the one Person of the man Christ Jesus, whose birth, growth and sufferings are thus salvific. But allowing that Nestorius thought in a way compatible with the orthodoxy of his day and later is one thing; that he expressed the complications of his logic obscurely and at times abrasively is another. He remains controversial: some of those modern writers who see him as orthodox, still prefer Cyril's approach to Christology.

The Formula of Reunion

Nestorius was replaced by Maximian, a candidate acceptable to the Alexandrian. Cyril and Memnon went back to their dioceses, not waiting for the imperial permission which followed them. Cyril put much effort, enormous sums of money, and some of his theological reputation into a reconciliation. The basis of the reconciliation between Cyril and John, the Bishop of Antioch, was the *Formula of Reunion*. This was a document which the Antiochene group at Ephesus had submitted to the Emperor, and was spelled out and accepted with a slight adjustment and his own interpretation by Cyril in 433, in a letter to John of Antioch (Cyril, *Ep.* 39 [CCC 313–17]). This letter was quoted in the Chalcedonian Formula, and has authority where that Formula is accepted. In the *Formula of Reunion* the Antiochenes first state their Christology in characteristic style: one Lord Jesus Christ, perfect (i.e. complete) God and perfect Man; begotten of his Father before the worlds as touching his Godhead, born of the Virgin Mary as touching his manhood; consubstantial with his Father in Godhead, and with us in his manhood. And 'of these two natures a union has been made. For this cause we confess one Christ, one Son, one Lord.' The movement is thus what Nestorius proposed, and what Chalcedon would follow: one person, understood in two distinct natures which combine in the one Christ. It is not Cyril's one heavenly Christ, with his flesh. But nevertheless they justify the use of *Theotokos* on the basis of 'this unconfused union' in the first of two conclusions drawn. The other conclusion is about the exegesis of New Testament texts: 'We are aware that theologians understand some as common, as relating to one Person; others they distinguish, as relating to two natures, explaining those that befit the divine nature according to the Godhead of Christ, and those of humble sort according to his manhood.' The main Antiochene body had not rejected *Theotokos* in the first place, so this irenic statement involved no serious concessions. For Cyril it was different.

Cyril possessed and used texts written by Apollinaris, but circulating under other more respectable names such as Julius of Rome and Athanasius. From these he had learned the Apollinarian formula, 'One incarnate nature of the divine Word' (Gk *mia physis tou theou logou sesarkomene*), and this undoubtedly represented his own view of incarnation: the unity of Christ rested in the divine Word who added flesh (that is a complete humanity with rational soul) to his own being. In that sense the union was 'natural' or 'hypostatic'. The Greek *physis*, in addition to the meaning of 'nature' which we understand in 'human nature', can also represent a concrete individual, as we might say 'being' in 'a human being'. If sometimes, as in his *Second Letter to Nestorius*, Cyril allowed himself to talk of the human nature, and even of its diversity from the divine nature in the union, still he does so in order to assert that the divine Word is the subject of the whole operation. In accepting the *Formula of Reunion* he subscribes to something which adopts the Antiochene pattern, the one Christ who is both God and Man; and with it, he accepts the language of 'two natures', and allows the biblical texts to be distributed, at least in some cases, between them, thus retreating from the ostensible position of Anathema 4. His supportive letter in no way softens these developments; he is more concerned to make it clear that this is not an addition to the Creed of Nicaea (which like the *Twelve Anathemas* it manifestly is), and that he is not guilty of the allegations that he taught that Christ's body came down out of heaven, or of confusing the Word and the Flesh.

Once peace was made between Alexandria and Antioch, the settlement was ratified by Maximian at Constantinople and by Sixtus III, who had succeeded Caelestine at Rome. But both John at Antioch and Cyril had dissident supporters. Some Nestorian loyalists withdrew from communion, and from their base in eastern Syria began the remarkable movement which led to a very widespread Nestorian Church, powerful in Persia and with settlements all over Asia until it was largely destroyed by Islam. Within the Empire John's best theologian, Theodoret of Cyrus (Cyrrhus), continued to campaign against the heretic Cyril, and like Ibas at Edessa was not reconciled till Chalcedon in 451. Cyril himself had to deal with those who said he had yielded to Nestorianism in conceding 'two natures' and not insisting upon 'one nature of the divine Word enfleshed'. In letters to his objectors Cyril defended himself. In a long letter to Acacius of Melitene he explains that the Formulary did not divide Christ as Nestorius had done, that the Antiochenes had denounced Nestorius and Nestorianism, and had asserted the *Theotokos*, and that he had not (as his Antiochene critics had demanded) withdrawn anything of what he had previously written. He thus implied, with some justification, that his past writings had allowed the two-natures formulation while asserting the one nature and the natural or hypostatic union. The careful and precise expression of his views here, as in the *Second Letter to Nestorius*, leaves little doubt that, given an intellectual and ecclesiastical climate free from the pressure to reduce Nestorius and Constantinople and to save his own position, Cyril could understand and come to terms with the Antiochene tradition. But characteristically at the same time he began a campaign to blacken the memory of theological heroes of Antioch, Diodore of Tarsus and Theodore of Mopsuestia, a campaign which would finally succeed in Justinian's Council of Constantinople of 553. For the time being it succeeded only in provoking the Antiochenes, though they did not break communion; but it did appease the dissidents on his own side. After his death open war was to break out anew.

21

EUTYCHES, LEO AND THE
COUNCIL OF CHALCEDON

New personalities

The death of Cyril in 444 brought a new faction to power in Alexandria. Dioscorus (Dioscuros) succeeded him, sustained by letters from leading bishops offering congratulations and advice. Even Theodoret seems to have hoped Dioscorus would share his own animosity to Cyril (*Ep.* 180 [*CCC* 319–21]). But though the new Bishop of Alexandria quarrelled with Cyril's family, he was to depart from his policy in a direction quite unfavourable to the Antiochenes. He campaigned to suppress 'Nestorianism', and in the process adopted a position represented by Cyril's earlier and sharper views: 'After the union, one.'

But first we must set the scene. Nestorius' successors at Constantinople had been disposed to a Cyrilline theology, especially Proclus (434–46). The Emperor was still the weak Theodosius II (408–50), now under the thumb of the eunuch Chrysaphius, behind whom in turn lay the influence of Eutyches, a venerable archimandrite (abbot) with deep anti-Nestorian prejudices. He was to cause the downfall of the new Bishop of Constantinople, Flavian (446–9), who succeeded Proclus. Antioch had a vacillating bishop Domnus (441–9), who leaned heavily on Theodoret. But the position of Rome was to be decisive.

Leo

Rome had a powerful bishop in Leo I (440–61), justly called 'the Great', who elevated the papacy both in theory and in practice to something like that awesome eminence which it has since enjoyed. The Western Empire was being progressively overrun by northern barbarians. Some of these were heathen, more were Gothic 'Arian' Christians, whose Christianity went back to the evangelistic policies of Eusebius of Nicomedia under Constantius II, when at the end of his life he had occupied the see of Constantinople. The

Gothic kingdoms stretched through the provinces of Gaul and Spain; North Africa fell to the Vandals between 429 and 439; Britain was lost. There was room for a strong pope, and it is no surprise that in 451 or 452 Leo himself negotiated with Attila the Hun, and is credited with diverting him from an attack on Rome. But before that other things had happened.

In Gaul, worldliness and feuding marred the life of the churches, while new monastically-based disciplines spread among the more serious. Hilary of Arles took it upon himself to carry out a campaign of reform, calling councils, deposing and replacing bishops, and carrying out other super-episcopal functions. Whether he knew that traditionally the bishop of Rome was consulted about Gallic matters, or was in close enough communication with Italy to do so, we cannot be sure. It certainly appears that some citizens refused to yield to Hilary's pressure; they had appealed to Rome, alleging that he was using force to impose unwanted clergy. In the event Leo got from the Western Emperor Valentinian III (425–55) a remarkable *Constitutio* (quoted in Leo, *Ep.* 11 [*CCC* 328–9]). This asserted that it was improper for any to go against the authority of the Roman see, 'inasmuch as the primacy of the apostolic see is assured by the merit of St Peter, prince of the episcopal order, by the rank of the city of Rome, and also by the authority of a sacred synod'. Rome's authority is thus based both on the primacy of Peter and on its civil rank. The 'sacred synod' may mean Nicaea, or Sardica, whose canons were in the West confused with Nicaea. But everywhere, 'we decree by this perpetual edict that it shall not be lawful for the bishops of Gaul or of the other provinces, contrary to ancient custom, to do aught without the authority of the venerable Pope of the Eternal City; and whatever the authority of the apostolic see has enacted, or may hereafter enact, shall be the law for all.' Hilary was confined to his see, which he was allowed to retain by grace and favour. But that was insignificant beside what Leo had achieved for the papacy.

In addition to such practical and imperial developments, Leo was to elaborate, especially in sermons on his own anniversaries and on the feasts of St Peter (or Peter and Paul), the theory that Peter had not only gone to Rome, the centre of a divinely-ordained empire, as primate of the apostles, but had bequeathed his specific powers to his episcopal successors there. So in Leo, as in every other bishop of Rome, Peter spoke again; and the bishop of Rome enjoyed the same primacy among other bishops as Peter had among the apostles. Previous bishops might have held parts of this theory; none had put it together so compellingly, or in such sonorous rhetoric. The Eastern churches were to feel the effect of Leo's expectations in the events that Dioscorus provoked, and Dioscorus himself would feel the weight.

Theodoret

In the Antiochene sphere of influence the government and Dioscorus both began efforts to check the advance of Theodoret's policies, by which supporters of Cyril were being harassed and removed. Ibas, Bishop of Edessa on the eastern frontier, had conducted a strenuous campaign against Cyril's theology ever since he succeeded the well-loved Cyrilline, Rabbula, in 435. Now he was charged with blasphemy, and though acquitted in 449, had constant riotous complaints against him in his city. Irenaeus, Bishop of Tyre, an old enemy of Cyril promoted by Domnus of Antioch, was deposed and replaced, to the humiliation of Domnus. Theodoret was threatened by complaints to Dioscoros against his doctrinal preaching, and he found it necessary to defend himself in 447 (letter in *CCC* 333-4). The next year he was inhibited by the government from conducting councils, and was confined to his diocese.

This controversy drew from him a neglected masterpiece of witty but scholarly christological polemic called *Eranistes* or 'Collector', because the Cyrilline opponent gathers all kinds of doctrinal rubbish. Theodoret's argument is in three dialogues: *Immutable* (Gk *atreptos*), in which 'Orthodoxos' proves to 'Eranistes' that the divine Word does not change in becoming flesh, but takes human nature upon him; *Unconfused* (Gk *asynchytos*), in which he shows that the two natures of Christ remain distinct; and *Impassible* (Gk *apathes*), where he argues that the godhead of Christ remains unaffected by his suffering and death. All these principles are negated by the sharply Cyrilline doctrines of his opponent, which are like those to emerge in the controversy with Eutyches. Two of the three principles would appear at a crucial place in the Chalcedonian formula. To his logical and biblical arguments Theodoret adds strings of patristic quotations, many of them otherwise unknown to us, but all from writers he thought would be congenial to his adversary; it is interesting to find him able to quote Apollinaris in his support. But Theodoret needed more than good arguments.

Eutyches

The case of Eutyches brought matters to a head. He was accused of heresy before Bishop Flavian of Constantinople by the Bishop of Dorylaeum, one Eusebius, who as a lay scholar had been active in the proceedings against Nestorius himself. Neither could be seriously considered a Nestorian sympathizer; but they may have begun to grow alarmed at the increasing influence of the Alexandrian party both theologically and ecclesiastically. The precise doctrines of Eutyches are obscure, but certain features stand out. He quotes Cyril's (Apollinarian) formula, 'One nature of the divine word', but without the word 'incarnate'. Two natures he acknowledged before the union, but one after. The flesh of Christ was not consubstantial with ours, but with God the Word. The last point set him at variance with the *Formula of Reunion*; but that document he repudiated, on the ground that only the Creed of Nicaea could stand. This would unsettle what had been painfully achieved after Ephesus, and was calculated to offend Rome, as it did. He was held (as Apollinaris had been) to believe that Christ brought his humanity with him from heaven, but that is not clear.

The 'Home Synod' met and in November 448 deposed him. Eutyches (who had previous connections there) appealed to Leo at Rome, as well as to the bishops of Alexandria and Jerusalem. Flavian also reported his troubles to Leo, who was to rebuke him for taking so long to do it. The emperor, Theodosius II, still advised by Chrysaphius, and angered by reports of troubles at Edessa which were blamed on the 'Nestorian' Ibas, commanded a council of bishops to meet at Ephesus on 1 August 449 to review the case of Eutyches. Ibas had been deposed, Theodoret was not to attend. With full imperial support, Dioscuros prepared to repeat the triumph of Cyril. Like Cyril, he would have the support of Memnon of Ephesus and the Asian bishops who resented Constantinople's encroachments, and his own body of monks and helpers. But even with the Emperor behind him, he had one fatal weakness: he had not convinced Leo of Rome.

The Tome *of Leo*

Leo took his time to appreciate the situation. Only when summoned to the council at Ephesus did he finally write. His letter to Flavian is generally known as *The Tome of Leo*; 'tome' (Gk *tomos*) merely means 'book', or in this case 'booklet' (*CCC* 336–44). It is in characteristically beautiful prose and confident judgement. It condemns Eutyches in uncompromising terms. Leo has perused the record of Eutyches' trial, he writes, and judges him 'very rash and extremely ill-informed'. If he could not read the Scriptures, he might at least have observed the universal confession, that is, the Creed (*CCC* 337). Leo then goes on to quote what is plainly the old Roman version of the creed (related to the so-called Apostles' Creed), not the Nicene; that in itself indicates his self-assurance as the heir of the prince of the apostles. The Creed makes it plain by the words, 'born of the Holy Ghost and the Virgin Mary', that he 'took our nature and made it his own'; otherwise he could not overcome our enemies, sin and death. In the following exposition, texts are listed which reveal the human descent of Christ from David and Abraham. In the conception of Jesus, the miracle of Mary's virginity in no way diminishes his fleshly reality: 'The Holy Spirit gave fruitfulness to the Virgin, but the reality of the body was received from her body.'

Leo explicitly states that Eutyches attributes to Christ 'the form of man but . . . not the reality of his mother's body'. The saving effect of the divine action depends on the coming together, by a divine act, of distinct natures:

> The distinctive character of each nature and substance remaining therefore unimpaired, and coming together into one person, humility was assumed by majesty, weakness by power, mortality by eternity; and in order to pay the debt of our condition, an inviolable nature was united to a nature capable of suffering, so that as a remedy suitable to our healing one and the same *Mediator between God and men, the man Jesus Christ*, was capable of death in one nature, and incapable of death in the other. (*CCC* 338–9)

The old doctrine of Irenaeus that Christ fights Adam's battle again as Man, and conquers as God, is applied to the new christological question, and the result is an uncompromising two-nature analysis.

Nestorius read it in his Egyptian retreat and thanked God (*CCC* 349). It follows that the human nature is whole and perfect, 'complete in what belongs to him, complete in what belongs to us', the manhood enhanced, not diminished, by the deity. So the Son of God stooped from invisible, eternal glory to exist visible in time. The union is real: 'Each form, in communion with the other, performs the function that is proper to it: that is, the Word performing what belongs to the Word, and the flesh carrying out what belongs to the flesh. The one sparkles with miracles, the other succumbs to injuries' (*CCC* 340). This plainly distributes the acts and words of Christ between the two natures, and it is followed by a sonorous series of biblical antitheses of exactly the kind which Cyril had appeared once to repudiate:

> The birth of the flesh is a manifestation of human nature, the childbearing of a virgin a token of divine power. The infancy of the babe is shown by its lowly cradle, the greatness of the Most High is declared by the voice of angels . . . To hunger, to thirst, to be weary and to sleep is obviously human; but with five loaves to satisfy five thousand people, and to bestow on the woman of Samaria that living water, a draught of which will cause the drinker to thirst no more . . . is without question divine. (*CCC* 340)

It is a different nature which says, 'I and the Father are one', and which says, 'My Father is greater than I'. Although in Christ God and Man are one Person, yet, 'The source of the shame that is common to both is one thing; the source of the glory that is common to both is another.' Various further scriptural passages follow, conspicuously Matt. 16.13–17, where Peter by divine inspiration identifies the Son of Man as the Son of God. In a last argument (ch. 6) Leo expresses surprise that Eutyches was not rebuked for asserting two natures before the incarnation, and one after; rather it was the other way about (one divine nature before, two when the manhood was taken). Leo proposes that Eutyches should yet have opportunity to repent, and names his own deputies, a bishop, a presbyter, and the able deacon Hilary of Rome, to attend on his behalf. It was a clear and emphatic judgement; but by the time Flavian got it, it was too late to save him.

The Council of Ephesus, 449

Dioscorus arrived in Ephesus and began the Council's work promptly. After the imperial letters of authorization were read, attention was at once turned to the proceedings of the trial of Eutyches at the Home Synod. Flavian and his supporters were not allowed to speak in their own defence. Eutyches himself was examined; he produced various patristic documents in his favour, some later revealed to be inauthentic, and testified that he believed that Christ took flesh from the Virgin. 'Two natures before the union, one afterwards', said Dioscorus, 'is it not what we all believe?' The bishops thought so, and approved the reinstatement of Eutyches. But there was more to follow. Assisted by Cyril's old ally, Juvenal of Jerusalem, Dioscorus deduced from what had been read that the judge of Eutyches, Flavian, and his accuser, Eusebius of Dorylaeum, had broken the decree of Cyril's Council of Ephesus: they had introduced another doctrinal standard different from that of Nicaea. They had unsettled everything, and become a scandal to the churches. They would therefore be deposed, and the Emperors duly notified (see the *Acta* cited in *CCC* 345). This was a frontal attack on the *Formula of Reunion*; but Dioscorus was playing for high stakes, and seemed to have all on his side. Flavian protested; Hilary the Roman deacon cried, '*Contradicitur*' (meaning, 'No!'), and fled. Bishops who two years later were anxious to vote the other way then alleged that Dioscorus used fraud (blank papers to sign) and menaces (armed troops carrying manacles); overawed the bishops surely were, even the Antiochene group. They voted almost unanimously in favour, and Dioscorus had his triumph. One nature had overthrown two, Alexandria had overcome Antioch for possession of Constantinople. Theodoret, Domnus and Ibas were all deposed, and the Twelve Anathemas of Cyril canonized. Flavian never recovered from the manhandling he received, and died the next winter in exile.

Meanwhile the defeated parties began to rally. Flavian wrote to Leo, appealing to him to intervene, both to rescue true doctrine and to restore legality (*CCC* 345–7). He claimed that the decisions were taken by bishops under duress, and that the majority still supported him, declared Eutyches an open Apollinarian, and alleged that when he appealed to 'the throne of the apostolic see of Peter, the prince of the apostles, and to the holy council in general which meets under your Holiness', soldiers tried to arrest him and he escaped in the tumult. All this was calculated to win Leo's support, though perhaps exaggerated. Theodoret also appealed to Leo (*CCC* 347–9). He gives a dramatic picture of his long career as pastor and theologian, converting and reconciling heretics, writing books publicly available which make his soundness clear. He will now abide by the judgement of the apostolic see, whichever way that goes. Words like these struck the right note for Leo, who saw his own view of his office acknowledged by the appeals. He had already given his judgement in his letter to Flavian, which had been ignored at Ephesus, and was unknown to the bishops there. He now began to write letters to those in the East who might be able to reverse the decision. He asked the Emperor for another council, and the emperor's sister Pulcheria for help in achieving it. He gave the second Council of Ephesus the name by which it is commonly known, the *Latrocinium* (literally 'Robbery' or 'Gang of brigands'; in English known as 'the Robber Council'). He negotiated with Anatolius, a creature of Dioscorus appointed to replace Flavian in Constantinople. Some of his letters were probably intercepted by Chrysaphius' agents. But the settlement was comprehensive and popular in the churches, as well as having full imperial support; it was nevertheless to collapse with a change of emperors.

The Council of Chalcedon, 451

On 28 July 450 Theodosius II was thrown from his horse and died. Pulcheria his sister took over the government, rapidly marrying Marcian, a distinguished soldier. Chrysaphius was put to death, Eutyches exiled, Flavian's bones honourably restored. Leo welcomed the new trend, but reversed his policy on a council; his *Tome* and the *Second Letter* of Cyril could resolve the matter. But the Emperor Marcian was determined to keep control, and called a general council for Nicaea; it finally met at Chalcedon. It was a mammoth council. Fifteen sessions were held from 8 October to 10 November 451. About 600 bishops appear to have been present at times; the Definition was signed by 452.

Dioscorus, who had gone so far as to excommunicate Leo on the eve of the Council, was put on trial for his conduct at Ephesus. The record of the proceedings alienated some of those who heard;

others, including former close allies like Juvenal of Jerusalem, saw the way the wind was blowing and forsook him (perhaps Juvenal was concerned with the status of Jerusalem). Dioscorus was finally left with only his Egyptian colleagues. The proceedings of Ephesus 449 were overturned, the condemnation of Eutyches upheld. Dioscorus was deposed for his unlawful action at the Council. Leo's *Tome* was read and approved, with some sharp questioning of those features which emphasized the distinct functioning of two natures in the one Christ (see above pp. 227–8). These misgivings were adroitly overcome by Theodoret, who had been restored on the condition that he disowned Nestorius. He found sentences from Cyril's more moderate writings, and especially the *Second Letter to Nestorius*, which seemed to agree precisely with each of the controverted passages of Leo.

Careful attempts were made to sift and study decisions and canons of past councils, and canon law reviewed and revised (see *CCC* 354–60). The most important canonical decisions however affected the see of Constantinople (*CCC* 361–2). Canon 9 allowed appeals from the decisions of local superior bishops (metropolitans of provinces) to the 'exarch of the diocese', which means the chief bishop of the major administrative division of the Empire (modern ecclesiastical usage has reversed the terms: dioceses were much larger than provinces). But as an alternative, appeal could be made to 'the Throne of the imperial city of Constantinople'; the bishop of that city thus had similar appellate status to Rome. Canon 17 confirmed this. Canon 28 reaffirmed the decision of the Council of 381 that Constantinople, as New Rome, deserved to enjoy equal privileges with old Rome in ecclesiastical affairs as it did in imperial. To this was added a reorganization, so that the imperial dioceses (major divisions) of Pontus, Asia and Thrace, and the barbarians outside the Empire whose churches were related to them, should be subject to the bishop of Constantinople and their metropolitans ordained by him. The see was thus greatly elevated, and the practice of interfering in the affairs of these neighbouring provinces, which had got both John Chrysostom and Nestorius into trouble, was justified. The status of Constantinople had already been the subject of letters between Anatolius and Leo. Leo might have granted some of the package, but when the Council was called his legates were directed to oppose any concession. Rome had not accepted Canon 3 of Constantinople

381, and after consideration Leo now annulled Canon 28 of Chalcedon (*CCC* 365-7): Anatolius was ambitious, and the canon contrary to the decisions of Nicaea (he probably meant the canons of Sardica, which were mistaken for Nicene). It was wrong to relegate the apostolic (Petrine) sees of Antioch and Alexandria to lower status than Constantinople. But the crucial point is the old one: Canon 28 had flagrantly based the claim of Constantinople on its imperial status, 'that the city which was honoured with the sovereignty and senate, and which enjoyed equal privileges with the elder royal Rome, should also be magnified like her in ecclesiastical matters'. The implication that the papacy derived its standing from the imperial character of its city, and not from Christ's appointment of Peter, was not tolerable.

The Chalcedonian Definition

It was in the context of the upgrading of the imperial city that the construction of the *Chalcedonian Definition of the Faith* (or *Chalcedonian Formula*) should be understood (*CCC* 350-4). The *Definition* was needed because the emperors were not content to let Leo's authority suffice. A unanimous christological settlement was desired, and this would be achieved by a formal declaration of faith. For obvious reasons it had to be based on things already agreed, but its method is very important for understanding how doctrine took its classic shape.

First the principle is asserted in section 2 that Jesus Christ passed the whole truth to his disciples, and that the Council is driving away the errors since implanted by the devil. It then goes on to reaffirm the faith proclaimed at Nicaea in 325, Constantinople 381 and Ephesus 431. These councils thus became, from the perspective of Chalcedon, 'ecumenical councils' of authoritative standing. Next, the two creeds, of Nicaea 325 and Constantinople 381, are set out. These had already been produced and discussed at an earlier session, the text of C being produced from some archive in Constantinople unknown to us (see above pp. 167-71). In the *Definition* the texts are adjusted to fit the theory outlined in section 3: C is N, but with some alterations to deal with 'those who impugn the Holy Spirit'. The 150 fathers at Constantinople had made this change, 'not as though they were supplying some omission of their predecessors, but distinctly declaring by written testimony their own understanding concerning the Holy Spirit, against those who were endeavouring to set aside his sovereignty'. Thus Constantinople sets the needed precedent for Chalcedon: no change to the apostolic faith represented at Nicaea, but dealing with new heresies by a further statement. So 'on account of those who attempt to pervert the mystery of the incarnation' (better, 'the economy' or 'the dispensation', Gk *oikonomia*, the regular term for Christ's presence in the flesh on earth), it has accepted 'the synodical letters of the blessed Cyril . . . to Nestorius and to the Orientals'. That means the *Second Letter to Nestorius* and the *Letter to John of Antioch* (CCC 295–7, 313–17), the latter itself embodying the *Formula of Reunion*; these are supposed to deal with the error of Nestorius, and 'for the explanation of the salutary creed' to enquirers. To these is added, 'for the overthrow of the impiety of Eutyches', the *Tome* of Leo, 'since it agrees with the confession of great Peter, and is a pillar of support against all heterodox'. All these documents are thus established as orthodox formulae. Some scholars both ancient and modern suppose Cyril's *Third Letter to Nestorius* to be understood also by the words quoted. If that is correct, the Council was much more Cyrilline than is usually supposed. But the best opinion is probably that the Council ratified that aggressive letter with its anathemas only insofar as it ratified the proceedings of Cyril's Council of Ephesus in 431, and did not intend it to be understood as annexed to its own *Definition*.

In section 4 the Council goes on to state its own position, first by disowning 'double sonship', the error attributed to Nestorius, and four errors rightly or wrongly associated with Eutyches: passible (suffering) godhead, confusion of two natures in Christ, a heavenly substance in the 'form of a servant' which Christ took, and two natures before, one after, the union. There follows a positive creed. This is based on the *Formula of Reunion* with some variations, and particularly with the insertion of a number of phrases from Cyril's *Second Letter to Nestorius* and from Leo's *Tome*. Our Lord Jesus Christ is 'one and the same Son', perfect (that is, complete) in godhead, perfect in manhood, which is itself a rational soul and a body. So the Antiochene principle of the one Christ with two natures is established, against the Alexandrian one divine Word with his flesh. It proceeds to assert that he is consubstantial with the Father in godhead, consubstantial with us in manhood, and that his birth is 'from the Father before all ages as touching his godhead, . . . from the Virgin Mary, the *Theotokos*, as touching his manhood' (there is only one verb in the Greek for his birth, *gennethenta*, though it is rendered 'begotten . . . born' in English). The process is then repeated: 'one and the same Christ, Son, Lord, Only-begotten, to be acknowledged in two natures, without confusion, without change, without division, without separation'. Here some delicate linguistic work was done. The traditional way to express the two natures in Greek was 'from' (or 'of') two natures' (*ek dyo physeon*); Flavian had used it in arguing with Eutyches. But the Romans were suspicious, especially since Dioscorus and Eutyches spoke of 'One from two'. So the continuation of the two natures was expressed in the more puzzling 'acknowledged in two natures' (Gk *en dyo physesin gnorizomenon* – there is no justification for the translation, '*to be* acknowledged . . .'). This might be understood in English as 'recognized as (someone) with two natures'; Greek uses *en* not only for 'in' but for the instrumental 'with'. Four adverbs are then added to 'with two natures'; two are from Theodoret's set: unconfusedly, immutably (Gk *asynchytos, atreptos*), and two are to avoid the imputation of Nestorianism: indivisibly, inseparably (Gk *adiairetos, achoristos*). Finally, in a pastiche from Leo and Cyril, it is made clear that the distinction of the natures is preserved in the union, but each keeps its characteristic features ('property') as they combine in the one person and substance (*prosopon, hypostasis*), not parted into two but one Son, Only-begotten, God, Word, Lord, Jesus Christ. This is to be set up as the only doctrinal standard for all, on pain of deposition for the clergy, and excommunication for others.

The value of the Definition

Even though the Egyptian contingent remained intransigent, and Chalcedon has been rejected to this day by the principal churches of Egypt, Ethiopia, Syria and Armenia in favour of Monophysite ('One-nature') Christology, its achievement was considerable:

> 1. The *Formula of Reunion* is upheld, and with it the principle that Antiochene, Alexandrian and Roman theology should all contribute positively to the understanding of Christ.

2. The error perceived in Eutyches is firmly set aside: his notion that to acknowledge Christ as God entails a humanity different in quality from that of other human beings. His manhood is complete ('perfect') and consubstantial with ours, like us in everything except sin. It is notable that the Monophysite churches mentioned above, when they came to formulate their dogmatic position under the leadership of skilful theologians like Severus of Antioch, anathematized Eutyches. Whatever else they would defend, it could not be any diminution in the human nature of Jesus Christ. This has not been true of popular Christian spirituality, which has often adored him as God, while evading the challenge of his earthiness.

3. At the same time markers are put down to exclude other earlier errors. Particularly Nestorianism is in mind, since division and separation of the natures is excluded, Mary is *Theotokos*, and there is only one Son, who is also God, Word and Lord. But Apollinarian ideas ('reasonable [= rational] soul and a body'; 'without confusion') are excluded, and Arian and Pneumato-machian ideas are excluded by the use and exposition of earlier creeds.

Attempts were made, especially by the Emperor Justinian at the Fifth Ecumenical council in 553, to reconcile the Egyptian and other Monophysites by interpreting Chalcedon in a strongly Cyrilline way, condemning some old Antiochene theology (Theodore, and writings of Theodoret and Ibas against Cyril). This failed, as did a later attempt to reunite on the basis of one Will in Christ (the 'Monothelite heresy'), and the Chalcedonian settlement was fixed in the canon law and theology of the imperial and papal churches of East and West; its principles also remained largely unchallenged throughout the Protestant Reformation.

In modern times the carefully balanced propositions of Chalcedon have offended those who looked for a purely spiritual or moral message: the living Redeemer is reduced to a metaphysical mummy. This has been true of Liberal Protestant interpreters (Harnack, Temple), of Anglo-Catholics (Prestige) and of advocates of 'Biblical Theology' (Cullmann). Among theologians of all schools there remain those who accept the Formula, but regard it as primarily negative, in that it states the limits within which

Christology may be discussed without falling into damaging error. Roman Catholics have stayed firm with the Formula officially, while practical devotion has centred elsewhere (as upon the Sacred Heart of Jesus). In recent times, however, as biblical study has encouraged concrete historical research into the origins of the faith and Jesus himself, one great theologian has suggested that only now can the Church begin to exploit the Chalcedonian principle of his full humanity (Rahner). At the same time ecumenical contacts have encouraged theologians to perceive the common ground between the Monophysites, whose exclusion begins at Chalcedon, and those who assert Two Natures. The Monophysites have survived under various forms of alien rule, and that fact alone must call in question whether the number of natures in Jesus Christ is a suitable point on which to divide the churches, when they all enjoy the light of God through the same Jesus Christ, and declare him complete in both godhead and manhood. The interpretation of Chalcedon remains an important part of theology.

22

THE HERITAGE OF ANCIENT THEOLOGY

The imperial Church

By 451 a great change had come over the Church since its birth four centuries earlier. The small body of believers, of those who had followed Christ and seen the risen Lord, Jewish in upbringing, had expanded by the middle of the fifth century to include members from Britain in the West and India in the East. In the beginning they had included 'not many wise, not many mighty'; by 451 not only was the emperor himself a Christian, but, after resistance and hesitation, the governing classes had followed the imperial example. Pockets of reluctance and opposition were to be found among certain noble families in the west and in the university centres of Athens and Alexandria. But for practical purposes the Empire was a Christian institution. To its people and officers, and so to the leaders of the churches, it was virtually the whole world. The institutions of the worldwide Empire would affect the shape of the churches, and the shape of their doctrine, even more than the Church's faith affected the way the Empire was run.

Since its beginnings the organization of the Christian Church had developed, and mirrored closely that of the Empire. At first the ministry of bishop, presbyter and deacon appeared in various forms, and these officers shared their powers and responsibilities with teachers, prophets, widows and deaconesses; by the year 451 the threefold ministry was fixed and universal. Other forms of ministry, especially those of prophets and teachers, had become functions of bishops, priests and deacons, and whatever part in them women had once played had disappeared. In the beginning each city had its own bishop, and he presided over his one congregation. By the fifth century areas of jurisdiction (later called 'dioceses'), though still based on cities, were spread over wider areas. The bishops themselves were organized regionally under archbishops, and the archbishops were in turn grouped under metropolitans, whose jurisdiction coincided with the geographical units of administration imposed by the Empire. The capital of the civil province usually housed the ecclesiastical superior of the region, or metropolitan. Over these metropolitans was an even wider division, that of patriarchs, though the name was not used till the sixth century. The five original patriarchates were Rome, Alexandria, Antioch, Constantinople and Jerusalem. Bishops of larger cities might have churches under them governed by presbyters.

If the ecclesiastical structure of the fifth-century Church owed much to the civil divisions of the Empire, since the days of Augustus the Empire had undergone massive reorganization, above all at the hands of Diocletian (284–305). He divided the Empire in half, each half being under the jurisdiction of an *Augustus*, and each *Augustus* having under him a *Caesar*. The four 'Tetrarchs' governed the whole of the Empire between them. Constantine too shared power with relatives, though his personality was triumphantly monarchical. After the battle of Chrysopolis in 324 he refounded the city of Byzantium as 'Constantine's City', Constantinople, to become his New Rome, with a Christian ethos. This broke with the tradition that had seen Old Rome and its gods as the centre of empire for more than four centuries; it also effectively divided the Empire into two geographical units, the wealthy and cultivated provinces of the east and the poorer western provinces, who during the next two centuries became increasingly subject to barbarian inroads. One consequence was the split between the Greek-speaking Church of the East and the Latin-speaking Church of the West. Lasting differences between the Eastern and Western Churches reflect this early divide. The Greek emphasis on argument and definition was matched by a Latin interest in order and structure. The Latins suspected the Greeks of being 'too clever by half', while the Greeks felt then and doubtless still feel that the Western Church is too dominated by the concept of authority. The different attitude to and practice of the liturgy both then and now reflect the different temperament that produced them. In the West the austere and brief Roman form came to prevail, at least officially, while the Eastern rites are flamboyant and long, and both, we must assume, very different from the practice of the first century.

Changes were also apparent in the demands made upon individuals. Early converts were coming out from their environment and taking on a new social identity, suspect and in some sense illegal. Adopting the God of Israel meant renouncing the gods and the religious fabric of the society around them. As disciples became more numerous, writers like the early apologists and the Alexandrians Clement and Origen sought an accommodation, finding in Jesus Christ a fulfilment of the best in Greek culture. Lactantius and particularly Augustine were to do the same for the Latin tradition, but much later; Tertullian and Cyprian were not like Clement and Origen. But fitting in with Roman society meant modifying attitudes, and Cyprian's lament over the loss of apostolic purity in the churches probably has truth in it (*De laps.* 5–6 [*NE* 215–16]). Attempts to impose or reimpose the strict discipline of earlier days, or a more advanced spiritual discipline, were constantly made by groups like the Marcionites, Montanists and Novatianists. But they were repudiated by the main body of the Church, which recognized its responsibility to a mixed congregation: even the steely Cyprian yielded, and allied himself with Cornelius of Rome in a policy of graded indulgence to the lapsed. The harder side of Cyprian was to re-emerge in Donatism, with its rejection of all sacraments but their own; but that was in turn firmly set aside by a state guided by the policy of Rome and Augustine. The problems caused by doctrinal division in the fourth century also led to greater tolerance towards clergy tainted with heresy and schism, and Athanasius himself led the way by unprecedented concessions at the Council of Alexandria in 362.

From the later third century some Christians' urge to forsake the bonds of Roman society, especially property and marriage, led to the flowering of monasticism, and a new spirituality. That too was not allowed to separate off from the body of the Church, but was forced back into service by dedicated bishops like Basil of Caesarea and Augustine of Hippo. Sometimes, as in the cases of John Chrysostom and Nestorius, the monastic ideals proved calamitous when applied directly to the management of a large episcopal administration. Monasticism also left one uncomfortable mark on Christianity, namely the belief that virginity was in itself superior to marriage, and not merely a different (and exemplary) calling. Augustine's personal experience, sensitive and powerful in its grasp of the divine grace in Jesus Christ overwhelming fleshly pride and rebellious intellect, unfortunately identified that conversion with the monastic vocation, leaving a residue of immense consequence, good and bad, for the Church afterwards. So did his woeful picture of predestination and hell, and the guilt of the newborn infant.

Doctrinal development

The Empire needed unity in the churches and coherent teaching and practice. The fourth and fifth centuries saw the theological basis of Christian doctrine receive a definite shape which remains basic for Christian self-understanding today. Numerous councils were held to deal with threats or resolve conflicts. We have followed the tortuous course of some of these debates. The four ecumenical councils of Nicaea (325), Constantinople (381), Ephesus (431) and Chalcedon (451) were those which in the end emerged as the norms for imperial religion and catholic truth.

The chief doctrines they stated were these:

i. that the Son is of the same substance as the Father;

ii. that the Holy Spirit shares the honour and dignity of the Father and the Son;

iii. that Mary is to be honoured as 'Theotokos', 'Godbearer';

iv. that Jesus Christ is fully divine and fully human.

The creeds and other statements of these councils used ideas and language sometimes perceived as very different in some respects from those of the New Testament. A typical example is given by Edwin Hatch, who at the beginning of his Gifford Lectures for 1888, published as *The influence of Greek ideas and usages upon the Christian Church*, spoke of the contrast between the Nicene Creed and the Sermon on the Mount: 'The one belongs to a world of Syrian peasants, the other to a world of Greek philosophers . . . The question why an ethical sermon stood in the forefront of the teaching of Jesus Christ and a metaphysical creed in the forefront of the Christianity of the fourth century is a problem which claims investigation.' For him, as for Adolf Harnack after him, the Church of the fourth and fifth centuries represents a betrayal of the primitive message of the New Testament, which is seen by them in primarily ethical terms. Similarly Harnack writes at the beginning of his *History of dogma* (p. 16), 'Dogma in its conception and development is a work of the Greek spirit on the soil of the Gospel.' Those who believe in Jesus Christ have to decide what they make of this apparent discrepancy.

Hatch and Harnack in various ways held that it was the moral claims of Jesus, the absolute and demanding morality of the Sermon on the Mount, which was the truth or 'essence' of Christianity as Jesus had made it known. Albert Schweitzer, a great theologian and critic before he became a medical missionary, saw Jesus as rather an apocalyptic visionary, and imitated his self-sacrifice with his own renunciation of European comforts for dedicated service. The Roman Catholic Modernists like Alfred Loisy and George Tyrrell found the key in the dogmas of the Catholic Church as symbols representing those other-worldly hopes and commitments which Schweitzer's Jesus taught and died for. They themselves had taken up and used the ideas of the great Anglican and Roman Catholic theologian, John Henry Newman, who had suggested in *An essay on the development of Christian doctrine* that Catholic doctrine develops and changes, though with an organized continuity like an oak-tree from an acorn. Newman's thought is very influential among modern Roman Catholics, who attribute the policies of the Second Vatican Council to his influence, effective over a century after he wrote.

All such ideas would have been unacceptable to the ancient Church, which held that the gospel had to be preserved and passed on exactly as the apostles gave it: we have met that idea in Irenaeus in discriminating truth from error (*Adv. Haer.* 1.10.2 [*NE* 112]), and in the Chalcedonian Definition, where it is given classic formulation in the very document which installed a new set of creeds (*CCC* 350). Sometimes an ancient writer is aware of the tension between continuity and change, like Vincent of Lérins, who argued in his *Commonitorium* about 434 that Christian doctrine, though essentially unchanging and universal, grows in expression and clarity (*CCC* 322–4). Gregory of Nazianzus was especially unusual in suggesting that there were real additions to doctrine, such as the deity of the Spirit (*CCC* 85–6). Orthodox, Roman Catholic and Protestant agreed with the Fathers on the immutability of doctrine, until the rise of historical criticism, particularly in the nineteenth century. To find an acceptable formula some reflection on the witness of Scripture may help.

The biblical basis

If we ask how the Church moved from the simple affirmations of the New Testament to the complex credal statements about hypostases, natures and consubstantial persons, we might begin by noting the powerful and sometimes paradoxical biblical texts themselves. 'Jesus is Lord' is a simple acclamation of primitive Christianity (1 Cor. 12.3; cf. Rom. 10.9). But that confession is itself said to be impossible without the inspiration of the Holy Spirit: 'No one can say, "Jesus is Lord", except through the Holy Spirit.' Further, the same Spirit inspires believers to recognize the Father: 'You have received the Spirit of adoption by which we cry, "Abba! Father!"' (Rom. 8.15). This 'Spirit of adoption' alludes to the idea that in calling God 'Father', as one does in saying the Lord's Prayer, the believer is made to share the status which Jesus Christ has. So there is a trinitarian *function* even in the earliest New Testament texts: 'To show that you are sons, God has sent the Spirit of his Son into our hearts, crying "Abba, Father!"' (Gal. 4.6). So God is glorified in and with his Son. Every tongue in all creation must in the end confess that 'Jesus Christ is Lord, to the glory of God the Father' (Phil. 2.11). This means that even in the New Testament Jesus Christ (the crucified and risen one) is regarded as the agent of all God's works, and shares his glorious titles. 'For us there is one God, the Father, from whom are all things and we for him, and one Lord, Jesus Christ, through whom are all things and we through him' (1 Cor. 8.6); these words form the basis of the later creeds, not merely verbally (the Nicene-Constantinopolitan Creed embodies phrases from it), but in its fundamental concept, that the one God functions toward the faithful through Jesus Christ. We should not underestimate the meaning of what the New Testament attributes to Christ. The idea that he was the biblical Creator, as the Image, Word or Son of God, is quite primitive (Col. 1.15–17; John 1.2–4; Heb. 1.1–3). The title 'Lord' might mean only 'Master' on the lips of disciples, but was soon used to interpret Old Testament passages where the same title was used of the God of Israel; and we find manifestations of God from the old Scriptures taken as manifestations of the pre-existent Christ not only in the Fourth Gospel (John 12.41 reflects Isa. 6.1), but in the Synoptics (where the Lord whom Moses and

Elijah met at Sinai is the transfigured Son of Mark 9.2–8 and parallels). So even if believers share his sonship by participating in his Spirit, he is 'uniquely Son', expressed as 'beloved' (Col. 1.13; Mark 1.11 par.) or 'only-begotten' (John 1.18 etc.).

Such thoughts as these came together in the elementary baptismal confessions of Christendom. Whether they were, as many from the start, explicitly trinitarian (Matt. 28.19; *Didache* 7), or simply in the name of Jesus as Christ ('Anointed King') or Lord, the sovereignty of the Father was implicitly confessed, and the working of the Spirit: it is no accident that at the baptism of Jesus the Father speaks of his Son while the Holy Spirit descends upon him; it is the clearest 'trinitarian' part of Mark's Gospel (Mark 1.8–11). But inevitably this complex of devotion and experience raised questions. Different attempts were made from the start to account for the divine status of Jesus. That he was a prophet like Moses, or an angelic being appearing as a man, could be dealt with quite early: more than a prophet, and physically human. The favoured solution used the Platonic notion of an intermediary between the Unoriginated Transcendent One and the physical world of change and decay, a 'second God' or 'Mind', conveniently designated Son or Word. While some version of this prevailed with most of the theologians of the first few centuries, it constantly raised new problems. If you identify the Son too firmly with the Transcendent (as the Modalists, Sabellius and Marcellus did), then even creation and providence, and certainly living and suffering as a human being, become inconceivable: he must therefore be a distinct *hypostasis* from the Father. But if you draw too sharply the distinction of the generated Son from the Unoriginated Father (as Arius and those like him were perceived to do), then he operated at a level less than God, and the glory of his saving work was seen to be diminished: he must be consubstantial, *homoousios*, in his essence not distinguishable from God.

The other puzzle, of humanity and divinity in Christ, was also inherent in the biblical testimony. The essential message was of the Crucified who was raised from the dead (1 Cor. 15.3–4; cf. 1 Cor. 2.1–2; Rom. 10.8–9). That raised the question, 'Who was the Crucified?', a question which in their various ways the Gospels answered. But they did so in the light of the glory of the risen and ascended Lord, and consequently they tell of a career suffused with divine power and light, which at times is at variance with the historical humanity.

This problem is present in all the Gospels, but most clearly felt in John, who simultaneously emphasizes Christ's divine supernatural powers and his concrete, suffering humanity. He is the Only-begotten God (or Son), the Word who is eternally in the Father's bosom (1.1,18), who knows all things (2.24–5; 13.1,3), controls his destiny (10.17–18), and performs stupendous miracles of creation and resurrection (2.1–11; 9.32–3; 11.38–44). Yet he became flesh (1.14), and suffers fatigue (4.6), thirst (19.28), grief (11.35) and perplexity (12.27). It is no wonder the Evangelist himself gets his narrative into a tangle when Jesus asks a simple factual question (6.5–6), or starts to make a simple petitionary prayer (11.41–2).

Such difficulties, apparent in the evangelists and particularly John, were just those which led the early church thinkers to various, and sometimes outlandish explanations. Not having the advantage of a critical view of the gospel narratives, they found themselves obliged either (like Theodore and Nestorius) to think that Christ kept switching from his divine character to his human and back again, or (like Apollinaris and Cyril) that the Word self-consciously adapted his outward behaviour at each moment to what befitted a man, so that he said things for the benefit of his followers which were strictly false, such as that there were things he did not know, or that he felt distress. Neither of these methods is to us satisfactory, and that is one reason we find it hard to get worked up about whether Christ was one combined Person of two natures, or one divine Nature with his humanity. The Chalcedonian Formula, like Leo's *Tome*, seems to have asserted both principles, even if Cyril's 'One Nature of the divine Word enfleshed' was only in the supporting documents and not in the text. If Chalcedon repudiated Nestorius unfairly, however, it did so because he appeared to say that Christ was a man divinely inspired, not God in a suffering humanity; and if Eutyches was misrepresented, it was because he divinized the flesh and left God too far from fallen mankind.

Finally we should perhaps note the central part played by liturgy in the development of doctrine. Above all the baptismal formula of Matthew 28.19, and the 'rule of faith' associated with baptismal teaching exercised a certain, if imprecise, pressure on the theology of the Church. Doctrine and worship are inseparable responses to what God has said to the world in Jesus Christ. And because true worship was from the start a spiritual sacrifice of the whole self in union with the sacrifice of Jesus Christ, obedience to Christ's law, and the deep commitment expressed in martyrdom and monasticism, constitute the outward testimony to the truth of the teaching, that God was in Christ reconciling the world to himself.

FURTHER READING

Constant reference is made in this book to the two companion volumes edited by J. Stevenson (new editions revised by W. H. C. Frend), *A New Eusebius* and *Creeds, Councils and Controversies* (London: SPCK 1987, 1989). These are abbreviated as *NE* and *CCC*, and reference is to *pages* of those books, *not* numbered items.

Useful for longer readings are: H. Bettenson, *The Early Christian Fathers* and *Later Christian Fathers* (London: Oxford University Press 1956/1970 and after); the first eight volumes of *Library of Christian Classics* (London: SCM/Philadelphia: Westminster Press [and Ichthys reprint] 1953 etc.); and the recent series *Sources of Early Christian Thought* (Philadelphia: Fortress Press).

For an introduction to the early Church, Ian Hazlett (ed.), *Early Christianity: Origins and Evolution to AD 600* (London: SPCK 1991) is full of useful information; for a short reliable history, Henry Chadwick, *The Early Church* (Pelican History of the Church 1) (Harmondsworth: Penguin 1967). For more detailed history try W. H. C. Frend, *The Rise of Christianity* (London: Darton, Longman & Todd 1984) or Hubert Jedin and John Dolan, *History of the Church* (London: Burns & Oates 1980) vol. 1 and 2. For doctrine: J. N. D. Kelly, *Early Christian Doctrines* (London: Longmans ³1978) and *Early Christian Creeds* (London: Longmans ³1972); J. Daniélou, *A History of Early Christian Doctrine 1–3* (London: 1964–1977). For Christology, Aloys Grillmeier, *Christ in Christian Tradition 1* (London: Mowbrays ²1975) is comprehensive. For reference, *Encyclopedia of Early Christianity*, ed. E. Ferguson (New York: Garland 1989); *The Oxford Dictionary of the Christian Church* (London: Oxford University Press ²1974); *Atlas of the Early Christian World* (London: Nelson 1958 and after). Frances Young, *From Nicaea to Chalcedon* (SCM 1983) is a readable guide to the writers of the later period.

Chapter 1: God and the gods

Robert M. Grant, *Gods and the one God: Christian theology in the Graeco-Roman World* (London: SPCK 1986). Robert M. Grant, *Early*

Christianity and Society (London: Collins 1977). W. H. C. Frend, *Martyrdom and Persecution in the Early Church* (Oxford: Blackwell 1965). R. A. Markus, *Christianity in the Roman World* (London: Thames and Hudson 1975).

Chapter 2: Community and morality

Early Christian Fathers (Library of Christian classics 1). Cheslyn Jones, Geoffrey Wainwright, Edward Yarnold, eds, *The Study of Liturgy* (London: SPCK; New York: OUP 1978).

Chapter 3: The message and the messengers

R. J. Coggins and J. L. Houlden, *A Dictionary of Biblical Interpretation* (London: SCM 1990); Bruce M. Metzger, *The Canon of the New Testament* (Oxford: Clarendon Press 1987); Bleddyn J. Roberts, *The Old Testament Text and Versions* (Cardiff: University of Wales Press 1951); Hans von Campenhausen, *Ecclesiastical Authority and Spiritual Power* (London: A & C Black; Stanford University Press 1969).

Chapter 4: Proliferation and excess

Walter Bauer, *Orthodoxy and Heresy in Earliest Christianity* (London: SCM 1972/Philadelphia: Fortress Press 1971); C. W. Hedrick and Robert Hodgson, eds, *Nag Hammadi, Gnosticism and Early Christianity* (Peabody, MA: Hendrickson 1986); Kurt Rudolph, *Gnosis* (Edinburgh: T. & T. Clark 1983); Bentley Layton, *The Gnostic Scriptures* (London: SCM 1987).

Chapter 5: Defence and definition

Henry Chadwick, *Early Christianity and the Classical Tradition* (Oxford: Oxford University Press 1966). R. M. Grant, *Greek Apologists of the Second Century* (London: SCM 1988).

Chapter 6: Tradition and truth: Irenaeus of Lyons

R. P. C. Hanson, *Tradition in the Early Church* (London: SCM 1962); John Lawson, *The Biblical theology of St Irenaeus* (London: Epworth Press 1948).

Chapter 7: Latin theology launched: Tertullian

T. D. Barnes, *Tertullian* (Oxford: Clarendon Press 1971); G. L. Bray, *Holiness and the Will of God* (London: Marshall, Morgan & Scott 1979).

Chapter 8: Sectarian religion and episcopal authority

Controversial discussions are not readily accessible in English; see however general books and G. Dix, ed., *The Treatise on the Apostolic Tradition of St Hippolytus of Rome* (reissued with corrections by H. Chadwick) (London: SPCK 1968); *Hippolytus of Rome Contra Noetum*, ed. and trans. Robert Butterworth (London: Heythrop College 1977).

Chapter 9: One Church, one baptism: Cyprian

Michael M. Sage, *Cyprian* (Cambridge, MA: Philadelphia Patristic Foundation Ltd); M. F. Wiles, 'The theological legacy of St Cyprian', *Journal of Ecclesiastical History* 14 (1963), pp. 139–149.

Chapters 10 and 11: Clement and Origen

Charles Bigg, *The Christian Platonists of Alexandria* (Oxford: Clarendon Press 1886); H. Crouzel, *Origen* (Edinburgh: T. & T. Clark 1989); R. P. C. Hanson, *Origen's Doctrine of Tradition* (London: SPCK 1954); S. R. C. Lilla, *Clement of Alexandria* (Oxford: Oxford University Press 1971); J. W. Trigg, *Origen* (Atlanta: John Knox Press 1983/London: SCM 1985).

Chapter 12: The rise of Constantine

T. D. Barnes, *Constantine and Eusebius* (Cambridge, MA/London: Harvard University Press 1981); N. H. Baynes, *Constantine the Great and the Christian Church* (Proceedings of the British Academy 1929/ reprint ed. by H. Chadwick, Oxford 1972); W. H. C. Frend, *The Donatist Church* (Oxford: Clarendon Press 1952); A. H. M. Jones, *Constantine and the Conversion of Europe* (Harmondsworth: Penguin 1962); Robin Lane Fox, *Pagans and Christians* (Harmondsworth etc.: Viking 1986) is valuable for the period before as well as for Constantine.

Chapter 13: Arius and the Council of Nicaea

R. C. Gregg, ed., *Arianism* (The Philadelphia Patristic Foundation 1985); R. P. C. Hanson, *The Search for the Christian Doctrine of God* (Edinburgh: T. & T. Clark 1989) covers the whole period to Constantinople; Rowan Williams, *Arius* (London: Darton, Longman & Todd 1987).

Chapters 14 and 15: Councils and controversies; Towards synthesis

H. Lietzmann, *A History of the Early Church 3–4* is particularly good, in addition to other church histories and Hanson. G. L. Prestige, *God in*

Patristic Thought (London: SPCK 1952); Charles E. Raven, *Apollinarianism* (Cambridge: University Press 1923); see also accounts of personalities in Frances Young, *From Nicaea to Chalcedon*, and histories of doctrine.

Chapter 16: Theodosius I and the Council of Constantinople

N. Q. King, *The Emperor Theodosius and the Establishment of Christianity* (London: SCM 1961).

Chapter 17: New spirituality: the monastic movement

Owen Chadwick, *John Cassian* (Cambridge: University Press ²1968); D. J. Chitty, *The Desert a City* (Oxford: Blackwell 1966); Philip Rousseau, *Ascetics, Authority and the Church* (Oxford: Oxford University Press 1979) and *Pachomius* (Berkeley/London: University of California Press 1985). H. Lietzmann, *A History of the Early Church 4* has a good final chapter.

Chapter 18: Origenism, Jerome and John Chrysostom

Chrysostomus Baur, *John Chrysostom and his Time* (London/Glasgow: Sands & Co. 1959; reprint Belmont, MA, 1988); J. N. D. Kelly, *Jerome* (London: Duckworth 1975).

Chapter 19: Augustine of Hippo

Gerald Bonner, *St Augustine of Hippo* (London: SCM 1963) is clear and thorough; Peter Brown, *Augustine of Hippo* (London: Faber 1967) is full and readable; Henry Chadwick, *Augustine* (Oxford/New York: OUP 1986) is brief and brilliant.

Chapters 20 and 21: Cyril, Nestorius and the Council of Ephesus; Eutycles Leo and the Council of Chalcedon

A. Grillmeier, *Christ in Christian Tradition* for all detail on Christology. *Cyril of Alexandria, Select Letters*, ed. and trans. Lionel R. Wickham (Oxford: Clarendon Press 1983) has an excellent introduction; see also J. B. Bethune-Baker, *Nestorius* (Cambridge: University Press 1908); G. L. Prestige, *Fathers and Heretics* (London: SPCK 1948); R. V. Sellers, *Two Ancient Christologies* (London: SPCK 1940) and *The Council of Chalcedon* (London: SPCK 1953).

INDEX